THE LIFE OF DAME GRACIE FIELDS

This is the first full-length biography of the much loved entertainer. Drawing on various sources Jean Moules shows us a woman whose public and private selves were almost complete opposites—the one extrovert and exuberant, the other shy and unconfident. We follow her life from childhood in Rochdale, starring on stage and screen, entertaining the troops, over-coming hostility to her wartime marriage to an Italian, bouncing back in the 50's, 60's and 70's with records in the hit parade, a triumphant last Royal Command Performance at 80, to the final honour, in the year of her death, of being made Dame Commander of the British Empire.

CONTENTS

OUR GRACIE

The Life of
Dame Gracie Fields

by
Joan Moules

MAGNA PRINT BOOKS
Long Preston, North Yorkshire,
England.

British Library Cataloguing in Publication Data.

Moules, Joan
 'Our Gracie' : the life of Dame Gracie Fields.
 —Large print ed.
 1. Fields, Gracie   2. Singers—Great Britain
—Biography
 I. Title
 784.5'0092'4   ML420.F46

 ISBN 0-86009-742-0

First Published in Great Britain by Robert Hale Ltd, 1983

Published in Large Print 1985 by arrangement with Robert Hale Ltd,
London.

Photoset in Great Britain by
Dermar Phototypesetting Co,   Long Preston, North Yorkshire.

Printed and bound in Great Britain by
Redwood Burn Limited,   Trowbridge, Wiltshire.

ACKNOWLEDGEMENTS

My thanks to my husband, Leon, for checking the original MS and for numerous journeyings in the interest of research.

To Wally Singer for compiling the discography, writing the musical appreciation, and locating so much helpful material for me.

To Roy Hudd for writing a foreword, and to the following for their assistance and, in many cases, generous sharing of memories:

Boris Alperovici—Clifford Ashton—Elis Ashton—Will Ayling—Lillian Aza—BBC Written Archives (Mrs Jacqueline Kavanagh), BBC Sound Recording, BBC Tape Unit (Margaret Cox), BBC Copywright (Stephen Edwards)—Bernard Braden—Irene Bevan—Broadfield School (Mr Cunliffe)—Stanley Clements—Russ Conway—Mary and Leon Davey—Florence Desmond—Dianne Doubtfire—Judy and Mike Davis—Jill Dick—Sir Anton Dolin—EMI Records Norman Empire—Harold Fielding—Joy and Frank Foster—J. Graham Garner—Cecil Gilmour—Nat Gonella—Alan Goode—Larry Grayson—Edna Grime—the late William Grime (Bill)—

9

Doris Hare—Hilda Harris—Margaret Hazell —Teddy Holmes—John Graven Hughes— Norman Jackson—Mr Jefferson—George F. Letts—Denis Lowndes—Geoff Love—*Manchester Evening News* (Mr Emmett)—Lord Bernard Miles—Dorothy Mitchell (Doris Paul)— Lady Morrison—Mona Newman— David Pluckrose—Mr J.B. Priestley—Hazel Provost—Ray Rastall—Red Funnel Group (Mr Monk)—Rochdale Library (Mr John Cole)—Rochdale Museum (Mr Pitman and his staff)—*Rochdale Observer* (Mr Whitworth and his staff)—Mrs Rushworth—Gertie Sammon—Semprini—Fred Shepherd—Donald Sinden—Bill Sowerbutts—Cyril Smith— May Snowdon—Rosalind and Neil Somerville—Annette Stansfield—Tommy Stansfield (Tommy Fields)—Patience Strong— John Taylor—Roy Taylor (Vitool Factory)— Barbara Timms—Dame Eva Turner—Derek Warman—Bob Watts—Joan and Kenneth Wells—Mary Whipp—Nell Whitwell—Paul Ward—Mr Wilde.

I should like to thank the following for their permission to quote copyright material: Associated Newspapers Group for an extract from an article by George Black from the *Sunday Chronicle* (1935). BBC written Archives for *A Pen Portrait* by J.B. Priestley (1947) and a letter from Kenneth Adams (May 1951). Mr Cunliffe of Broadfield School for various quotes from some of the children's work. The *Daily Express* for extracts from reviews and other material. The *Daily Mail, Portsmouth Evening News, Portland Oregon* and*Seattle Times* for reviews of concerts. The *Tacomo News Tribune* for reviews. EMI for a passage from record sleeve written by Norman Newell. *Lancashire Life* (the Whitehorn Press) for an extract from 'What Rochdale Means To Me', written by Gracie Fields in 1956. The *Manchester Evening News* for an extract from Eric Wigham's article published in 1936, and for reviews of concerts. Mr R. H. Naylor for a 1933 horoscope. Mr J.B. Priestley for permission to quote *A Pen Portrait* (1947) Red Funnel Group for the story of the paddle steamer *Gracie Fields'* last voyage. The *Rochdale Observer* for an extract from the 1933 report of Charity Week, for a report of the Portrait Fund and for a report of the Freedom of Rochdale. The *Observer* for part of Miss C.A. Lejeune's article on Gracie (1939). The *Southern Echo* for a report of the launching of paddle steamer *Gracie Fields*. Noel Gay Music for 'I'll Always Love You'.

I should like to thank the following publishers for their permission to quote from the books mentioned: Hutchinson, *I Had To Be Wee* by Georgie Wood (1948) and *Me and The Mediterranean* by Naomi Jacob (1945).

FOREWORD

by Roy Hudd

I first met Gracie Fields in my agent's Mum's front garden. I'd better explain. My agent is Morris Aza, his Mum is Lillian Aza, Lillian Aza is the widow of Bert Aza, Bert Aza was the brother of Archie Pitt. Archie Pitt was Gracie Fields' first husband. My agent was Gracie Fields' nephew. Do not pass 'go', do not collect two hundred pounds!

I'd called at Mrs Aza's house, which was also her and Morris's office, to see if he might have found me a week's work, anywhere! As I walked up their garden path Mrs A was sitting having a cup of tea with another comfortable white-haired lady. 'Hello Roy,' she said, 'this is Grace. Grace, this is Roy Hudd, he's a comic.' Grace jumped to her feet and held out her hand. 'Hello love, so you're a comic. Are you as funny as you look?' Well, there's no answer to that is there! Dame Gracie Fields, CBE!

To write a few words about Gracie is not easy. What can I say that hasn't been said already, a thousand times more eloquently?

I can only say, in cold clinical terms, that she was, quite simply, the greatest female artiste we have ever produced. She was an actress, a comédienne, a singer of comic and serious songs and a breaker of box-office records from the London Palladium to the Batley Variety Club. She made over three hundred records, she was the *first* British film star, and she stayed at the top of her profession for over sixty years. She was, before the word had even been invented, a superstar. But there was more.

OK, she was a highly talented performer with great technique and expertise, but there were, and are, lots of others to whom we gratefully give our applause. But to how few do we give our love? We did to Gracie. Why?

Perhaps it was because she never changed. Not her material, of course. That was always up-to-date, as far as we would let it be. On one of her last television interviews she just spoke the words of 'Send in The Clowns' and it sent shivers down your spine. How I wish she'd recorded that one. No, it was her personality, attitude and outlook that never changed. She was honest, down-to-earth, and stood no nonsense. She genuinely cut right through all the pomposity, all the 'don't come near me I'm so special' trappings that surround a public figure.

When, in 1979, she was made a Dame

Commander of the British Empire she said, 'So now I'm Dame—wonderful, as long as they don't call Boris Buttons!'

She learnt her trade the proper way, by dedication, perseverance and hard graft. In today's world of plastic entertainment and stereotyped personalities she stood out as a 'one off'. She was the real thing. The eighteen-carat genuine article.

You must forgive me the purple prose, I don't do it very often but when I do it's from the heart. Gracie Fields touched my heart when she sang love songs and my funny bone when she sang comic ones. I was a fan. Joan Moules was a fan too. Joan's book tells the Gracie Fields story and has lots of quotes from fans. Perhaps they tell us more about the real Gracie than facts ever can because, despite the public image, Gracie remains an enigma.

How could she be so unaffected by the overpowering adulation that surrounded her? Why did she seek seclusion and yet lead total strangers in a sing-song at the drop of a hat? Why was she like putty in the hands of the three men in her life? Some answers came through to me between the lines of *Our Gracie*.

But I loved *my* Gracie and Joan Moules' book has gone a long way in explaining to me just why I did. Thank you Joan, and thank you Gracie.

15

For Gracie

I could write a million words
Yet none of them convey
The magic that you gave to us,
Impossible to say.

You *were*—and we were there,
Some of the crowd who saw,
Who heard, and felt, and loved you so,
Were rich, and now are poor.

I won't write a million words,
I'll let it go with two,
Bless you, Gracie—rest in peace,
The words—simply, thank you.

PROLOGUE

Dame Gracie Fields became something of a legend during her eighty-one years on earth. When the house where she was born was demolished to make way for a new factory one of her fans took the latch from the door and sent it to her in Capri. He knew she would understand why he had done this. For although so much of her heart was in the Mediterranean island where she lived for over forty years, a bit of it never left Rochdale in Lancashire, and all of it stayed in England and with her 'ain folk'.

She was straight as a die, and she was pure Lancashire. Although she left there when she was sixteen, Gracie remained a Lancashire woman all her life. It was this that made her bargain in Capri, refuse chipped cups and insist on a bag for her purchases. It was the Lancashire in her so tough and so gentle at one and the same time. The two sides of the coin were hardly ever shown to a greater degree than in Gracie. The Lancashireness of her was a strong element of her character.

Her 'ain folk' were made welcome wherever she was. 'I come from Rochdale' were magic words which opened the portals of her home to them. But it was not always and only Lancashire folk who stole her heart. None of her husbands was from her own county, two of them were not even from her own country, and many of her dearest friends were from other parts. Yet still she was, and remained, a Lancashire Lass some-where deep inside her—she knew this and was proud of it; it gave her a sense of belonging, and there were times when she desperately needed to feel she belonged somewhere.

She had her faults—thank heaven she did; she also had so much heart, so much love (that often misused word) and an abundance of talent, pride and humility.

So many people said to me during the writing of this book, 'She made you want to be good,' and I know what they meant—I had felt it so strongly myself. She was not a 'goody-goody' but a *good* person in the truest sense of the word. As she grew older, this seemed more pronounced, or maybe she just let the mask slip a bit.

When she heard a disc jockey announcing a number with the words, 'I think you *might* find it amusing,' she said, 'I don't want to be "amused"—I want to be *moved*. Make me laugh, make me cry, but make me *feel*.'

Some time in the future someone will say, 'Gracie Fields—didn't she sing comic songs?'

Yes, she did sing comic songs. She also sang romantic ballads, sacred songs and what she once described hesitantly as 'some of the semi-classics', because she did not want folk to imagine she was getting above herself. But listen to them on her records and you will hear a little of the magic she created. Add to that her wonderful personality and the warmth of her reaching out to her audience—'It's like an invisible silver thread between us,' is how she described it.

Sometimes people need courage, faith, belief...Gracie gave it to them. Some force, a glow, a vitality—probably a bit of hers, but she gave it out and people responded to her talent, her artistry and that part of her which somehow supported them and gave them the incentive and the courage they needed. That is not putting her deep appeal too strongly.

She never lost touch with reality, and she was tremendously human. Her confidence offstage was a frail thing which she covered well but which often left her lonely.

Gracie was a communicator, who got through to people of all ages and in all walks of life.

Here then is her story, which began in Rochdale and—I was going to say ended in Capri, but it did not end: it is still going on; her photograph is in so many, many homes; her voice is heard on old gramophones, modern record-players and tapes. Some of her songs have become part of our language, and her memory and inspiration linger in the hearts of her legions of fans and friends of all ages.

CHAPTER 1

The Early Years

It was bitterly cold in the bedroom above the fish and chip shop in Molesworth Street, Rochdale, but nineteen-year-old Jenny Stansfield was sweating. She was in labour with her first child, and on 9 January 1898 her daughter Grace was born.

Grace was a bonny baby, her mother was as proud of her as any other first-time mum, but she had dreams that not every mother has, dreams which could not have come true for her if Grace hadn't had the talent, the personality and, above all, that wonderful voice. In later years Grace herself said this—and never forgot to thank God for her voice.

She was christened in Rochdale parish church—St Chad's, on 2 February 1898—the same church where her mother and father were married a year earlier.

Jenny was born in 1879 and baptized Sara Jane Bamford. Orphaned at ten years of age, she went to live with an aunt in Rochdale. She also worked fulltime in the cotton mill at that tender age.

Her aunt, who was religious and strict,

sent her to Sunday School in the mornings and afternoons on the Sabbath, and to the Band of Hope several evenings a week. Jenny used to play truant whenever she could and go to the music hall instead. It was held at the Old Circus in Rochdale, and she dreamed of becoming a performer there herself. She had a good strong voice and a lot of push. When she was fourteen she left her aunt's and set up house with two friends from the mill, so as to be free to sing and dance and go to the music halls as much as she wanted.

Fred Stansfield, Gracie's father, was an engineer, first on a cargo boat and later, after he and Jenny married, with Robinsons, a Rochdale firm.

They lived with Fred's mother over her fish and chip shop at first, but as soon as Fred had a rise they moved to a place of their own. This was the pattern of Gracie's childhood—each time there was sixpence a week more wages, it meant another house—always in Rochdale, but 'We're going oop!' Jenny told them all.

Within a few years Betty and Edith arrived. As the eldest child Grace often had to help with her sisters. She also spent a lot of time with her grandmother, who was known locally as 'Chip Sarah'. Grace was fond of her grandmother. 'I remember her looking like a gaudy Queen Victoria. She loved bright

24

colours as I do,' she said later.

'Chip Sarah' told her earnest little grand-daughter a bit about her own life when they talked together. At six years old Sarah had worked in the coalpits, opening the heavy doors which sealed each shaft, to let the pit ponies pulling the coaltrucks through. Later she went into service—that was where she met Fred's father. Later still she had bought a barber's shop for £15, sold the stock and refurnished it as a fish and chip shop.

By the time Grace was ten, the three girls had a brother, Tommy, and Jenny recognised that her hopes and dreams for the stage lay in her children. Already Grace had one of the loudest and most melodious voices in the neighbourhood, and she and her sisters were encouraged to sing wherever they went—by their mother if not always by the neighbours. Remembering her early days many years later, Gracie said, 'We often used to play in the cellar, and one day Mumma fixed up a blanket as a make-believe curtain, saying, "There, now you can play theatres".'

And they played theatres, Gracie said, 'You didn't scrap with my mother—well, *I* didn't. We charged our audience of course; entrance fee was two buttons, and the seats were a stepladder turned on its side.'

Rochdale then, in the early 1900s, was a busy mill town. There were fewer motor cars;

only the very rich could afford them, and in any case many fought shy of this noisy, modern monster. Mostly it was horse and carriage for the mill owners, and trams or Shanks's pony for the rest. The trams ran through the centre of the town, and young Grace Stansfield used to hang onto the back of a tram when it started and run with it until, due to its speed, she *had* to let go.

They had few toys except ones they made themselves. Grace had a bogie, a handmade truck, which she used to pile her sisters and brother into and pull round the streets. Rochdale is very hilly, and they often used the 'bogie' as a sledge, whizzing down the hills to the danger of anyone walking by.

'Mostly though it was quiet in the daytime,' Gracie recalled. 'When the mills were working, there were few people on the streets.'

She was not supposed to, but she went paddling in the canal. She made friends with a girl called Edith Mitchell whose father had a boat there, and he sometimes took them for rides in that. She learnt to swim in the canal too, against parental rules, but right from a small child she loved the water.

She knew from an early age that she would go on the stage, because her mother told her so—knew also that if she wasn't talented enough, or professional enough, she would finish in the mill.

The mills dominated the skyline of Rochdale—their chimneys standing tall and proud above the town. They manufactured cotton, wool and rayon and sent their products all over the world. Barry Cockcroft, writing in 1956 (when Rochdale still had forty mills working), said about Gracie's voice, 'The high note on the second "Sally" is the one the mill girl has to hit if she's to make herself heard in the next line of the noisy doubling department. It has a quality peculiar to the cotton mill.'

The Pennines circled the town, giving escape from the noise and grime of industry. A short walk or a penny tramride and there were the hills, the fresh, fragrant air and the freedom of green, green space.

In each house they lived in, Grace and her sisters slept together, all three in one large bed. Strangely she wasn't the most mischievous of the family—that title went to Betty. I say strangely because, from the public figure most of us know, it would be easy to imagine her as the leader of the gang; but as a child Grace, as she was known then, was very shy and seldom spoke up for herself.

When she was seven, Gracie took part in a time-honoured custom. Each street had its maypole, and she was all set to join hers when her mother said, 'Nay, lass, tha'll have thy own pole.'

The three Stansfield girls—Grace, Betty, Edie—and Gracie's best friend at school, Ruby Rylands, helped to decorate a broomstick with brightly coloured ribbons and paper flowers. Gracie's sense of showmanship was evident even then, for she knew a girl who 'looked classy', she said later, and, with the promise of being allowed to hold the 'Maypole' and given the title of 'May Queen', the child put on her best silk frock and went with them.

Gracie held the box and led the singing, and at the end of that day they had 530d (old coinage), which works out to £2.25p—not much today, but more than a family's weekly wage then. Gracie sang all the songs she knew, sang them at the top of her voice, and the others followed her lead as she rattled her collecting box and roamed the town. 'I led them outside every pub,' she said years later, with a twinkle in her voice, 'and I knew plenty because I used to go with my Dad to his allotment and we often stopped off on the way.'

There were three theatres in Rochdale at that time, the Hippodrome (which used to be the Old Circus), the Theatre Royal (originally the Prince of Wales) and the Empire (eventually showing silent films with a 'turn' in between.)

Jenny not only worked in the mill, and in the kitchens of some of the big houses, she also got a job in the Rochdale Hippodrome. This was to scrub every Sunday—and she took her eldest daughter with her.

'For that day we were both in Wonderland,' Gracie said later, 'and Mumma's ambitions for me had full rein as we moved around the theatre when we had finished.'

Jenny's next venture was taking in theatricals' washing; again it was Grace who helped her do it. They hung it in the kitchen at night and took it down early next morning because neighbours were likely to come in at any time during the day.

'They'd see if you needed anything if they were going to shop, bring in a bit of stew if you hadn't been well—you all helped each other in those days,' Gracie said later. 'So the theatre washing had to be a secret. Jenny had her pride.'

When the washing was ready to be returned, they ironed it between them, then packed it up and walked down to the Hippodrome. They timed it so they could stand in the wings and watch the show.

'Three times a week,' Gracie said, 'once to collect and twice to deliver. Jenny thought it wouldn't hurt to take in an extra performance. When we reached home I had to mimic everything I'd seen for the others.'

None of the houses in Baron Street, where they were living then, had indoor sanitation, and once a week Gracie used to clean out the backyard lavatories for the neighbours. She did six at a halfpenny each, and she sang while she was doing them. Her mother encouraged her to sing *loudly,* and she had a powerful voice even then.

One day after school, as she was scrubbing away and belting out the songs she had heard the night before at the Hippodrome, a woman popped her head round the door.

'I've been listening to you. You've got a wonderful voice. Where do you live?'

Grace told her, and the woman said, 'Let's go and see your mother. I think you should go in for the singing competition if she'll let you.' The woman was a music hall singer called Rose Bush, who used the name Lily Turner on stage, and she was lodging along the road. Gracie was seven years old, and it was a blow when the family discovered that no one under eleven was allowed to sing in public any more. Not for long though. Gracie was tall for her age, so Jenny simply made her look older with a more sophisticated hairstyle and grown-up clothes. When she was ready, Lily Turner gave her the only singing lesson of her life. She taught her the song, 'What Makes Me Love You As I Do?', and she tried to get her to sing the 'h' in

30

'what'—without success, for Gracie sang 'wot', and after many frustrating attempts she managed 'quat'.

'It'll have to do,' said Lily. 'There's no time to practise any more.' They went down to the Hippodrome, Jenny, a tall seven-year-old child who looked—almost—like a young lady, and Lily Turner.

Gracie tied for first place with two others who were much older, and won 10*s* 6*d*.

After that she took part in many local charity concerts, usually earning herself a tuppenny pork pie or two by the end of the evening. When Lily Turner next had work, she took Gracie Stansfield with her.

To get to the theatre in time they had to catch a bus or train before school finished, and her dad wrote a note for the teacher that day to say she was sick. This became the pattern whenever they were appearing a few miles away, to enable them to leave in time.

At first Grace sat in the gallery, and when Lily had sung her song, she stood up and sang it back to her; but people didn't always realise that this was part of the act, and one day a woman sitting next to Grace thought she was trying to interrupt the performance, and hit her on the head with her umbrella. After that Lily had her protégée on the stage with her.

When Lily Turner left the stage to get married, Grace auditioned for a place with Clara Coverdale's Boys and Girls. There were a lot of juvenile troupes in the theatre in those days—most of Clara Coverdale's were between fourteen and sixteen, and although Grace fitted in for height, she *was* only ten years old. The others resented having such a young child with them, and, on the pretext of teaching her some of the acrobatic dancing which she would have to do, they made certain she wasn't in a fit state to appear the following day.

'They strained the ligaments of my legs and arms,' Gracie said later, 'and bruised my bones—I was in agony and simply wanted to go home. But I knew I had to stick it out—you didn't give in at the first setback, not if you were going to be an actress you didn't.'

Aching, and crying as silently as she could with the pain, Grace sat on the edge of the bed while the three culprits she shared the room with slept. The swellings and stiffness grew worse as the week progressed, and she was sent home without once setting foot on the stage.

Probably Clara Coverdale decided not to accept such a young child again, no matter how promising or keen she was.

Grace's father was for sending her into the mill and forgetting about 'all this theatre nonsense', but her mother won the day. She had dreamed of a stage career practically since she was born, first for herself and then, when that hadn't materialised, for her family. Grace was the eldest—she had talent; you didn't need to be her mother and possibly a bit biased to see *that*. Someday her Grace would be a star.

Jenny Stansfield was a very determined woman-everyone who knew her said that. She wasn't afraid of hard work, and she did it all willingly, sure that at least one of her children would make it; possibly they all would, but there was time enough for the others after she had Grace launched.

The next troupe was called 'Haley's Garden of Girls', and these too were much older—between fourteen and eighteen; Grace still hadn't had her eleventh birthday. Being the youngest, she was the only one who had to go to school each day—a different one in each town they played—and before she could become used to the routine they moved on and she was fitted in somewhere else. It was a lonely life for a little girl, with no time to make friends of her own age at school and considered too young to be included in the theatre group outside working hours.

Because of their extra years the others sent young Grace on all the errands for them. One day, when she took a jug of hot water upstairs to the bedroom, she found the landlady's son in bed with one of the girls. Embarrassed, she turned to go, but fearful she would talk and get them into trouble, the girl leapt from the bed and pounced on her.

'Here,' she shouted to the boy. 'Come on, I'll hold her.'

'Somehow,' Gracie says in her book *Sing As We Go,* 'I scratched and fought myself free and ran in silent terror to my bedroom where I shoved a huge chest of drawers that only my panic gave me the strength to move, in front of the door. I wouldn't let anybody in all night.'

The following morning Mrs Haley got someone to break the door down. Grace was a twitching bundle of nerves with St Vitus Dance. Imagine what that night must have been like! Ten years old, and terrified almost out of her mind, completely alone in an alien place with the horror of what nearly happened...

They took her to Rochdale Children's Convalescent Home at St Anne's on Sea, and slowly she recovered. When she returned home, she went as a halftimer—mornings in the mill and afternoons at school one week, and vice versa the next.

Grace was a cotton winder, but often the other girls minded her frames so she could entertain them. Above the noise of the factory she sang her heart out, and when the overseer was on the way round, they warned her and she went to work again.

On morning shifts she had to be at the mill at six, which meant rising just after five when the knocker-up came tapping at all the bedroom windows in the street with her long pole; then she would have a cup of tea—all her life Gracie enjoyed her cup of tea; then out into the street, wearing clogs because they were sensible footwear on the cobbles, and cheaper than boots, a shawl over her head and shoulders against the early morning cold, and carrying two tin cans, one containing bread and the other tea, for breakfast, which was at eight o'clock.

After three months Grace got the sack. 'My work was being neglected,' she said.

In between local concerts Grace worked in a papermill and as an errand girl. She joined the 'Nine Dainty Dots' for a while, and everyone who remembers her from those days says, 'She was always singing and clowning.' She used to sing, whistle and turn cartwheels at Bob Brierley's cloggers on Milnrow Road and usually had her clogs mended free; and she did her impressions of George Formby (senior) and Gertie Gitana for old Fred when she came in from school or mill.

'Old Fred' was like the man who came to dinner and stayed to tea and supper too.

Originally he came to them for a week while waiting for his relatives to take him to live with them when he could no longer look after himself properly—and he never left. He thought the world of Grace and encouraged her all he could.

It was old Fred who heard that singer Jessie Merrileas, who was comedian Jack Pleasant's wife, was sick and unable to appear at the Hippodrome one night. Jenny went down to the theatre with Grace, and they booked her as a substitute. A hastily printed poster went up on the billboard: 'Tonight—Young Grace Stansfield, Rochdale's Own Girl Vocalist.'

She was paid 35 shillings for that week and was booked for the following one. That was when Jenny insisted on Grace staying at home and looking after the family, while *she* went to the mill. 'That way you're free to take any theatre work that comes along,' she said.

Grace was now thirteen, and the rest of the family consisted of Betty, Edie, three-year-old Tommy, their father and old Fred.

Not many jobs came up. It was a time of great wealth and equally great poverty in Britain. King Edward VII had died the year before, after a lifetime of waiting for his nine years on the throne, and then his son George V reigned with the beautiful, regal-looking

Queen Mary. A census taken in 1911 showed there were 9,171 actresses in the country. What chances against those figures would there be for a skinny thirteen-year-old with no previous theatrical background?

Gracie mothered her family, wrote for auditions, sent her one professionally posed photograph to an agent. It was returned two weeks later cracked through the centre where someone had folded it in half, and scrawled across the bottom were the words, 'Hardly suitable.'

CHAPTER 2

The Touring Years

When Gracie was fourteen she was offered
4 shillings a week with Charburn's Young
Stars. This was another juvenile troupe, and
she had to get to Blackpool to join them. The
fare was 4 shilings—she would not be paid
until she had worked a week—and they
simply did not have the money.

'Dad refused to pay,' Gracie said later.
'He hoped I'd finished with "all that nonsense".'

'Get a job in the mill where tha'll get
regular wage.'

Old Fred came to the rescue; he had no
money in his pocket either, but he had read
in the paper details of a singing competition
in Middleton that evening. Her friend's aunt
went with her and paid the bus fare.

The first prize was 5 shillings and Gracie
won, but the audience would have none of it.

'She's not a Middleton girl,' they shouted.
The judge gave her the second prize of
2s 6d. 'No, she's from Rochdale.' He made
another effort with the third prize of a shil-

ling, but to no avail: the few miles between the towns were an insurmountable boundary.

'It was hard not to cry,' Gracie said later, 'but I wasn't going to let them have the satisfaction of seeing that.'

On the way out the judge caught them up and, diving his hand into his pocket, gave Gracie 5 shillings.

'You should have had the first prize—you *won* it, Middleton girl or not,' he said.

That is when Grace Stansfield became Gracie Fields. Many people claimed the idea as their own, but Gracie said it was on the advice of a theatrical manager who said her real name was too long. Her mother played around with several possibilities, eventually settling for Gracie Fields.

She stayed with the Charburn troupe for almost two years, and in that time she danced, sang and acted in the comedy sketches. The 4 shillings a week were increased to eight, most of which she sent home to her mother, along with the notices from each town they played. As Gracie had a good mention in every one, Jenny decided that the time had come for her to branch out on her own.

She found work where she could, but it was sparse; she filled in with errand-girl jobs, anything which would bring in a few more pennies, and Jenny argued fiercely against her going back to the mill whenever it was mentioned, which was often, as more months went by without her finding regular theatre work.

Then Mr Ernest Dotteridge in the Palace in Oldham booked her for a week. She was fine until the last night, when she had a different song to sing. She forgot to tell the band, who played the old one while she sang the new. Anyone who had heard Gracie do this routine since will know how funny it can be when she argues with the conductor, finishing by saying, 'I'll win, you'll see,' and overriding, almost drowning the band with her powerful voice. But that first time wasn't a routine—it was real, and the manager dropped the curtain on her.

Ernest Dotteridge was generous. He wrote, saying, 'We must not condemn a good week for one bad performance. I can offer you a season with Cousin Freddy's Pierrot Concert Party at St Anne's on Sea.'

Gracie was reluctant to accept because she had set herself a target of £5 a week, and this was three. Also she had indulged in some childish showing-off when she was at St Anne's in the convalescent home a few years before—telling the staff how big she was going to be once she got back to work.'

Jenny looked aghast when Gracie questioned it. 'We need the money—£3 is better than nowt,' she said. 'You'll go to concert party.'

It was valuable training for Gracie because that was really where she discovered how good she was as a comedienne, and how to enjoy it.

Fred Hutchins was the man who developed her comic talent in the beginning. Gracie said he taught her three important lessons. Not to mind being laughed at; to be a generous performer; and timing.

In the first show she did with him, she had to ad-lib until he touched her with his 'magic' wand, when she had to freeze and become like a statue. She was so good he let her carry on, and never used his 'magic' wand at all.

She had one season with Freddy and his Pierrots, then she was back home and looking for work again.

At pantomime time she landed a small part. It wasn't a happy show, and when she had an enormous success with one of the songs, the principal boy objected and it was taken out. Fred Stansfield had an accident at work and was in hospital, and Gracie knew she had to stick it out and send home what money she could.

There was a show on Boxing Day, so Jenny sent Betty to spend Christmas with Gracie as they could not all be together.

'It was a terrible Christmas,' Gracie

remembered years afterwards. 'Dad was very ill, mum desperately worried over everything but determined we should all carry on; I was homesick, miserable with the pantomime, hurt by the jealousy that abounded each time I had a song, then to put the finishing touches Betty and I bought two oranges as a special treat for Christmas afternoon—we picked out two of the largest ones we could find—and they were as bitter and sour as the rest of that horrible Christmas. They turned out to be not oranges at all but grapefruit.'

When the pantomime finished, Gracie was out of work again. Her father was still in hospital, and even old Fred was poorly. They broke up boxes the greengrocer gave them for firewood, and huddled round the warmth in the evenings, longing for the warmer weather, but more than anything praying for something to turn up. Nothing did, and Gracie resigned herself to going back to the mill, if she could get 'set on'.

Then old Fred was taken bad and had to go to hospital. He had pneumonia and died a few days later. In an envelope with Jenny's name on was his will. He'd left her £100, his insurance money. 'Tha knows best how to spend it,' he'd written on the accompanying note.

When she had paid for the funeral, settled the debts and stocked up the larder, Jenny took Gracie to a Manchester studio to learn extra tap-dancing steps, for she knew she would need every bit of stagecraft she could get, to succeed. The instructor was Corlette, and his fee was 2s 6d for thirty minutes. Gracie had six weeks, and in that time she learnt the basis of all the dancing and acrobatics she was to do later in her films.

She did the rounds of agents again—a week's booking here, another there, still nothing regular. Her father came out of hospital, and then Mr Percy Hall, a Manchester agent, offered her a six-week engagement, with an option for ten years at no less then £5 a week, and if she earned more, the balance to be divided between them.

From the beginning of the First World War in 1914, Gracie sang to the soldiers, the wounded in hospitals in the area, and the refugees who were housed in some of the larger places nearby. With a friend, Marion Greenwood, who belonged to Jackson Troupe, she went one evening to entertain Belgian refugees at a big house just outside Rochdale. She met Nell Whitwell there, and the two young girls became friends.

Nell's father was a freemason, and when there was any entertaining needed for a masonic party, Gracie was usually part of it. One day she was playing the piano and singing to a group of elderly people, and a lady who was using an ear-trumpet crept nearer and nearer to the piano. When she was so close that Gracie could feel her breath on her cheek, she turned and blew down the ear-trumpet. The woman heard that all right— she almost hit the ceiling! Gracie was naturally impulsive, and on stage, be it at the church hall or the Palladium, she lost the shyness that plagued her offstage and was game for anything.

She often stayed at Nell's home in those days, and she became fond of her whole family, as they did of her.

'Only once was I ashamed to be with her—in fact I pretended I wasn't,' Nell told me. 'That was when she had to telephone her agent in Manchester. I didn't realise that Grace had never used a telephone before, and we went together to the old post office in Rochdale. The boxes were all down the side, and I went to buy stamps whiles she was phoning. Suddenly I heard this voice, terrifically loud it was, shouting into the instrument. Her agent must have told her to speak quietly, for she stopped so quickly, but everyone in the post office had turned to look at her.'

Years later Gracie remembered that incident when she wrote to Teddy Holmes, her friend and often her pianist. It was after the 1954 radio show she did:

'Nice to know that the Christmas Radio Show wasn't too bad. I certainly felt I did a lot of screaming, much too much now that it's over. It's like the first time I ever did any telephoning—I made such a noise I could be heard from Capri to Rochdale, and I guess I made as much noise this time as that first 'phone call. For this I am sorry if I deafened you.'

The memory of that first telephone call obviously stayed with Gracie. 'She was very hurt at the time,' Nell said. 'She went quiet and she looked so—so vulnerable.'

Gracie went on singing, to refugees, to the wounded in hospitals, and on the music halls. Sandy Powell recalled working with her at a little cinema at West Houghton, near Bolton.

'I think it was called The Electric Palace. Gracie was nearly sixteen and I was thirteen. I remember that there was great excitement one night because word got round that an agent was out front. It was Percy Hall, and he came round afterwards and booked Gracie...'

The Stansfields were living in Whatmough Street by then. They were still moving around.

'I reckon I lived in nearly every street in the town during those early years,' said Gracie later.

Once she was working fairly regularly, Gracie fulfilled one of her ambitions and bought a travelling basket. She was very proud of this. It was kept in the hall and was always neat and tidy. It was a habit she never lost—folding her clothes and keeping everything orderly.

She was full of energy and enthusiasm for the theatre and taught Edie and her young brother Tommy the latest song-and-dance routines. They were still at school, but, with a borrowed straw hat and walking-stick for a cane, Gracie had them doing, 'Tell Me, Pretty Maiden, Are There Any More At Home Like You...'. She was very severe, making them practise until they had it exactly right.

When Percy Hall procured her an audition for a revue, *Yes, I Think So*. Gracie was overjoyed. She got the part—regular work at last, or it would be if the show did well.

The revue's comedian was called Archie Pitt: but Gracie didn't think he was funny on stage, and she felt in awe of him off. He was bossy, and, although she didn't *have* to take notice of what he thought and said about her act, it was difficult not to listen because he was so absolutely engrossed in the mechanics of the theatre.

While *Yes, I Think So* was touring the

Manchester area, Jenny had arranged for Gracie to lodge with people she knew through mutual friends. They were cheap digs, but they were three miles from the theatre, and Gracie walked each way to save money on tram fares. Archie persisted in questioning her as to why she was staying so far out and never believed her answers that she was with friends.

'It's false economy to try to save on cheap lodgings,' he told her. 'I'll fix you in with me when we move to Preston.'

Even though she was away from home quite a lot touring, Gracie was still very much under her mother's influence. One morning, while she was working in Manchester, she went into Rochdale and called on her friend Nell Whitwell. She was playing the piano and singing, for the sheer enjoyment of it, when Mrs Stansfield came to invite Nell and her mother to the rehearsal in Manchester that afternoon. On seeing Gracie there, she walked straight over and gave her a back-hander that almost knocked her off the piano stool.

'You should be rehearsing, not mucking about here—get back to the theatre this minute,' she said.

Gracie went home most weekends, unless she was working too far away, and Jenny would make her impersonate the stars she had been working with—this time for the neighbours to hear. Imitations came easily to her, and she was amazed to find that people had been on the bill with two years previously hadn't changed.

'They paused for breath in exactly the same place, never altered their phrasing....'

She decided that when she became a star she would change it. 'If somebody was mimicking me, I'd do something else. I wouldn't be stuck—would never give exactly the same rendering....'

Yes I Think So toured for eighteen months; Gracie celebrated her sixteenth birthday with that show and tasted champagne for the first time in her life. Archie bought it for the party he gave to the cast, and Gracie asked everyone present to sign her autograph book. Archie wrote: 'To Cracie Fields; one day you are going to be a big star.'

Her name on the posters and billboards was in very small print, but she did well in the show—so well with her songs that there was jealousy among some of the others, and the manager would take away any song that proved too successful and give her a new one to work on.

'It was good experience,' Gracie said later. 'It taught me how to turn a mediocre song into a good one with vocal acrobatics, although at the time I didn't always think that way.'

When the tour ended, Percy Hall had another revue lined up for Gracie Fields, but Archie wanted her to join the company he was about to launch. Jenny thought this would be a good idea too. She never found Archie a great comedian, and she told him so, but she recognised his flair for managing.

Gracie, the least keen of all, produced her trump card—her contract with Mr Hall, but Archie wasn't worried over that. 'I can deal with him,' he said. He bought Gracie's contract for £12, which at that time he didn't even have in hard cash. He made an agreement to pay the money in instalments once he had his own show on the road. If he could be as persuasive as that with an agent, what chance did seventeen-year-old Gracie stand? Especially as her mother, who was the other dominant force in her life then, approved wholeheartedly.

Jenny and Archie didn't like each other much, but they had one strong ambition in common—getting Gracie to the top. That she had the talent to reach the highest rung of the theatrical ladder neither doubted, and they knew also that she would work; what they had to chance were the breaks every performer needs.

'Right,' Archie told Gracie. 'It's fixed. Your mother approves, and I've got your contract from Hall; we're in this new show together now.'

Gracie held out her hand. 'It's a bargain,' she said, and that was the only business contract they ever had. No papers were signed, there were no rules or conditions. A handshake sealed their partnership for a show as then only half written.

'That's what we'll call it,' Archie said triumphantly, *'It's A Bargain.'* Archie's brothers joined them in this show. There were three of them—Bert, Pat and Edgar, and although their name was Selinger, Archie had changed his to Pitt, and the other three to Aza, which was the trade-name of a manufacturer whose cloth they advertised in their stage suits.

They started off in *It's A Bargain* as 'The Three Aza Brothers', doing a comedy act, but this was altered fairly soon afterwards to two. Bert Aza became the company's manager and later went on to manage Gracie's professional life until he died in 1953, when his wife, Lillian, took over. Edgar died in 1970, and Pat lived well into his nineties.

Mona Frewer, who had been in *Yes, I Think So* with them, came into *It's A Bargain* as leading lady, with Gracie as second lead. It was Mona who, watching Gracie from the wings as she mimicked

Charlie Chaplin, went for her when she came off to thunderous applause.

'Any monkey can do imitations—that's just stealing other people's material.'

Shocked and hurt at the vehemence of the words, Gracie gave up doing her impressions on stage from that night.

'Gracie was easily deflated,' Lillian Aza said. 'Even when she had been at the top for years, a million people could tell her she was wonderful, but if one person said she wasn't, *that* was the one she listened to.'

Gracie liked Mona Frewer. 'I understood how she felt,' she said. 'I'd have felt the same in her shoes, because Archie had cut *her* number to let me do the Chaplin impression. I'd worked hard to get it right, but I never did it again, not on stage, anyway.'

In later years, offstage, Gracie was a great imitator and could probably have earned her living in a one-woman 'Mike Yarwood' type show.

It's A Bargain ran for 2½ years, and, as they became old enough, both Gracie's sisters joined the show. They were a talented family and had been brought up with the idea of showbusiness as a career. Jenny was ambitious to better them all—if it had not been the theatre, she would probably have still tried to get them away from working in the mill, which would have earned them a lot of

51

money in those days. With her own theatrical dreams and her family's undoubted talent, she never needed to look elsewhere for a different career for them.

It's A Bargain went into theatres and halls all over the country. It tested the dedication of its performers to the utmost, because often Bert Aza went ahead to the next town they were playing to get an advance on their salary to enable them to pay the company's fares to their destination.

In his book *Our Gracie,* he tells of the 'deathtrap theatres, draughty, ill lit and insanitary dressing rooms, fire buckets for washbasins, interminable Sunday journeys, scratch meals and dingy lodgings,' and of halls without pianos, let alone bands—and houses with twenty people in front. Gracie learnt her craft touring with these shows. Bert Aza says in his book, 'Gracie was superb in these romps, and her natural flair for burlesque had plenty of scope.'

In a letter written in 1917 to Doris Paul, who had left the show the year before to be married, Gracie said, 'We are working such terrible places, they make one feel very miserable. Thank goodness we have better work coming in.'

It was at this period that Gracie began wearing clothes with a Scottish flavour.

'We have been out shopping all day,' she

reveals in the letter to Doris. 'I'm going in for Scotch outdoor things, looks good—nice Tammy and socks, and a nice Scotch coat....'

Mona Frewer left the cast through ill health, and Gracie, who had often taken Mona's part as well as her own on days when Mona was too ill to play, became the leading lady.

Halfway through the run Annie Lipman joined the show as a chorus girl. She was really a musician, but as they didn't have an orchestra to conduct at that time—all taking turns at playing the piano when they were not on stage—she turned her hand to anything that needed doing. One of her greatest assets was her enthusiasm. They all needed this, especially on the bad days. She and Gracie became friends, and Gracie took her when she visited her own pals around the north.

Archie Pitt was Jewish. He had tried several careers, as a shop assistant, a commercial traveller, then he began entertaining in the pubs in London, going on to working men's clubs up north. He realised he would not make a fortune in that line, and he became interested in the theatre—he recognised talent in the raw, and in Gracie he saw the beginnings of something very big, and he had the courage to foster it.

Clarkson Rose, that inimitable man of the theatre, and great, great pantomime Dame, says in his book, *With A Twinkle In My Eye,* 'Mr Archie Pitt observed many of the old-world courtesies. If he went to a show and saw an artiste that he would like to book, he would not communicate with the artiste until he had first contacted the artiste's employer. In several instances he booked artistes from *Twinkle*, and always paid me this courtesy.

'In management he had high ideals. He studied the welfare of his people quite outside the ordinary managerial spheres. He had a savings scheme for his companies in which he encouraged thrift, and made tangible contributions to that thrift himself. His companies were run with discipline and law and order that was refreshing.'

In later years Gracie's view of Archie was obviously and naturally coloured by their unhappy marriage, but she always acknowledged that he had channelled her talent in the right direction.

'He took over where my mother left off,' she said, 'and he did it with her full approval. I was young, pliable, and very used to doing as I was told at that time.'

When *It's A Bargain* finished, another revue written by Archie, called '*Mr Tower of London*', began.

54

CHAPTER 3

Mr Tower of London

Mr Tower of London was an incredible show. Gracie said that in the beginning it was poor, but thay all worked on it. It became famous and ran for nine years. In 1918, when it started, the Great War was almost over, but there was no money about and the country was till in a state of depression. The 'fit land for heroes', which never quite materialised, was talked about with optimism by the politicians and scepticism by the people. *'Mr Tower'* started life at the Coliseum, Long Eaton, Nottingham, on 28 October.

It toured the country, playing in whatever theatre or hall would book it, and they improved it as they went. The company travelled thousands of miles with that show, and it was estimated that seven million people saw it.

Mr Tower was a revue which starred Gracie, and in its cast were most of the Pitt and Fields families, Archie was the boss, 'the guvnor' they all called him later, but during the *It's A Bargain* and *Mr Tower* days, it was

'Daddy Pitts'. He signed photographs to the cast as this, and referred to the girls as his daughters. Bert was the business manager, and he and Archie were the ideas men, but it was Gracie who carried them out, often with Annie Lipman's help. She did most of the training for the show, drilling the chorus girls and getting the whole thing shipshape.

Gracie sang a lot of songs, and took part in numerous sketches. In one of these she had on a short frilly apron. Gracie was quite a tall lady, and she was laying the table and singing; she was also doing crazy acrobatics with her legs, hoisting them in and out, putting one behind her then suddenly giving a funny little kick with it. Her long, thin legs were sometimes a source of embarrassment to her, so she turned them to her advantage in the sketches by using them to make people laugh. She sang as she moved about the stage;

There's no-one like mother to me,
No matter how good she may be,
I fly over the land and the sea'
There's no-one like mother to me.

The audience rolled about laughing at her antics. Another sketch involved Gracie and company being locked in the chamber of horrors at the waxworks. Yet another scene took place on top of a bus, and, to keep it fresh and the others on their toes, Gracie often ad-libbed.

When they were playing in Rochdale, she asked Nell Whitwell if she would be a passenger on the bus. At that time Nell had been out a few times with a man called Bob, whom they all knew, and in the middle of the bus scene Gracie said 'Cos our Nell's courting Uncle Bob, y'know. She's a bonny lass—Uncle Bob thinks so anyway.'

Another sketch took place in a courtroom. Archie was the judge, and one night, when he asked the name of the prisoner, she said, 'Tom Whitwell' (this was Nell's father), and the cast had to follow through with this name to keep it sounding right.

She often did this, bringing her local friends into the act, and sometimes she would mimic Nell on the stage, especially about how she was at getting up in the mornings when she was not feeling her brightest. Gracie knew this because, before the touring days, when she was still living in Rochdale, she had often stayed at Nell's house after the theatre, and they slept in Nell's bedroom and talked until the small hours.

She had great reserves of dynamic energy —Nell said that after two shows a night, and often a matinée too, Gracie would come in and leap right across the bedposts—she seldom got into bed by the normal method.

Gracie used to say she inherited her vitality from her mother, and anyway she 'couldn't ever do nowt'.

Certainly she was always working, and, as the show began to make money, she bought black silk material in the market very cheaply and made underwear for herself and the chorus girls. She used to embroider red roses onto the panties and slips to make them beautiful and more exotic-looking, and the girls loved them.

She liked dressmaking and sometimes said that if she hadn't been on the stage she would have enjoyed being a dress designer. (Many years later she did design the stage clothes for some of her tours.) When *Mr Tower* eventually went into the West End, it was Gracie and her sisters who made new dresses and hats for the show (under the collective name of Madame Roberts), because she thought theirs were too shabby for the Alhambra after all the touring years.

'They were wonderful days,' she said later. 'We would rehearse in the mornings, then back to the digs for lunch, which we had already bought and taken into the landlady to cook. Then the afternoon was free. Most of the girls went to the pictures, but I nearly always used to go on the tram as far as it would take me. Usually the trams ran into the country and I loved it. I'd breathe in all the lovely fresh air, then back on the tram and get ready for the show in the evening.'

Her young brother Tommy, joined the company when he was thirteen, and one of his tasks was to sell Gracie's photograph to the audience for a penny a copy. In many of these photographs she has her hair styled in 'earphones', which were very fashionable during that period.

She bought Tommy his first pair of long trousers when he joined *Mr Tower of London*. They were playing in Bolton, and she took him to a tailor there and had him try on top hat, tails, the whole outfit.

'You look really smart,' she said, 'Like Fred Astaire.' Tommy worked with Gracie many times, long after Betty and Edie had given up showbusiness and were concentrating on their own families.

They toured the British Isles. 'All the geography I never learnt at school I caught up with during that show,' Gracie said.

When they were in Ireland, so many people could not buy tickets that they started knocking the door down to get in. On hearing the pandemonium from her dressing-room, Gracie opened the window to see what it was about. When she knew, she said, 'Don't worry, I'll give an extra show on Saturday afternoon. Listen, when this house goes in, you can book for it. Just tell the management you want tickets for a matinée on Saturday and I'll be there.' Already she knew that it was *her* audience.

Gracie had many funny stories about *Mr Tower of London*—not surprisingly, for she played in over four thousand performances. One, which she told in her book, *Sing As We Go,* is about the 9 a.m. show they put on for miners coming off the night shift. They did a show at *any* time if there was a paying audience for it.

'I was so tired,' she says, 'that when I saw rows of sooty faces turned up to me, their smiles gleaming white in contrast when they laughed, I staggered off into the wings and said to Archie, "How ever did you manage to get so many chimney sweeps at this hour of the morning?" '

When they were touring and had to make the often long train journeys from one town to another each Sunday, they met the other companies, all of them dressed up to the nines to let each other see how well they were doing. Often they would settle down in the carriage and play cards. Gracie knew only one game—pontoon, and she always won.

'She was terribly lucky with cards,' Tommy said. 'She'd start to play, then take over the bank and win all the way. When she had taken everyone's money, she used to lay it all over the table and say "I've had enough now—share it amongst you, I'm going to have a rest." '

Mr Tower of London moved from Selby in Yorkshire to the Queen's Theatre in Poplar, London, during the railway strike of 1919, so the company travelled with all their props on the back of a lorry. It was cold and foggy, and it became colder and foggier as the day wore on. The driver lost his way more than once. (They hadn't been able to travel on the Sunday for the simple reason they could not obtain transport until early Monday morning, or they would not have cut it so fine.) It was past five o'clock in the evening when they finally arrived, cold, tired but triumphant—to find that the manager of the Queen's had engaged another revue because he thought they weren't going to make it! However, they *had* made it, after a particularly gruelling journey, and in one hour they had to offload and be ready. They were ready, and the applause pushed the memory of the nightmare two-hundred-mile foggy ride into the 'put it down to experience' category for them.'

Night after night, as Gracie had them rolling in the aisles with her comedy and brushing tears from their eyes with her songs, managers and agents came along to see this girl who had caught the public's imagination with her work. One of them, Archie Parnell

61

(his brother Val Parnell later became manager of the London Palladium and a good friend of Gracie's), offered her £100 a week, then £200—she was earning about £28 a week at that time because all the profits were being ploughed back into the business. But it was only her he wanted, not the entire show.

'It was tempting,' Gracie said later, 'but there were the others to think about. It was a family show really, we were all in it, Edie, Betty, Tommy, Bert, Archie, Annie Lipman...I wasn't sure if after all these years being with the company, I'd be any good on my own again.'

The show went on and on and on...It made money—after all the struggling years when Bert and Archie had accepted bookings in the worst theatres in town (and in those days there were a lot of very rough ones) on a percentage of the profits. When they had worked unceasingly, and believed completely in the ultimate success of the company, they were proved right. But it was Gracie the people wanted to see and hear. It was that liquid voice which soared so effortlessly up and up and up, taking you with it until you were floating somewhere above ordinary life, somewhere among the gold and silver of the universe, that they came to applaud.

In those days Gracie's ambition was to get

£200 in the bank for her mother, then get married, have a family and settle down to a home life of her own. In her autobiography Gracie says of her marriage to Archie, *Mr Tower of London* was in its fourth year of touring. In its fifth year I married Archie Pitt. Archie insisted.'

It is a sad little statement, and although those last two words may *sound* incredible, when you remember that for nine years, since she was sixteen in fact, Gracie had been used to doing as Archie told her, it is not surprising.

She said no at first, because she didn't love him, and she knew he didn't love her; and she went on saying no for many months. She met few men outside her work. There had been a brief romance with the brother of a friend, but mostly life had been all theatre since she was a child, or very nearly so, and she was used to Archie. Sometimes a little afraid of him, but used to him. Ever since that attempted rape when she was ten years old, Gracie had felt wary of men, and to a certain extent Archie was the known quantity.

He told her he was afraid she would marry someone quite unsuitable and ruin all they had worked for. Her mother was pleased; her father said, 'It's up to you, lass.' Years later she told Florence Desmond, 'I wasn't in love with Archie, but he was the boss and I was afraid if I didn't marry him he'd give me the sack—and I had all the family to keep.'

Gracie was a strong character, but she didn't like fights. It went even further than that—sometimes she simply could not bear fights. Lillian Aza has said that she considers Gracie *always* let the men in her life dictate to her, and she knew Gracie for over sixty years. Gracie herself, when talking of that marriage, compared it to 'a black existence—the whole thing is like a black hole.'

When asked outright in an interview why she married Archie Pitt, she said, 'Because I didn't know anything else. I'm—perhaps I'm a bit sloppy. It sounds silly to say it, especially to everybody who seems so able to stand on their own feet. My mother could, yet I can't bear anybody arguing over any thing. They all said, "It's perfect—wonderful." It was just one of those things that happened. My mother didn't *tell* me to do it—we all have free will, but it turned out badly for both of us.'

Although she was twenty-five, Gracie was fairly naïve in those days. Life was mostly work, and the goal towards which everyone seemed to be pushing her was stardom. She wanted this herself—by that time she was more ambitious—but she wanted other things too, and a home and family of her own were high up on the list.

Whatever finally induced Gracie to marry Archie, neither of them ever pretended that it was the love-match of the century.

The ceremony took place at a register office in Clapham in April 1923. Archie was forty-three, eighteen years older than his bride.

Life went on much the same after they were married as it had beforre. Gracie still drilled the girls, and now that they were making more money she often hired a coach and took them all out into the country for a picnic. She bought cricket sets and footballs and packed several hampers with food. After rehearsing they settled down to enjoy the rest of the day in the fresh air, and Gracie's voice rang joyously across the fields or murmured gently as she wandered under the trees.

Irene, Archie'd daughter by his first marriage, was about seven then.

'When my father told me he was going to marry again, I said—"Are you marrying Auntie Gracie?" '

Irene was pleased—she spent holidays from school touring with the company, and a few years later, when she was old enough, she appeared with them.

Eighteen months after Gracie and Archie's marriage, Sir Oswald Stoll booked *Mr Tower of London* for the Alhambra Theatre, Leicester Square, to fill in a spare week.

The Alhambra stood (it was demolished in 1936) where the Odeon Cinema is now. In 1925 it was one of the leading theatres in London and had seen George Robey and Violet Loraine in *The Bing Boys Are Here* and *The Bing Boys On Broadway* and had staged ballets, variety, revue and opera. In 1925 and 1926 it was also the theatre chosen for the Royal Command Performance.

To the *Mr Tower of London* company, a booking for the Alhambra seemed like heaven. Practical Gracie looked at the stage, then at their ten chorus girls, and decided they needed more.

'We can only afford two more,' Archie told her grudgingly.

'All right, two more, and we'll spread 'em out a bit,' she agreed. It was for this West End début that she recostumed the show, but it was the same show they had put on throughout the country. Archie wrote new sketches from time to time, and they introduced topical items, but that was all.

They were nervous on the first night of the Alhambra opening—all of them. Gracie tried to keep them calm, but it wasn't easy. When Evelyn Laye sent her a good-luck telegram, she said it nearly finished her: '...After all Evelyn Laye was a big star.' All her life Gracie thought there were brighter stars than herself—this wasn't a put-on act; she knew her own worth, yet found it difficult to accept.

'I always knew I had more, much more than most,' she said once in an interview with the BBC when asked if she had known she would go so far.

On that night in 1925 she came down a stairway on the stage of the Alhambra behind a huge white fan, opened her mouth and poured forth notes that sent shivers along the spines of those present.

The reviews in the following day's papers confirmed what the provinces had known— as Gracie humorously said many years later, 'They proclaimed me a star!'

The cash really started to roll in then, and Archie launched several companies which he sent out on tour, one with Betty Fields, who was a tremendously talented artiste too but who later left the stage and did excellent sculpturing work and also patented many of her own inventions; one with Edie and Duggie Wakefield, the man Edie had married, and yet another with Tommy. Gracie stayed in London, enchanting audiences twice nightly.

Jenny and Fred Stansfield had moved to Islington a few months before, when Fred was offered a job there. He had been reluctant to accept, but Jenny encouraged him.

'After all they are all working more that

way now than up north. It will be a good base for the family,' she said.

Although Gracie and Archie were married, they had no home of their own—they lodged with the rest of the company as they always had done, and the Stansfields' house was still home to them all, wherever it was.

CHAPTER 4

The Hectic Years

James Agate said of *Mr Tower of London*
at the Alhambra, 'If some impresario doesn't
snap her up quickly Miss Gracie Fields will
go back to the provinces where they know
her worth, and London will be the loser.'

Life changed rapidly. There was still hard
work, but now it was earning very substantial cash for the Fields and Pitt families.
Gracie's Auntie Margaret, who was really a
second cousin of her mother's, came to be
her dresser.

Everyone, it seemed, wanted to meet
Gracie Fields. Archie loved the fame, but
Gracie was frightened. She had worked for
this since she was a child entering the competition at the Rochdale Hippodrome; for
years she and her family had dreamed of the
day when they would play the top theatres
in the land. What came next?

Every night the audience, wherever she
was appearing, clapped and cheered, and she
was terrified in case she could not live up
to their expectations. Yet the moment she

walked onto the stage, *any* stage, she knew she could. It was offstage she was scared.

'I've never done a show when I haven't been a bundle of nerves and a bunch of butterflies,' she said later. 'I somehow think I put as much nervous energy into the bit before the show as I do when I'm out there in front.'

Her husband had no such qualms. He was supremely certain they could keep this up. Now that she was more in the public eye than ever before, Gracie became nervous of doing the wrong thing. Archie took it all in his stride, but she needed longer to adjust to such a different lifestyle. When, on Archie's orders, she had a chauffeur-driven car to take her to the theatre, she would send the driver home afterwards because she didn't like to spoil his evening.

Gracie said there were four beings of tre-mendous importance in her childhood. 'God, the King and Queen, and the Mayor of Rochdale, in that order.'

When *Sir* Gerald du Maurier sent an engraved calling card to her dressing room with a request to see her, she wasn't sure of his ranking. Not that she ever treated people differently from each other—she gave her attention to dustmen and dukes, chars and countesses, but she did like to create the right impression and get it neat and tidy in her

70

mind.

Sir Gerald asked her if she would play 'Lady Weir' in *S.O.S.*, his next play to be put on at the St James Theatre. She told him she would need to think about it: she was a music hall artiste and, tempting as the offer was, she didn't feel sure.

He sent her the part to read, and she said yes. Archie, Bert, her mother, they were all worried—here she was, one of the biggest names now in music hall, accepting a part in a straight play. But it worked. Whatever reason Sir Gerald du Maurier had for asking Gracie Fields to play opposite him (and some said it was a gimmick), she did him proud.

It wasn't a long part—in fact she 'died' in the first act—but Gracie proved herself a competent actress.

Her fans went to see the play because of her—many leaving after the first act and following her to her next venues. This, while being both complimentary and embarrassing to Gracie—'It's a bit rude,' she said—also made it more difficult to judge the audience's reaction to her as an actress.

Gerald du Maurier, one of the last of the actor-managers, was fifty-five then but still with the image of a matinée idol. He usually fell in love with his leading lady, and Gracie was no exception. The first time he kissed her, after she had dined with him and his family at Cannon Hall in Hampstead, she said, 'Don't be soft, lad, you're older than me dad.'

'He got used to me,' she said later, 'but I didn't understand then how sensitive he was about the loss of youth—and anyway, even if I had, it didn't seem right when I'd accepted the hospitality of the family.'

Gerald du Maurier took Gracie out to lunch every week and bought her flowers and little gifts, and they became very fond of each other. She understood that his attentions to other women never detracted from his love for his wife, and she enjoyed the romance of being entertained by a man whom half of London were falling over themselves to know.

He was so very different from most of the men she had met up till then—suave, debonair and yet with a devastating passion for practical jokes that belied his image. He played one on her: suddenly throwing onto the table a box from a very well-known jeweller, 'Wear it for me,' he said, and as she opened it, 'It only cost £700...' Without looking further, Gracie slapped him round the face—hard. It says much for both their senses of humour that, when she realised that it was a fake—a mock-up diamond ring costing less then a pound—she laughed with him, and they stayed good friends.

Because she was on stage only during the

first act of *S.O.S.*, Gracie went on to play the second-house music hall at the Alhambra, and then a late-night cabaret a the Café Royal. She was paid £100 for *S.O.S.*, £200 for her Alhambra appearance and £300 for the Café Royal Show.

At the Café Royal she met Noël Coward (he told her to get rid of the 'kiss curl' in her hairstyle), Beatrice Lillie (forty years on, she along with Cilla Black, persuaded Gracie to accept a booking at Batley when she was seventy) and writers and artists—including Augustus John, whose studio in St John's Wood she eventually bought.

Although everything Gracie touched in the theatre now seemed to succeed beyond everyone's wildest dreams, her private life was very unhappy. She and Archie, never madly in love, had less in common now—success had driven them further apart.

'We reacted to it in such different ways,' Gracie said. 'Archie lapped it up like a kitten with a saucer of cream. He was at home with it and I wasn't. That was the great difference between us. If we had been happy together maybe we could have ironed it all out, but we weren't, and never had been. We shouldn't have married really—we were totally wrong for each other.'

Archie bought a plot of land in Bishop's Avenue, Hampstead, and had a house built

73

there. He called it 'the Tower' after the show which had been the turning-point for them professionally. It had twenty-eight rooms, a bathroom for every bedroom, a huge ball-room, a lift and a staircase fit for a palace. Archie loved it, and Gracie hated it.

'The only place then that seemed like home was the middle of a stage,' she said.

Archie liked monkeys. 'He had what almost amounted to a passion for monkeys,' his daughter Irene told me. He always had one about the place wherever he lived; it had the run of the house, sat to table and ate with them. In the Tower Archie had several, which had the freedom of the large garden too, and he also had his parrot, Mac, who had been part of the household for years.

Annie Lipman moved into the Tower with them, and, although it was Gracie who posed with Archie for the publicity photographs, it was Annie who shared his life.

Now the Musical Director for Pitt Productions, Annie was small, dark-haired and as hard a worker as any of them. She enjoyed the opulence of the Tower and wasn't over-awed by any of it. Gracie was. All her life she did things for herself: if an ashtray needed emptying, she did it; if something needed making, putting away, scrubbing out, and she was there, she got on with the job. The servants who shooed her out of the kit-

74

chen, the butler who hovered over her, the housekeeper who said she was really a Russian princess, terrified Gracie. 'I feel a bit like a real life Cinderella,' she said. Amid all the splendour she turned her sitting-room into a small retreat with furnishings which reflected her love for homy, comfortable surroundings and bright cheery colours.'

Home Chat, one of the leading magazines of the day, ran a feature on Gracie's new house—'The last thing the Tower reminds me of is a *home,'* Gracie said privately.

Two paragraphs seem significant in that account now. First, the description of Gracie's bedroom: 'Really adorable it was— a tiny room (compared to most of the others), furnished in a French style, of the Pompadour period. Green and gold taffeta curtains and bedspread, beautifully embroidered in pastel shades. Then a truly feminine dressing table painted in gold with a triple mirror to match. Softly shaded silk lamp shades in shell pink completed this pretty picture.'

The other telling paragraph is this: 'When I asked Gracie Fields how she liked her new house, she said, "Of course I love it. It's beautiful", and then, her inimitable humour sparkled and she added, "but the sad thing is, after all you can only live in one room at a time!" '

Was she remembering all the little houses of her childhood, the three in a bed and the parlour where you were all together? She didn't want to live like that again, but this was too far in the other direction. Yet she was trapped—trapped in marriage to a man she didn't love, and trapped with an 'image' —a word she disliked—which was only one aspect of her many-sided character.

She needed people—all her life Gracie *needed* human contact—sometimes she *had* to get away before it overwhelmed her, but never for long. 'People Who Need People' was a song she often sang later in her career —it was true for Gracie.

Sometimes she returned from the theatre at night and went into the staff sitting-room to perch on the arm of a chair and chat. The ostentatiousness of the Tower was too much for her to accept when she was so unhappy, but she could unwind after the show with folk who were in tune with her, whether they were rich or poor, beautiful or ugly, just as long as they *cared*.

Right from the start Gracie had a tremendous affinity with the human race. Most of us have our own small circle—she reached millions. Probably the part of her that did this would have done so even if she had not been in show-business. She said once, half jokingly, half seriously, 'I used to think I'd be a missionary....'

She wanted to help people, but without intruding, and because of her singing she was able to do this. In a letter to her friend Wally Singer in the 1960s, about not being an opera singer, she says, 'Maybe it's best, I think, possibly I've given more happiness, more fun, and had more myself this way....'

During the thirties she topped the bill at every leading theatre in the country. She laid foundation stones, opened theatres, stores and cinemas, and people flocked to watch. In her professional life it seemed she simply could not go wrong. She brought her own happy-go-lucky style to these ceremonies, kneeling to lay foundation stones and smooth them in properly, pretending to lick the cement from the trowel ice-cream fashion —'Got to make a good job of it!'—climbing the scaffolding with the workmen and singing to the huge crowds who always gathered where she was.

Extra police were drafted into the area when Gracie Fields was there officially, to control the usually good-natured crowds who waited hours for a glimpse of her. People *expected* her to play the fool, and, as she often said, 'You can't disappoint the customers.'

She was 'a natural' but in that period of her life she probably felt less like being funny than at any other.

'Because it was of my own making you see. I had all this wealth, all this glory, yet I was so very unhappy; and that seemed wrong when there were so many folk who had much greater cause to be than I did.'

So she carried on clowning and singing and found in her work the solace of a job well done, the warmth of a relationship with not one but thousands of people at a time—her audiences.

1928 was a year for firsts: first straight part, first commercial record cut (she had made some in 1923, but they were not released) and her first Royal Variety Show.

The Royal Variety Show was in March at the London Coliseum, and from that often hard to please audience she received a heart-warming ovation.

The record was 'My Blue Heaven', and on the flip side was 'Because I Love You', which she burlesqued. This was the pattern for future recordings—not all, but many, of Gracie's records have a serious song on one side and a comic one on the other.

She began her recording career with HMV and during the next fifty years recorded on every important label in the business. The early records cost a shilling, and millions were sold throughout the world.

In 1898, the year of her birth, the record industry, although twenty-one years old, was still in its infancy commercially. Improvements in the technique of cutting a disc were swift during the following decade, and during the 1920s electrical recording was introduced. By the 1930s, when Gracie was recording abundantly, the gramophone and radiogram were important features in many homes.

Gracie recorded right into the 1970s, and the last two records came about when she was at a party and was asked to sing. But let Norman Newell, who has worked with her many times, tell the story himself:

'I was attending Lillian Aza's birthday party. Gracie and her husband Boris were present, and as I had not seen them for some time it was a most happy reunion. Gracie hadn't changed at all—she was the same happy-go-lucky friendly personality she has always been, and before many minutes had elapsed word spread around the restaurant and fans were coming from all directions to greet her, and she had a pleasant word for them all. It was not long before someone said, "Sing us a song Gracie," and she stood up in the restaurant and sang, unaccompanied—at least unaccompanied until the waiters and customers joined in.

'It was a magic evening, the kind one wishes could never end, and I said to my host, Teddy Holmes, "If only we could capture an evening like this on record.''

'He suggested to Gracie and Boris that before returning to Capri the following Sunday, she should make an album with audience participation, and I could not believe my good fortune when Gracie agreed to this suggestion. When word got round the demand for tickets to be present was incredible, and the atmosphere in the studios was so electric that one felt one was attending a magnificent party. If only the running time of an album allowed for the inclusion of Gracie's introduction, her asides, and her banter with Geoff Love. It would have been wonderful not to have to edit the tapes to the vocal performances only.

'Gracie has always been indescribable. She was unique—one of the most wonderful personalities with whom I have ever worked.'

It is a good sing-song record; and Gracie had a good voice for a woman of seventy-seven—she sounds like someone in her early sixties, but, if you want to hear an echo of the voice that shot her to stardom and kept her there for fifty years, listen to some of her earlier recordings.

Most of the experts I have spoken to put her peak in this respect between 1925 and 1950. And that's a long time for a 'peak'.

In February 1933 Gracie made her four-millionth record for HMV, and they gave a party for their best-selling star. On the menu was Lancashire hotpot, red cabbage and broth. The waitresses were dressed in clogs and shawls. In addition to the heads of HMV and the Mayor and Mayoress of Rochdale, her parents and several of Gracie's oldest friends were invited. As a novelty there was a singing record invitation and menu.

CHAPTER 5

Capri

In 1928 a show called *Topsy and Eva* (the musical story of *Uncle Tom's Cabin)* came to the Gaiety Theatre in the Strand. It starred two American girls, the Duncan Sisters, Vivian and Rosetta. One week after the opening, Rosetta was taken ill and rushed to hospital. Gracie who was rehearsing for *The Show's The Thing,* stepped in at the last moment to keep *Topsy and Eva* open. She had met Vivian and Rosetta and liked them, so, when Vivian called into Bert Aza's office to ask Gracie if she could possibly help, Gracie never hesitated. With a single-mindedness which many envied her, she learnt the part in twenty-four hours and proved to be a huge success as black-faced Topsy.

Crowds waited outside the famous Gaiety stage door for her and chaired her down the Strand, alternately singing and cheering. She stayed in the show for two weeks, playing to packed houses every night, took not a penny for doing so and, when Rosetta left the hospital, returned to her own rehearsals.

Her sister Betty had introduced her to an artist and a writer some months before, and these two were to influence Gracie's life. The artist was John Flanagan, and the writer Henry Savage. On the first night they met, at the Café Royal after her cabaret act, they talked for a while, and suddenly John Flanagan said, 'I should like to paint you.'

Gracie was embarrassed. She thought artists only painted beautiful people, and she didn't think she was beautiful. Years before, her mother had put her hair in rags to make it curly, but Gracie never thought she succeeded, either in making her hair curly or in making her beautiful. Her features were strong and, when she grew older, gentle. In the late twenties they didn't have that gentleness, except perhaps sometimes when she was singing certain songs or when she was with a real friend. Mostly, in the publicity pictures, she had 'character': a strong chin, high cheekbones, vigorous hair, a high forehead, a singer's long, slender throat, and good legs and ankles—those long legs that had been an embarrassment to her in her teens, that she hadn't known what to do with, were now an asset.

She met John Flanagan again and agreed to let him paint her portrait. He was Irish, and Gracie said he had one of the saddest faces she had ever seen. 'Big brown eyes, dark hair, and a wistfulness in his expression that sometimes caught you unawares.'

Gracie and John fell in love. She and Archie Pitt were still together then, but two days before *The Show's The Thing* opened in 1929, they had another row.

'It was terrible,' she said, 'and the tension of it all drove me to do something I'd never have contemplated under normal circumstances. I packed a bag and left.'

She went to Victoria Station and boarded the boat train for France, where John and Henry Savage were on holiday. On that long journey on her own, each mile taking her further from her homeland and nearer to the man she loved, she had plenty of time to think, and she knew she could not do it that way. Without leaving the station she telephoned her family from Paris.

'It's all right, I'm coming back,' she said, 'The show will open on time.' Then she phoned her husband.

'I never asked you to leave in the first place,' was Archie's comment.

'I cried a lot on that return journey,' Gracie said, 'everything seemed such a muddle, and I was desperately unhappy, but I knew by then that I had to go back and sort it out properly. I couldn't just walk out and let everyone down.'

Two days after her return, *The Show's The Thing* opened at the Victoria Palace, and people flocked to see it. From the career point of view, Gracie's skies could not have been bluer—but for 'the inner person' life was painted in dark colours, except for the splashes of warmth and brightness of those audiences; they didn't know about the turmoil of her feelings—on stage with her audience everything else was forgotten, and there was only that deep and instant rapport between them. Afterwards she was alone again inside herself.

The Show's The Thing ('an apt title', Gracie said later) ran for eighteen months, and when it finished she moved out of the Tower, acknowledging that her marriage had irretrievably broken down.

'We never loved each other,' she said much later, 'yet I had hoped it would work out. Somehow it didn't seem right to mess things up.'

There was no legal separation; they just ceased to live together. The Tower was offered for sale, and Archie and Annie Lipman set up house together, while Gracie moved into a studio in St John's Wood. She also bought a caravan to use when she was on tour, preferring a place where she could brew a cup of tea to an hotel.

In the climate of the early thirties a divorce

would not have been good for her spiralling career, although in retrospect she was so adored by the people that it might not have made any difference. In any case she did divorce Archie in 1939, and it wasn't her divorce that sent her flying from the top of the pedestal but the nationality of the man she subsequently married...

After *The Show's The Thing* finished, Gracie took the train again to France, where Henry and John were both working and 'absorbing atmosphere', but she never had any intention of staying there, because she had been reading Norman Douglas's book *South Wind* and had developed a great yearning to see for herself the island it featured.

She had read a lot since the time she discovered the great joy to be found in books, which was not until she was in her teens. (Almost every photograph taken of Gracie as she boarded a ship, or plane or train shows her with a book, a scarf and either a box of chocolates or a bouquet of flowers in her hands).

While John and Henry were in the south of France, Gracie had been reading books about islands.

'They all fascinated me,' she said. 'Maybe I needed the seclusion of an island at that time, I don't know, but I found myself longing to have a place somewhere away from the crowds, away from the pressures and stress of too many people. For a while, after reading Somerset Maugham I fancied Tahiti, then I thought maybe it was *too* far from all I loved; but Capri, which was called Nepenthe in Norman Douglas's book, was only in Italy —with the money I was earning now I could get home quickly from there if I needed to.'

Gracie arrived in the French village where John and Henry were living, but, instead of staying there and enjoying it with them, she wanted to whisk them both off to Capri.

'Neither of them were keen,' she said, 'but sometimes I can be a bit of a bully I think, and anyway John was so glad that I was finding my feet so to speak, because by then he knew, more than most, how difficult life had been, and so they agreed to come.'

In spite of the fact that Gracie and John loved each other, she hadn't been free, and John, although he was selling pictures, wasn't making anything like the sort of money she was.

They went to Capri, and at first glance it simply seemed a very beautiful island. They explored it from the harbour up to Anacapri, and, on the day they planned to leave, the driver of the carriage taking them to the boat asked if they had seen 'the little seashore'—

'la piccola spiaggia'.

When they told him they hadn't, he took them there. It was the most uninhabited part, and when she saw it, Gracie knew she had found her Shangri-La. Here was the beauty and peace, the *feeling* she had sensed before she set out.

They stayed for ten days in the place that some years later Gracie bought, added to and eventually made her home. It was owned by an Italian—Marchese Patrizi, who lived there with his wife and sixteen-year-old son.

During that idyllic holiday—the first real one Gracie had ever had (unless you count her weeks recovering in the St Anne's convalescent home), Henry wrote—mostly about cats, which were his speciality, John painted and Gracie relaxed and dreamed.

Capri in those days was a little-known island—even the now-famous song about it hadn't been written. Travel was usually by horse-drawn carriage, or on foot along the steep, winding paths, bordered by oleander and bougainvillea; past the perfect bay of Marina Piccola and the Faraglioni Rocks, looking like a jumbo-sized version of the Needles off the Isle of Wight. The island, which is a vast limestone rock, is four miles square—Mount Tiberius (1,100 feet) and Mount Solaro, the highest point at 1,700 feet, affording a marvellous view of the whole.

Gracie, already in love with John, went on to fall in love with Capri. Some years later she was to write to a friend about it: 'It's the most wonderful spot in the world, almost unbelievable. God was good to me when He guided me there.'

John knew how famous she was, had seen the adulation she inspired, and could visualise a little of what life might be like married to someone who could, and *did*, command such Intensity from others. Gracie's brother Tommy says that she tried to give him too much.

'She could afford to buy him paints and canvases, build him a studio, and he didn't want this. It frightened him to consider staying in one place for ever more—he felt it would stifle his work...'

Lillian Aza says that he could not accept *her* fame, and Barry Norman commented, in his television profile, 'In every way perhaps she was just too rich for Flanagan.'

After they parted in the late thirties—and at the time the world knew nothing of their romance—a friendship remained, and, when John needed money for a nightclub he wanted to open, and later for a film he was producing called *Riders of the Night,* it was Gracie who financed him.

Before she left Capri that first time, Gracie

had asked Ettore Patrizi, the young son of her host, who spoke a little English, to let her know if there was ever any property for sale there. A year or so later he wrote to her saying that his father's place was for sale, and Gracie began the long negotiations which resulted in her buying the area of cliff and beach which included what she described as 'the long, low, shanty-like shack' where she had stayed with John and Henry and the Patrizis on that first visit.

When she knew for certain that it was hers, she was in Rochdale, in the kitchen of her old friend Bertha Schofield, whose first reaction was, 'Eeh Grace, does your mumma know?' Even though Gracie was now thirty and a married woman, this was the immediate thought of those who knew the family well.

Gracie *hadn't* mentioned that particular transaction to her mother, and when she told Bertha this she was even more astounded.

'Best be careful how tha tells her, or she'll give thee a reet good clout,' was her comment.

After writing the cheque for her newly acquired property, Gracie had £25 left in the bank—'And my voice,' she said when talking about her first venture into property buying, something she admitted she liked doing, and from which she later made a great deal of money.

'Buying buildings gives me a thrill,' she said years afterwards, 'and I love it.'

Now that she actually owned a bit of property on her magic island, she set about turning it into a home.

She had bought many interesting pieces in the Portobello Road market and learned a great deal about furniture and pictures from John Flanagan; in addition she knew what she liked, and in her final choice this was what influenced her. Gracie never bought something because someone else said it was good. 'It may well be,' she said once, when someone was trying to persuade her toward something she wasn't happy about, 'but it doesn't appeal to me.' That directness that was so much a part of her nature intermingled with her natural charm, which so often turned a refusal into an apologetic compliment.

CHAPTER 6

The Film Years

Gracie's film career began in 1931 with *Sally In Our Alley,* and it was in this film that her signature tune was born.

Gracie disliked filming. She felt claustrophobic when the heavy doors were closed and locked before shooting, and she missed the immediate reaction of a live audience, but *Sally In Our Alley,* which was adapted for the screen from the stage play *The Likes Of 'er,* by Miles Malleson, was a huge success, and she went on to make fourteen more films.

Most of them disappointed her as representative of her talent. 'They always wanted me to sing,' she said, which of course wasn't surprising, but Gracie would have liked to have acted more in her film life.

She fought her family and managers when she was offered the lead in *Holy Matrimony.* She admitted to being easily swayed: 'Sheer laziness, sometimes,' she said, 'but I was always glad I stuck to my guns over that film. I adored it, the words were rich, it was a *real* story. Some of my films were built around a few songs, and although they were successful they weren't good, not what I'd really call good.'

They were also hard work. She had to be at the studio at six in the morning and often did not leave until eleven o'clock at night.

'And it was doing the same thing over and over and *over* again,' she said. Ideally she liked doing things once. Lillian Aza told me: 'We called her "one-take Joe", but she used to say about some of the others. "There's twenty-take Charlie and thirty-take Fred—it drives you mad." '

Sally In Our Alley was a hit with the public, and many people feel that it was the very best film Gracie made. It had all the ingredients for appeal: laughter, sadness and drama. It had Gracie singing—'Sally' was the song on everyone's lips when the film was released, and became the one associated with her forever after.

'Sally' was written by Will Haines, Harry Leon and Leo Towers and almost did not get into the film at all. It started life as 'Gypsy Sweetheart', the music written by Harry and Leo, and Will Haines (who was usually called Bill) started the lyric as 'Mary, Mary', which he discarded in favour of 'Sally, Sally'. While he was writing it, someone came into his office; he looked up and said, 'What

93

rhymes with smiling?'

'Beguiling.'

When they took it round to Gracie in her dressing-room at the Metropolitan Theatre in Edgware Road, she turned it down.

'I think it's more the sort for a man to sing,' she said, then suddenly remembered that the title of the film she was doing was *Sally In Our Alley*. 'Tell you what, show it to Archie—I'm doing a film and it might fit in.'

Archie didn't care for the last line, so they all played about with it until Annie Lipman came up with, 'You're more than the whole world to me.'

'Sally' became so much a part of Gracie Fields that letters were often addressed to her as 'Sally, London, England', and they were delivered without delay.

Gracie says in her book *Sing As We Go,* 'I have sung Sally all over the world, in peace and war, triumph and disaster, but never in such nightmare conditions as that first time, in the film studio. I was supposed to be in a coffee house when I was singing it, and to get what they called "the right smoky atmosphere", they decided to burn brown paper. The fumes made the technicians sneeze, and each time one of their muffled sneezes was picked up on the sound track we had to scrap that recording and start all over again.

'I can't remember how many times we had to do it before it was recorded properly, but I can remember standing there, my eyes streaming with the smoke from the burning paper and the glare from the baking kleig lights, and all the camera, sound, and lighting crews going red in the face and working like mad to get it all in the can before they either coughed or choked.'

It became one of the most famous signature tunes of all time. Every orchestra worth its name knew it, errand boys whistled it, and, if Gracie appeared anywhere in public where there was anything from a piano to a fullscale band, they struck up with 'Sally'.

Gracie often grew tired of the song, but, as she said more than once, 'It appeals to so many. We have all said, or wanted to say to someone we love, "Don't go away, you're everything to me", and "Sally" says it for us most beautifully.'

All Gracie's early films were made in England, most of them at Ealing Studios, and whatever *she* may have felt about the lack of storyline in them, there is no doubt about their cheering-up qualities.

Gracie's art flourished in an impoverished time, when so many were out of work and really 'on the breadline', when the word 'poverty' meant exactly that, in its stark reality. It was the days of the means test (introduced in 1931), when, if you applied for unemployment money, it was refused while you still had more than a table, chairs, a bed and a cooking stove. The piano, a feature in so many homes then, was often the first thing to go—it had no practical use; but if people had 6d left at the end of the week, they went to see Gracie, either in person at one of the many Hippodromes or Empires boasted by almost every town, or at a cinema which had probably been an Empire a few years before.

Sing As We Go, Love, Life and Laughter, Looking On The Bright Side, Look Up and Laugh, Keep Smiling—the titles were optimistic, and the films lived up to that optimism.

'Whenever there was a Gracie Fields picture showing, I would be there. My word, if you were down in the dumps when you went in, you were a different person when you came out. It put new life into you,' said Ethel Lord, one of her fans from those days.

Basil Dean and Maurice Elvey directed those early films, and, according to many who worked with him, Basil Dean didn't have an easy manner for comedy. Gracie said to John Loder, her co-star in *Love, Life and Laughter,* 'John, how *can* I be funny when Basil's watching me so seriously all the time?' John Loder suggested she meet Monty Banks, who had directed his last film. The result of that meeting was that Gracie's next four films (apart from *The Show Goes On* in 1937) were directed by Monty Banks.

Meanwhile Basil Dean had shown that it wasn't only the glamorous Hollywood stars and lavish productions that made money and drew the crowds to the cinema. Gracie's fooling around and trying to put wrong things right, and her breezy cheerfulness, epitomised the way so many of her audiences would like to be. The fact that her buoyant approach was part of her offscreen personality too brought them even closer. Watching the rushes of her own pictures in the studio projection theatre during the silent close-ups of herself singing, she said, 'Eeh, what a fool I do look—let's have a tune with it,' and proceeded to sing with her image on the screen.

In one scene in *Looking On The Bright Side,* which called for drinks, Gracie suggested they should be the real thing to be truly authentic. 'Coloured water isn't the same,' she said. They used the real thing. 'We shall probably have to change the title to *Looking On The Tight Side,'* she quipped when she watched the reaction!

Looking On The Bright Side has a moving story connected with its title song. Howard Flynn wrote it after a two-year stint in hospital, where he had had several operations. He was in continual pain, and then he became deaf and a further operation was decided on to try to rectify this.

From his hospital bed Howard wrote:

I'm looking on the bright side
Though I'm walking in the shade,
Sticking out my chest, hoping for the best,
Looking on the bright side of life.

One of his publishing friends visited him the day before the operation and said he would show the song to Gracie.

The operation was successful, and Howard slowly recovered, while the song he wrote from the depths of his pain went round the world to cheer and inspire millions of people who heard it.

Another interesting snippet concerning the same film is the fact that the biggest set built in English pictures up to that time, 1932, was made for this one. It consisted of a block of tenement flats named Parkers Piece (where Gracie lived in the film), and she had to throw copies of her sweetheart's new song to the people below.

Margaret Hazell, who worked at Ealing Studios in those days told me that, when the crowd of extras often could not afford to eat in the canteen on the little they earned, Gracie told them to go ahead and have what they needed and she would foot the bill.

'They used to troop in and say, "Gracie will pay", which she did the whole time they were there.'

When *Queen of Hearts* was finished, she gave everyone at the studio a present. For each of the ladies there was a leather photo-frame with a still from the film inside it, and for the men an engraved fountain pen.

Gracie's films always did better in the provinces than in London, and while the critics were quick to praise her as a performer, many of the stories had a rough ride. Here is a part of a review of *Sally In Our Alley* when it was showing at the Leicester Square Theatre:

'Against a background most aggressively cockney, the chirpy, sentimental, jauntily capable personality of Gracie Fields contrives dominatingly to overshadow the faults of this sketchy talkie. Lancashire rises triumphantly above a story that is a story in name only, and direction which is not worthy of Maurice Elvey, even though he is handicapped by the weakest of plots. Elvey, with admirable commonsense, declines to fight a losing battle with a poor narrative, and confines all his efforts to placing Gracie Fields in the limelight and keeping her there.

'He succeeds in this without much trouble, and Gracie does the rest with all her usual enthusiasm. The result is a talkie which never begins to be a film but is sound entertainment of the roast-beef-and-yorkshire-pudding variety.

'Just to add a little diversity to the film, a newcomer, Florence Desmond, gives a fine performance as a quite unmoral, screen-struck waif; and thereby demands for herself the future attention of producers who want a girl with acting ability and personality. The rest of the cast is just competent.'

The review finishes with the remarks, 'You'll like Gracie Fields and a few scenes of the picture which are really well done. There is enough entertainment here to help you to forgive the weaknesses.'

The Leicester Square Theatre was at that time doing what it called a '50-50 Show': Gracie Fields in *Sally In Our Alley* on the screen, and Jack Hulbert, 'exclusive song and dance show on the revolving stage', live. The prices of admission ranged from 1*s* 6*d* to 8*s* 6*d*, and *all* seats were bookable.

Gracie made her Ealing Studio films on a share of the profits basis, and as all her films did well in cinemas around the country, she made more money than by taking a set salary. Basil Dean said in 1933, 'In cinemas where three day runs were the rule, *Sally In Our Alley* stayed for three weeks.'

The only British comedy star who came near Gracie in the thirties was George Formby (in the forties he surpassed her box-office drawing-power), who began his film career with Basil Dean in 1934.

The film magazines and comics all featured Gracie—*The Film Star* telling 'the long complete story of Gracie Fields new picture' in several issues. *Film Pictorial, Picturegoer* and *Film Weekly* presented her frequently, with interviews, pictures and reviews. No matter how poorly the critics rated the story of the picture, and mostly they did, they awarded it marks for 'entertainment value'.

'The public go to these films to see and hear Gracie Fields,' one critic wrote, 'the story doesn't matter to them.'

Although the stories were, for the most part, flimsy and unreal, Gracie's personality breezed through the pictures—she made people laugh and actually believe that the most lowly of a factory's employees, the poorest down-and-out, the humblest citizen of the world, could with cheerfulness, song and a dash of down-to-earth common sense, solve not only her own problems but those of the community in which she was involved.

Later she made four films in America, all in quite a different tempo from her English ones.

Holy Matrimony, the one she did with Monty Woolley in 1943, was adapted from Arnold Bennett's *Buried Alive*, a case of mistaken identity between a famous artist and his valet, the ensuing romance and repercussions.

We're Going To Be Rich, in 1937 (in America it was called *He Was Her Man),* co-starred Victor McLaglen and Brian Donlevy and was a story about the South African gold rush.

Molly and Me, which she made in 1945, was again with Monty Woolley. In this she is an out-of-work actress who becomes a housekeeper and revolutionises the big house. There is a lovely scene in a pub with Gracie and her friends singing to a concertina

Madame Pimpernel, which was called *Paris Underground* in America, was not a type usually associated with Gracie. It was the story of two women (Constance Bennett and Gracie Fields) who were resistance workers during the war. Gracie had a real chance to show her acting capabilities in this film, and she came through with flying colours, giving a superb and moving performance.

In 1936 *(Madame Pimpernel* wasn't made until 1945) Eric L. Wigham, in the *Manchester Evening News,* wrote the following article, titled, 'You Fans—Why Not Give Gracie A Chance.'

'I write this to the hundreds of thousands of Gracie Fields fans, to the hundreds and thousands who love her as few stars have been loved—and who are preventing her from reaching the greatness of which she is capable.

'It is your fault that Gracie's screen work is known only in this country. It is your fault that her films are all just laughable hokum instead of penetrating pieces of life. Gracie is an actress of genius—but you will not let her act—you will only let her sing and fool about.

'The other day I saw her new picture, Queen of Hearts. It is at least as funny as anything she has done—and as unreal. The story so incredible that one can regard the picture as little more than a series of music hall sketches. Each of them is brilliant in itself, but there is no unity.

'It will be tremendously popular of course. You will all go to see it and spend a happy, laughing evening. But it will be very trivial and easily forgotten. But even in that musical farce there are moments when Gracie, by a single sentence or expression, brings reality into the story. I remember the expression on her face when she leaves her nagging mother and goes up to her bedroom in her poor home. Or a scene near the end when she is going to star in a new show and her father brings a bunch of violets to her dressing room.

'If we could only see her in a real piece of life, full of strong emotion and of humour that has a human basis, she would be tremendous. Gracie is the most real person that we have met. She can give us the films of the people which have been so conspicuously absent from the British schedules, and which have been the foundation of the great film industry in America. She has never ceased to be one of the people, and as one of the people she could make us laugh and cry.

'But you will not let her. Do you, her admiring fans, ask what you have done to prevent her? I will tell you. Whenever there is any suggestion that she should do anything but her usual mixtures of song and farce you raise an outcry.

'In straight films Gracie would, I believe, sweep through the cinemas of America carrying all before her. She has the humanity and reality which the American audiences like. But she will never do it in the type of film you are insisting on her making.'

Most of the critics, after two or three films said, 'She is good—please let her have a better story next time.'

Gracie herself wanted to do more acting—not to give up singing but to do a play or film without music sometimes, as she did in *Holy Matrimony*.

'You had real words to say which the

author enjoyed writing, and so you enjoyed them too,' she said of this script.'

She won an award on American television for her part in Barrie's *The Old Lady Shows Her Medals,* in 1955, and high praise from the critics whenever she had the slightest chance to show her paces in the acting field.

James Agate said in 1934 after seeing her at the Palladium: 'No other music hall artiste could invest this howling defiant drivel with such exquisite pathos and sincerity. This fine actress could play Carmen or any role. She should be given a chance to play St Joan.'

Because of her magnificent voice Gracie suffered from typecasting. In the singing films her personality was so strong that it came through. In many of the films they never changed her name even—the character she played was simply called Grace, or Gracie. If she had been able to get into a part, as she indeed did in *Holy Matrimony* and *Madame Pimpernel,* she would have submerged this forcefulness into the role. Today, I believe a producer would take a chance and let her do both types of film. She did two completely different styles of singing on stage—from the sublime to the ridiculous—and although people argued over it, they flocked to see her. It is a matter for regret that the actress in Gracie wasn't given a vehicle worthy of the talent more often.

Nevertheless, her films gave great happiness to vast numbers of people. They were right for the times—helping folk to keep cheerful against the dark background of the Depression. 'Come on, luv, your chin's touching your knees,' she used to say to her friend Nell Whitwell in her own poor days, if Nell looked miserable. In her films Gracie said just that to everyone who ventured into the cinema.

Filming earned her a great deal of money, and it seemed that the more reluctant she was to do it, the more she was offered. She said many times that she felt imprisoned in the film studio and found all the waiting about and repeats tedious. She used to tell a story about dancing up and down a flight of stairs every morning for *eight weeks:*

'I never saw the finished film until a year afterwards. When it came to that scene, the sight of those stairs so exhausted me that I felt I'd done the whole thing over once more, and when I got up to leave I found my knees were so weak that I had to sit down again.'

This was a slight exaggeration, but Gracie could always tell a good story. She did all her own stunts: 'Basil Dean insisted, and after all, I was being well paid.'

She received £50,000 a picture for four films from 20th Century Fox, and the newspapers reported that, although Mae West was the highest-paid actress in the USA, Gracie Fields was the highest paid in the world!

Gracie accepted the American contract for two reasons, one highly practical. At the time she owed a lot of money in tax to the Inland Revenue, for during the preceding boom years she had spent heavily, buying property and settling money on her family. The second reason was that, having once been so poor, she 'felt it would be wicked to turn away such an offer'.

The film critic C.A. Lejeune said of her, 'She was the art, like Chaplin, of touching an accessory and bringing it to life. She can sing Walter like a pantomime dame, The Sweetest Song in the World and make it sound like a Victorian posy, and Music Maestro Please and make it—almost—resemble—high dramatic art.'

The same lady, writing in the *Sunday Observer* in 1939, said Gracie was, 'a star of the theatre, the radio, the films, and now television, she is as much part of English life as tea and football pools, our green hedged fields and the Nelson column.

'She has been mobbed by more crowds and held up more traffic than any other film star except, possibly, Robert Taylor. She has had to slip out of buildings by fire escapes and be rescued by police in a Black Maria. She has been decorated at Buckingham Palace and sung to workmen up a scaffolding. She is enormously kind and endlessly generous.

'Rich people send her roses and poor people knit her teacosies. When she comes in front of the tabs to sing her final number the house roars like a great hungry beast and won't let her go.

'Someday the best English film biography ever made will be done on the life of Gracie Fields, and I hope that Gracie herself will be the one to do it. There will be nothing sentimental about it—a sheer story of hard work done with humour and courage. In its way it will be the complete English microcosmography of the twentieth century, a story of north and south, fame and the inarticulate, of the people who work and move in the front page limelight and the others who live behind lace curtains and an aspidistra in a suburban row.'

CHAPTER 7

With a Smile and a Song

'The Aspidistra' was, of course, one of Gracie's famous songs. It was written by Jimmy Harper, Will Haines and Tommie Connor, three names which constantly crop up in Gracie's numbers. Tommie Connor says the inspiration for it came when he was walking along a London street and saw a woman by her window with a huge green watering-can.

'As I watched her watering an equally huge plant, I thought—my goodness, that's the *biggest* aspidistra in the world. I knew at once it was the title for a song, and I began working it out in my head. By the time I got to the tram, the first verse was written, and I finished it as soon as I reached my office.'

He contacted Jimmy Harper, who wrote the music, then Bill Haines showed it to Gracie. The rest is history.

It was a good song, and the fact that Gracie and some of her fans who weren't as keen on her comic songs grew sick to death of it, in no way detracts from its merits as a comic number.

This type was more difficult to find than any other. Gracie could sing ballads already in existence, but the funny numbers were more specialised. The three names above are on many of the comic song music sheets, plus Harry Castling, Noel Forrester, J.P. Long, Leo Towers, Maurice Beresford, Robert Rutherford, Leslie Elliott, Noel Gay, Desmond Carter and Reg Low.

Bill Haines owned the Cameo Music Publishing Company and was associated with many of Gracie's songs. Although others could have sung them, because she never bought them outright, they seldom did. Mostly the songs were written with Gracie in mind, and her interpretation was the one that prevailed.

Not many comedy songs *look* funny in print—the words need the light and shade of a human voice. Max Kester says that 'Turn 'erbert's Face To The Wall Mother' put a roof over his head:

'The money I made from that song enabled me to put down a deposit on my first house, yet at the time Gracie wasn't too keen about the number.'

'Well, I'll try it,' she said, 'but I'm not sure. Not sure at all.'

Gracie gave most songs three or four airings, and if they hadn't caught on then, she threw them out. One which she used to sing in the earlier days was ' 'enery, 'erbert, 'epplethwaite', but she stopped doing it after a while because she said it was so difficult to time.

'Some folk laughed more than others,' she said, 'and we couldn't get it right. You've got to time properly on the variety stage or you overrun.'

This was the old music hall tradition—never overrun, for others have to earn their living too. Gracie was always the complete professional. She listened to advice, although she didn't always take it, often preferring to trust her instinct (which seldom let her down), but she kept the unwritten rules.

Although many of her comedy numbers *were* loud, not all of them involved screeching. 'Walter', 'He's Dead But He Won't Lie Down', 'She Fought Like A Tiger For 'er Honour'—they made folk laugh, and Gracie sang them with gusto, but not everything was so high-pitched. In 'The Co-op Shop' she raced the band with good effect, and it was very topical when she was singing it.

There was gentle comedy, satirical comedy and the simple comedy of everyday things. 'Got To Keep Up With The Joneses' (whose title speaks for itself and must surely find an echo today), 'The Nudist' (the tale about try-

ing to buy a birthday present for a nudist—
'A watchchain would look silly, draped
across the front of Willie...') and 'I Took My
Harp To A Party (and nobody asked me to
play)'—it has happened to so many of us at
some time, maybe not with a harp but with
our own particular equivalent.

When Gracie was urging us to 'All Talk
Posh', there was a greater division in the way
people spoke and lived than there is now.
Music hall has always been a working-class
entertainment, and Gracie was a wonderful
music hall artiste. Her songs and sketches
were about the lives of everyday folk, ordinary people who worked and married and
brought up their families—about people who
'got on', and people who had bad luck,
about babies and marriage, arguments and
making up, about poor people who wanted
to be rich, town people who wanted to live
in the country, and some people whose
dream was to live anywhere as long as they
had a roof over their heads.

When Madame Tetrazzini heard Gracie
singing at the Lyceum, she asked her to sing
the aria from *La Traviata*.

'I was in a panic,' Gracie said at the time,
'never having had a real singing lesson in my
life—I had learnt all the arias from listening
to Galli-Curci's records. I couldn't understand any of the Italian or French, so I'd

sung comical gibberish, intermingled with the real thing. But I loved Grand Opera, and I loved Tetrazzini's voice too much to want to ridicule great music in front of her. To me opera was only for singers who were properly trained. I should have loved to learn, but when I was young we didn't have the money for lessons. When I understood operatic music more I wouldn't attempt it unless I could do it perfectly.'

Gracie sang the aria in the role of the character she was playing in that particular sketch—a charlady, and afterwards Madame Tetrazzini tried to persuade her towards opera, 'but I stayed where I knew I belonged,' Gracie said, 'although I always cherished the memory.'

The great operatic diva Dame Eva Turner said in 1982:

'In my opinion she had an exceptional voice which she used to great advantage. Her sense of timing was excellent, and she never unduly abused her voice which is evidenced by reason of the length of time it served her. Right up to the end of her career she was able to "fill the bill" and "put it over".

'I recall she once asked me whether she made a mistake in not becoming a "serious singer", and at that time I told her in view of her great success in her particular field, she had certainly done the right thing by working on the lines she did. I do think, however, she could have made a career as a ''serious'' singer, had she so wished.'

Gracie worked with few props, often without any. She didn't need them. All that was necessary for her was an audience, and all that was necessary for them was Gracie.

On stage she usually had a simple setting; a piano, the stage drapes and in her hands a scarf, often matching her dress.

Gracie never wasted time on stage; the audience had come to hear her sing, and she got on with the job quickly in true music hall fashion. She used to stop the welcome applause with her famous whistle and go straight into the songs. Often she wore round her shoulders a white fur, which she threw across the piano after the opening number. 'Only wore it for swank.' 'Hope someone dusted the piano,' or 'You've all seen it now so I needn't bother,' she'd say. Song followed song, and if the audience clapped too loud or long, she whistled for 'hush' again or told them to 'Cease, cease.'

Steadily she worked her way through from the hilarity of 'The Rochdale Hounds' to the comic pathos of 'The Birthday Song' and the little boy whose day was less than perfect. Nervously twiddling her scarf, with slightly pouting lips, she told of the frustrations the

six-year-old suffered, and how he reacted—
'Then I showed 'em if I could be sick or
not—*every room.*'

From the rollicking fun of 'The Spaniard
That Blighted My Life' she went on to the
sending-up of 'Oh I Never Cried So Much
In All Me Life', then a sudden switch to the
drama of 'The Nuns' Chorus', or the peace
of 'Ave Maria'. No messing about here—
Gracie always sang the sacred songs straight.
Then she would be fooling about with her
voice, doing 'cod opera', throwing her long
rope of pearls round her neck in a mock
choke, yet as she hit those high notes you
knew what opera had missed. Next a romantic number, and just as you are feeling all
misty-eyed, she decides to burlesque it and
instead has you almost crying with laughter.

Her voice was versatile—the range and
depth of her singing were amazing: from
comic numbers to romantic; from simple to
sophisticated; from innocent to saucy. She
got away with some daring lines during the
twenties and thirties, possibly because no one
could really take offence at them for she
made them such fun.

In 1933 at the Holborn Empire she said
to the vast audience (three thousand people):
'Right, we'll forget we're at the Holborn
Empire. Imagine we're in our front room
and we're having a bit of a "do". We've had

a nice tea—some boiled ham and lettuce, and a tin of salmon, and we're all right now,' and they sang and sang with her, just as though they really were at a 'bit of a do' in their front room. She could reduce the biggest theatre to everyone's front room, and turn everyone's front room into the biggest theatre.

Let's imagine for a moment that we have gone to the theatre to see Gracie. In the foyer her picture smiles at us from the posters. We go to our seats, buying a programme on the way, and settle down to read it.

The overture, then two young dancers open the show, a pianist, a comic, a magician, a tenor, and a couple of acrobats...as the theatre fills with people, you can sense the excitement in the atmosphere. Smiles are exchanged with folk we have not met before, and, as the orchestra files in, the packed theatre fairly hums with anticipation.

It is a good bill and we applaud well, but most of us are there to see Gracie, and when the safety curtain falls during the interval, we know we have not much longer to wait, for she is doing all the second half.

Everybody is back in their seat as the orchestra strikes up, 'Sally, Sally...'. The curtains open, and Gracie comes on singing... 'Pride of our alley...'—the applause is thunderous, but her voice soars above it, 'You're

116

more than the whole world to me. Thank you, thank you very much,' and she launches immediately into a quickfire medley— 'Sing As We Go'—'Walter, Walter, Lead Me To The Altar'—'Pedro The Fisherman'—'I Never Cried So Much In All Me Life'— 'Roses Of Picardy'...

Her expressive hands tie her scarf round her head for the next number, and when she takes it off again, she runs her fingers through her hair, using them as a comb. A stillness comes over her, and the theatre is hushed and reverent as she sings 'Ave Maria'. Everything mean and small leaves you until you are one with all the goodness and beauty in the world. 'Amen...A...men...'

Absolute silence while we return from that glimpse of heaven in her voice, then the solid sound of thousands of clapping hands. Gracie holds her own hand up, 'Enough,' she says. 'We're now going on a trip round the world, and if you know the words you can join in,' and she transforms herself quickly into an Irish Colleen, a Scots lass, French, Spanish, Italian—'It's Lancashire Italian,' she says with a laugh, speaking 'off' for a moment, and it isn't just her accent which is good, it's her gestures, expressions—for the duration of the song she becomes that person completely.

Sometimes she talks to us in between

numbers, in her surprisingly deep voice.

'A long time ago I brought a song back from New Zealand with me,' and in a cracked and wheezy voice she sings the first line of 'Now Is The Hour'—then, briskly, 'Well, we're *not* going to sing that one.' The laughter mingles with her next words, and by the time she really *is* singing her sign-off song, 'Now is the hour for me to say goodbye...', we are still clapping and cheering.

She blows kisses, and the curtain comes down on another performance. We talk to each other as we jostle for the doors. We go out smiling, humming, revitalised for the coming days. We smile back at her picture in the foyer, and if there is time before the last bus or train, or if we have come by car, we might go round to the stage door and join the crowd waiting for her; and for days afterwards we are carried along by the memory of that wonderful evening.

This is how it was so many times for so many people; this is why Gracie's concerts were always sold out. It is hard to describe to any who never saw her what a performance by Gracie was like. In modern parlance I suppose you would say it 'turned you on, got you high'. Her voice held all the joy and sorrow in the world; the richnesses, the sadnesses—it was all there in the depths and tones of Gracie's singing.

She made you think of stained glass windows and great cathedrals, of every man, woman and child—their loves and hates, joys and sorrows. Her art was simple and great—great with the simplicity of goodness and understanding.

One critic wrote, 'Her performances aren't so much a theatrical occasion as an emotionally charged reunion.'

Another (Anthea Goddard) talked about her 'ripe voice—from poignant sob to hysterical falsetto, and suddenly to a disconcerting unladylike hoot. Gracie has never lost the art of knowing exactly when and how to dissolve the tears into laughter. Just as the sentiment of "Sonny Boy" or white-haired granny is at its stickiest she saves the situation with that piercing hoot, then launches a vocal attack on the biggest aspidistra in the world.'

She was such an original—when she sang a song it was *hers*—whether you liked it that way or not. She sang 'Waltzing Matilda' slower than most—'It's too pretty to rush through,' she said, 'so I do it slowly.'

When she sang 'Over the Rainbow', she sounded as *unlike* Judy Garland as possible. In 'White Christmas' she echoed the longing for an English Christmas. You may prefer one recording to another, but Gracie never tried to sing a song in the way it had been sung by someone else. It was always *her* version—even if somebody else was associated with the song. A critic once said, 'They go into the sieve, and come out as Gracie Fields numbers.'

She stayed true to her earlier prophecy of sometimes altering the phrasing—singing it just that little bit differently to the last time. 'Well, your mood isn't always the same, and naturally your interpretation varies...'

It didn't stop the mimics, and her manager issued a statement to the effect that they would sue anyone impersonating Gracie without permission: 'We don't wish to stop the sincere artiste, only the many cruel caricatures which are being perpetuated....'

Gracie's control of an audience was complete. I believe that, if she had told them to stand on their seats, all those physically capable of doing it would have done so; but Gracie would never have made people look silly—not to that extent. She controlled them with love, with the mutual desire to have a good evening's fun which she, and they, knew she was going to lead. There need to be leaders in most things, and Gracie could do it without appearing to.

She was a natural; she respected her audience, knew they wanted the fun of her comedy *and* the beauty of her serious voice, and knew too that she was capable of maintaining this balance.

George Black wrote in the *Sunday Chronicle* in 1935, 'Seven years ago I took over the London Palladium and to have Gracie Fields on my opening bill was great good fortune, for I had always seen in her the living em-bodiment of all the great traditions of var-iety. Marie Lloyd at the top of her career was never more popular than this ex-mill girl had become. Her power over the laughter and tears of an audience was greater than that of Elsie Janis* or Florence Mills.**

'I studied Gracie as she worked. That was something I had often done. From the day I had first seen her at Barrow-in-Furness long before, when she was quite unknown—I had tried to discover the secret of her charm and power. It eluded me then, and even today I cannot say wherein it lies. What she has is so peculiarly her own that none can copy it. It is something that cannot be learned in schools of acting. She breaks all the rules and can never do a thing wrong.

'She broke a cardinal rule that night. Any manager could have told her that to turn her back on the audience and walk upstage

* American actress, singer, lyricist, producer, mimic, 1889-1956.
** Negro singer and dancer, 1895-1927.

before the applause and laughter were over was one certain way of ruining an act. She did it and it was one of the most remarkable things I have ever seen her do.

'With her back still to the audience she paused a moment and began to sing. The crowd, prepared to laugh again, were brought to silence by the clear, liquid notes—that "third voice" of hers—of a plaintive melody, "Three Green Bonnets."

'At exactly the right moment, known to her by instinct, she turned her head, then her body, and began to walk slowly down the stage, singing. The house was hushed, breathless. As the last notes died away I heard a gasp. And I, who had been a hard-boiled showman since boyhood, and thought I knew all the tricks of the trade, felt what the audience felt. For here was no trick. This was blazing sincerity—a heart speaking to the hearts of the world.'

Wally Singer, a friend and fan of hers from Brighton, says he has listened very closely to Gracie's voice, and tried to analyse it; the nearest he can get is that it was like a finely tuned violin.

There was the other side, the people who 'could not stand Gracie Fields' screeching', but they were few against the hundreds of thousands who loved her voice.

She has been called 'common'; if making

folk laugh with no matter how loud a voice is common, then she was. But if they, the common people, understood her humour, they also understood her other side and were more reverent than a church congregation when she sang the sacred songs.

When the critics chastised her for rock and rolling to 'Born To Be Your Baby' at a Royal Variety Show which was televised, she said, 'The public expect me to mix it up, now serious, now larking. I always have and I always will—that's me. These TV critics—they don't understand that I'm not singing to *them*, but to all the folk in their family parlours. I can't do things by tricks—I have to feel it or nowt happens.'

She sent up the rich and poor equally—she had personal experience of both sides of that coin, and although she was rich for the greater part of her life, she never forgot the poor days.

Her voice has been variously described as 'a unique and glorious soprano' and 'the great coloratura of the century'. It was an operatic voice, yet, because of lack of funds when she was young, she never trained for the opera. By the time she had enough money, she thought it was too late, and she was established in a different field.

Some thought it almost a sin to waste that glorious voice on numbers a lesser one could do; musical comedy would have been another possibility yet she never did it. Would her personality have shone through whatever character she was portraying? I do not think so—I believe she would have absorbed the character and acted the part. C.B. Cochran was going to team her with Richard Tauber once in a musical at the Lyceum, but that idea fell through, mostly because it was the period when Gracie was getting to know Monty Banks and wanted to be free of further long-term commitments for a while.

Eventually she was a one-woman show, combining all the fields in her performance. She misused her voice to a devastating extent without any disastrous results. No matter how she croaked and wheezed in some of the comedy numbers, when she wanted a good note she achieved it. It was a powerful voice, carrying to the farthest corner of great concert halls even before the days of the constant use of the microphone. 'She made the Palladium stage her own. She explored parts of it which other singers, rooted to their microphones, never visit,' said the *Daily Express* reviewer in 1948.

Her diction was good: 'I can't abide not being able to understand the words,' she used to say, 'I've been to concerts when you'd have thought they were singing a lot of gibberish—or a foreign language.' She laughed at the memory of her own Lancashire Spanish and Rochdale Italian.

'OK if you do it for laughs, but not out of laziness. Folk pay their money and *should* be able to understand what you're on about.'

Gracie could sing in several languages. 'You can learn a song without being able to speak the lingo,' she said. Nevertheless, when she went to France, to the Apollo Theatre, Paris, in 1928, she sang her songs to the French waiters at the Café Royal first, to check the sound, and many of the reviews commented on 'her perfect French accent.'

On a tour of Wales she learnt Welsh from a Welshman, and she put her knowledge to good use when she was in Christchurch, New Zealand, at a civic reception, by singing in Welsh when she discovered the Mayor's original hometown.

From her early days she was a good mimic, and she was always a great professional, so she worked at and polished her accent and pronunciation when singing in another language, and the unsure part of her nature encouraged her to joke with her audience about it.

'Ee, that were a difficult line to learn.'

'We'll take a deep breath and hope for best.'

'How are we doing—all reet?'

And the voice, and the accent, came across

perfectly and with an ease and assurance that made light of the preparatory work she always did in pursuit of giving good value 'to the customers'.

'I wanted everyone to go out happy and feel they've had what I would call a good meal. I wouldn't like to go on and think—I'm just going to do that show, and they've got to take it or leave it. I couldn't do that ever—I have to give everything I've got then I can sleep happy.'

CHAPTER 8

Honours and Awards

For many years in the early thirties Gracie did a week's work in Rochdale for local charities. I have the programmes for 1931, 1933 and 1934 in front of me as I write, and they are an incredible record of how things were and what she did to help.

They begin with an official welcome, then two concerts a night at the Rochdale Hippodrome, the daytime spent visiting hospitals, old people's homes, the Infirmary, the crippled children, then the Nurses Home, the Boys Home and the Blind People's Institution. The week always included the Mayor's Ball, and in addition to the items printed in the programme Gracie fitted in all sorts of extras, visits to small groups and individual people which had no place on the official list.

The money raised from all these activities was £1,673 in 1931, £1,117 in 1933, and £1,629 in 1934 (a phenomenal amount of money in those depressive times, and from an area that was amongst the hardest hit with unemployment), and these amounts were divided among many causes ranging from young people to old. In both 1933 and 1934 the People's Service Guild received over £500. The Guild established workshops for various crafts, to help the unemployed, and Gracie visited the centre and talked to the men. She had been poor and out of work, and she understood and did something about it.

Her sympathy was of a practical kind, and she gave not only money raised through her concerts and appearances but her time and interest. When one man said to her, 'We *are* trying to look on the bright side,' she answered sadly and genuinely, 'It must be hard sometimes, lad.'

Perhaps the best indication of the way Rochdale felt about Gracie then is shown in the following extract from the *Rochdale Observer* in 1933:

'There were tears in Miss Gracie Field's eyes as she stood on the Rochdale Theatre Royal stage on Saturday evening at the conclusion of her week's performances on behalf of the funds of the People's Service Guild.

'From Monday until Saturday Gracie had given her best unstintedly, and when the town as a whole, with the Mayoress as spokeswoman, tried to tender adequate thanks, the Lancashire girl broke down. For a few moments she was unable to speak. Her stage presence deserted her as she heard the few earnest words of thanks for what she had done for her less fortunate townspeople. She tried to hide the tears but could not do so.

'In that moment she was indeed "Our Gracie"—never have the hearts of an audience gone out to her more than they did then. Rochdale was deeply touched by the love of a great daughter who, in her immense success, refuses to forget her humble home, and she in turn was openly affected by the sincere regard of the townspeople for herself.

'The Mayoress, addressing Miss Fields, said, "It is with deep affection and a keen appreciation of your loving devotion to our town, and of the self sacrifice you have shown to us this week that I ask you to accept from us our abundant thanks. Tonight Rochdale is at a loss to know how to say thank you. We really do not know how to put into words our love for you, and we have been wondering how we can express this love and this gratitude in a practical way.

' "You have shown us how to give. Every minute of your life seems to be spent in giving, and we wonder if we can have the privilege of sharing with you in this giving, and helping you to care for the little ones you are providing for at your orphanage at Peacehaven which we know you are about to open.

' "Would you accept from your people of Rochdale this cheque for £100. It is only a small contribution to your funds. We add to it our loving wishes for the success and welfare of that home and pour into it a "thank you" which comes from the hearts of all Rochdalians who not only honour you and are proud of you, but who love you.'

'Loud applause greeted the speech of the Mayoress. Miss Fields, as she rose to reply, wiped tears from her eyes. Words simply refused to come, but her involuntary silence was more expressive than the most eloquent phrases. The audience understood and all hearts went out to this citizen whom success has left unspoiled.

' "I don't know what to say",' stammered Gracie, then she added, "I just say I am happy I can do it."

'The whole audience then joined in the singing of For She's A Jolly Good Fellow, and Miss Fields, in a voice a trifle more composed said,

' "I am sure I do thank everybody. I have really enjoyed myself this week. It has been wonderful." Then, tossing up her head she remarked, "And thanks for sending me home with a red nose."

'Gracie was the first to leave the stage, and uttering "goodbyes" as she left, ran through the wings to her dressing room.'

In 1933 Gracie opened an orphanage at Peacehaven in Sussex. This was because the Theatrical Ladies Guild (now the Variety Artistes Ladies Guild) needed somewhere for the children of actors and actresses who had either died or were ill and temporarily unable to provide for them. The home was to 'keep, clothe and educate needy children of professional people until they reach an age where they are capable of looking after themselves, to give them a happier, sunnier outlook on life, and to strive to maintain that outlook after they leave it to make room for other little ones.'

Gracie's mother and father, her manager, Bert Aza, her two sisters, Edie and Betty, and their husbands were all present at the opening ceremony, as were many celebrities of the day—music hall artistes Charles Coburn, Robb Wilton, Norman Long and Charles Austin, and Sir Harry Preston and Dominions Secretary Mr J.H. Thomas. Gracie made a little speech, then the guests all had tea in the large dining-room before departing.

Twelve children were the nucleus of the orphanage, which was originally the first house Gracie had bought for her parents. They had found it 'a bit far from pub and fish and chip shop, lass,' so she bought another one for them nearer to the good things of life, and, with additions, the first house became the Peacehaven Orphanage. The Guild ran it, and Gracie financed it until 1967, when it closed through lack of children needing it. The two remaining were found homes in the area, and the house was sold (it is now an old people's home).

The number of children fluctuated through the years between twelve and twenty-five. Gracie went to see them frequently and kept in touch with the matron about the welfare of her charges.

'I should like to *be* the matron,' she said once, 'I suppose that sounds funny, but it's true; I love kids and I'd see they were all one big, happy family.'

Most of her visits were private ones—when she lived in Telscombe (during the latter half of the thirties), it was near enough for her to pop in for a while, and she did this often. When she broadcast, all the 'repeat' fees went to the orphanage, and when she was asked to open anything, from a store to a cinema or holiday camp, she usually asked for the fee, whether it was £15 or £250, to go to the orphanage fund.

* * * *

Many things have been named after Gracie: a ship, aeroplane, theatre, cocktail, rose, once even an elephant and a horse.

The horse, a London dray, saved Charlie Gardner's life once. For thirteen years Charlie and Gracie delivered beer to the pubs on their round. One day, outside the White Horse in Shoreditch, Charlie was taken ill. He managed to climb into his seat before collapsing, and Gracie realising after a while that something was wrong, nudged Quota, the young horse in the traces with her, who hadn't been on the rounds as long, and set off back to the depot. It was a mile through busy roads and three sets of traffic lights, where she had to wait because they were red, and when she reached the brewery she whinnied and made a fuss until someone came to see what was wrong. Charlie was taken to hospital, and a few weeks later he and his horse Gracie were back together on the rounds they knew so well.

Gracie's ship was launched on 8 April 1936 at Southampton. *Gracie Fields*—a 393-ton pad-dle steamer was built by John I. Thorneycroft. She cost £35,740, and her captain was N.R. Larkin.

As the *Gracie Fields* glided into the water, her namesake led the crowds who were watching in 'Sing As We Go'. Several thousand people watched the launch, and Gracie, from her position by the microphone, gave those at the back a running commentary on the scene from where she stood.

Two hundred guests sat down to a luncheon afterwards at the South Western Hotel, where a novel feature was the naming of the tables after principal marks in the waterway served by the ships of the Red Funnel Company. The top table was called Southampton Water, while the others became the Solent, Spithead, the Needles, Cowes Roads, Sandown Bay, St Catherine's Point and Christchurch Bay.

The Red Funnel Company, whose flag is blue, green, red and white, and whose first four ships were named *Sapphire, Emerald, Ruby* and *Pearl*, presented Gracie with a brooch in the shape of the flag and incorporating the four gems (the colours of their flag), and she treasured and wore it frequently until it was stolen when she was in America many, many years afterwards and never recovered.

An easy-to-remember poem shows the arrangement of the flag's colours:

Blue to mast, Green to fly,
Red on deck and White on high.

Gracie also received a silver christening mug and a lifebelt inscribed with the name of her ship from Sir John Thorneycroft, and from the Portsmouth and District Lancashire

Society an ornamental clog, inscribed 'To Our Gracie with best wishes', and an enormous bunch of red roses.

Gracie Fields was on the Southampton to Isle of Wight service, and soon after her launching Gracie took all the children from her orphanage for a trip in her.

On 15 July 1939 the steamer was involved in an incident with a flying boat. As she was leaving Southampton for Ryde, filled with holiday-makers, at the mouth of Southampton Water an RAF flying boat from Calshot struck her foremast and crashed into the sea alongside, with its starboard wing shattered. No one was hurt, although several passengers suffered shock. Jagged pieces of metal from the ripped wing were showered onto the ship, which had her foremast snapped off and her port bow damaged.

The *Gracie Fields* was called up for war service on 22 September 1939. Putting on her warpaint at Dover, she was used, as many paddle steamers were, as a minesweeper, serving with the 10th Minesweeping Flotilla.

At 2100 hours on 27 May 1940 she left Dover for Dunkirk, arriving at 0300 hours on the following day. She proceeded to transfer troops from the shore to the waiting HMS *Calcutta*. After a few trips between the shore and HMS *Calcutta*, she sailed home to Margate with 281 troops on board.

The following day she returned to Dunkirk and took about 750 troops off La Panne beach. She was starting back across the Channel when she was attacked by dive-bombers off Middle Kerke buoy. Hit amidships by a bomb, she was unable to stop her engines and was continuing underway at six knots when her helm jammed. A small craft, *The Twentie,* secured alongside, transferring as many wounded and others as she could carry. Another craft, the *Jutland,* then steamed alongside, secured and took off more troops. After she had pulled away, low in the water beneath her human cargo, HMS *Pangbourne,* already damaged by near misses, and with twenty-four casualties aboard, went alongside, took off eighty troops and, after a difficult manoeuvre, took the crippled paddler in tow.

At 0130 hours on Thursday 30 May 1940, the *Gracie Fields* reported that she was sinking. *Pangbourne* took off the stricken ship's crew, slipped the tow and abandoned her. The last call from the paddle steamer *Gracie Fields* came from 51° 20′N, 02° 05′E.

Gracie said when her ship sank, 'It makes me feel sad, but as J.B. Priestley wrote, "she went down doing her duty".'

The hybrid tea-rose named for her was deep buttercup yellow and won a gold medal for its breeder, Mr George Frederick Letts of Hadleigh, Suffolk, in 1938, when it was introduced.

It had fine, glossy leaves which were mildew-proof, produced vigorous growth and was free flowering and an ideal bedding variety. It had a rich, fruity, sweet-briar scent, and sold, in 1938, for 2s 6d a bush, 24 shillings a dozen. At 2s 6d a bush it was among the more expensive roses in the catalogue, but it proved very popular.

It takes up to ten years to breed a new rose, and 'Gracie Fields' was raised from original stock of 'The Evening News' and 'Daily Mail'. George Letts sent Gracie a bouquet of 'her roses', and she sent him back a photograph of her with them. Although he saw and heard Gracie many times, George Letts never met her. 'She was always my favourite,' he said, 'I admired her tremendously.

In January 1938 the *Rochdale Observer* launched a 'Portrait Fund'. They asked people to send a shilling, or as many shillings as they could, towards a portrait of 'Our Greatest Townswoman'.

In a little over a month, more than thirty thousand readers had contributed 15,046 shillings, making a total of £752, and forty-five-year-old James Gunn, later knighted as one of Britain's most eminent artists, was asked to paint the portrait which now, when it is not on loan to art galleries in different parts of the country, hangs in Rochdale Art Gallery.

Typically, when it was unveiled and presented to her, Gracie said, 'I feel that this is the most magnificent tribute that has ever been paid to any artiste. I am very, very happy and thrilled. You have proved now that you *do* think something about me—and I think something about you too.' Laughing, she added, 'I took three weeks off specially to pose for this picture, otherwise it would never have got done and Rochdalians would have said, "Hey! You've got our shillings—stop mucking about." '

Gracie gave the painting to the art gallery right away. 'He's made me quite nice looking,' she quipped.

Thirty years later, when she was appearing at Batley Variety Club, Graham Garner, a Rochdale taxi-owner, drove her over to Rochdale to see her Auntie Margaret, who had not been well. As they went past the gallery, Gracie said, 'There's a painting of me in there.'

Graham asked her if she would like to go in and see it.

'Yes, please,' she answered quietly. Her husband Boris, her friend Ada Schofield and her sister Edith were with her. As they looked at it, Graham said,

'Do you remember when they gave you that at the Regal Cinema,* and you stood against it and said, "Is it like me?" '

Gracie looked wistful. 'I remember,' she said.

1938 was quite a year for public recognition. She was awarded the CBE, the first woman variety artiste to receive it.

Waiting with the other people in the Ballroom at Buckingham Palace, Gracie said afterwards, was 'like something you read about, a wonderful fairy story—I watched a man being knighted, and believe me I felt a long, long way from ordinary life at that moment.'

The crowd waiting outside the palace cheered her as she came out with her medal. Shortly afterwards she was given the Order of St John of Jerusalem for her work for hospitals and the Red Cross, the first actress to receive this, not lightly given, award. The Priory in Clerkenwell is the headquarters of the Order in England, and it was there that Gracie was invested as an Officer Sister of the Order; she left with the eight-pointed cross pinned to her dress, driving through the beautiful, historic Gatehouse whose pavements were lined with her fans. A typical 'Gracie incident' happened then. She saw a

* Now ABC

little old lady peering round the corner of the arch where no one was supposed to be, and she asked for her car to be stopped, alighted and showed her the cross, which she wore frequently and treasured for the rest of her life. Many years later, on hearing of a friend's recognition also, she commented, 'Sisters in the service of mankind.'

In May the town of her birth gave her the highest honour it could bestow on a citizen. The day Gracie received the Freedom of her hometown lived forever in her heart. She loved Rochdale—the Rochdale of her childhood and youth especially, because a lot of her memories were there.

Many moving and inspiring words were spoken that day, great crowds cheered her, and the nation 'listened in' to a lively interview conducted by Richard North, who was described as 'the travelling radio reporter' of the North Region staff. The broadcast also went out on Empire Transmitters to her admirers in Australia, New Zealand, Canada and South Africa.

When the ceremony was over, Gracie went onto the town hall balcony to receive the cheers and good wishes of the thousands of people who were packing the streets below. From the many lovely moments of that day (when she admitted softly, 'I'm all nerves'), three items above all else *show* us Gracie,

I think. The last part of her reply to the Mayor: 'Wherever I go in this big world of ours, this casket is going to go with me. I shan't need it to remind me of Rochdale, because I couldn't forget it if I tried. But it is going to go with me wherever I go, and from the bottom of my heart I thank you very much indeed. Thank you.' The other two were not words but deeds. Gracie had a rug made by the Disabled Men's Handicrafts Ltd and presented it to the Mayor before she left the town hall. The wool rug bore the Rochdale coat of arms. Also she suggested, and gave, three performances for local charities after the official presentation, before leaving for London around midnight on that historic day.

After the solemnity of the citation Gracie had lunch with the Mayor and city dignitaries. Then she lightened the proceedings by riding round the town on a fire engine in full fireman's gear, before going to the theatre for the first of her charity shows.

Eighteen years later, in 1956, when Rochdale celebrated its centenary as a borough, the magazine *Lancashire Life* asked her what Rochdale meant to her, and she wrote:

'You ask what Rochdale means to me— perhaps you will think my answer strange, but to me Rochdale means "first". In Rochdale I first opened my eyes. In Rochdale I first cried—first laughed—heard the birds sing for the first time, I sang too for the first time in my life. I was even spanked for the first time in Rochdale. And in Rochdale I wore my first pair of clogs.

'My first, and almost my only schooling took place in Rochdale at the Parish Church School. My first tram ride around the town, my first swimming lessons in her baths, and when very young, slipping into the Ship Canal along with the other children for an extra swim during the hot summer days.

'My first job was as an errand girl for a confectioner's shop—for this I got a shilling a week and my mother complained that it cost her *two* shillings a week to have my shoes repaired after all the walking I did on the job.

'My first song on a stage was sung at the Old Circus in Rochdale where now stands the Hippodrome.

'My first job as a winder was in Pouches old cotton mill way down off Oldham Road. My work since then has meant travelling the world over, to great places and small, but "Home" to me always means Rochdale and its gradely folk. My memories are ever sweet and homely. I see all Rochdale's lovely parks and gardens, the beautiful walks all so near—Healey Dell, Hollingworth Lake, and

142

all the rest.

'On my travels too I am reminded so often all over the world of home, whenever I see the machinery and products of Rochdale proudly stamped with the names of her great manufacturers. Once, in Naples, one of the Cirio people—they make jams and sauces—told me that the machinery in their factories came from Rochdale. You can just imagine how proud that made me.'

She took great pride in the town of her birth and early years, and, although she left it when she was sixteen and never returned there to live—'I probably would have done if it had been by the sea,' she often said jokingly—in the years before the war she went back frequently, always staying with her old friends the Schofields, who ran an off-licence in Milkstone Road.

She returned after the war too, but less often, although she always was, as Rochdale's current Member of Parliament Cyril Smith once said, 'Rochdale's greatest ambassadress'.

She mentioned the town in concerts, broadcasts and other countries, from east to west, north to south, and anyone who had ever heard of Gracie Fields always knew she originally came from Rochdale.

'Where do you live?'

'Rochdale.'

'Ah—Gracie Fields' town,' is a common occurrence for the natives of the town in conversations with other folk all over the world.

CHAPTER 9

Illness and Divorce

In 1953 Gracie toured South Africa. There had been a delay on the film *Queen of Hearts* when one of the actors was ill, and the film was only finished and 'in the can' at three o'clock on the morning she sailed.

For a few days she rested, then she began rehearsing for the South African concerts. Gracie, superstitious over some things, wasn't over colours, and she wore a dark green dress on her arrival in South Africa.

'Friends told me it was an unlucky colour,' she said later, 'but it wasn't so for me.'

Her brother Tommy went to South Africa with her. 'Her reception was phenomenal,' he told me. 'I'd never seen anything like it. Every usherette from every theatre and cinema—all lined up with bouquets of flowers, bands playing...we drove from the docks in open cars, right through the whole of Cape Town, and there was the ticker tape flowing down, and thousands of people who had taken the day off work to welcome

145

Gracie. It really was an incredible experience.'

That tour of South Africa was a surprise to Gracie too. She thought she would have to win them over but found that many people were already committed fans.

'I was totally unprepared for my reception in South Africa,' she said later, 'and their welcome unnerved me.'

They had heard her records and seen her films, and when she did a thirty-minute act for her first show in that country, the critics complained that it wasn't nearly long enough. Gracie said, 'All the criticism, instead of being directed at me, was somehow thrust onto the orchestra. It just shows you the advantage of having a reputation. If the show was a flop it couldn't be Gracie Fields—it must be the miserable, anonymous orchestra.'

She did a typical 'Gracie' thing then— invited the critics to come back at her expense and she would put on a 'better show'. She told them she had been nervous after such a welcome and hadn't realised that they expected a longer performance, but that it had nothing to do with the orchestra and was entirely her fault. When she left Cape Town, that orchestra gave her a silver plaque which said, 'To Our Gracie from the orchestra', and there wasn't one of them who would not have followed her anywhere to play for her.

While they were in South Africa, Gracie saw as much of the country as she could, visiting gold and diamond mines and talking to as many people as possible.

'I'll always remember going to the diamond sorting department and holding piles of the stones, just letting them trickle through our hands,' Tommy Fields said, 'and Gracie laughing and saying how rich she felt.'

They toured from Cape Town to Johannesburg, and at each station crowds were wating to catch a glimpse of Gracie, and so she sang from the observation platform at each stop along the line.

She was in South Africa for Christmas 1935, and the BBC arranged for her to broadcast a message to people in Britain, but they could not get through, and, as it was to be 'live' and not a recorded message, there was nothing to be done. The tour was so successful that it was extended by six weeks.

On the day she returned she went into Broadcasting House for a short interview. The announcer simply said, 'Here she is— just back from South Africa,' no names or long, elaborate lead-in, and Gracie's voice went into thousands of rooms with her usual greeting, 'Hullo everybody...'

In 1930 she toured America. 'I was a flop for the first three days,' she said, 'and most unhappy. I didn't feel right.'

Many British artistes have not done well in the USA, and vice versa. Humour especially does not always travel, but she was a singer as well as a comedienne.

Always nervous before she went on, and with some critics saying that the Americans would never understand her accent, she had many qualms, but Gracie enjoyed a challenge too, and by the end of the first week she really *did* have a success on her hands.

'The first three days *were* a flop,' she insisted, 'but I worked on it.'

'She has a voice packed tight with soul-appeal, a gorgeous sense of comedy-values and a versatility in delineation that is rarely combined in one individual. She had the Palace mob at her feet and trailed off in a dizzy array of encores. These United States will hear plenty more of the Lancashire Lassie,' the American newspaper *The Billboard* enthused wordily.

This kind of thing always frightened Gracie. 'In America they billed me as *Gracie Fields—The Funniest Woman In The World* well that petrified me for a start,' she said. She always did have a wonderful reception in the USA after that.

Her brother Tommy was in New York several years after the war when Gracie was working at the Plaza Hotel, doing five shows

148

a day.

'I'd never seen her work in America,' he told me, 'so I went along. When she came onto the floor, I was absolutely amazed because everybody stood up and applauded. She had a terrific reception even before she opened her mouth.' She sometimes chided her audiences for doing this. 'You shouldn't clap too soon, you'll put me off; wait and see if I'm worth it.'

Everywhere it was the same story: streets lined with her fans, Gracie standing up in an open car so as many as possible could see her; whenever she went on tour, in England or abroad, it was like a royal progress. She felt a duty to the people to let them see her when they obviously wanted this so much, but she was frightened when they mobbed her.

Once, outside a theatre in Britain when this happened, she opened the car window when she had reached safety, and really went for the crowd.

'You *know* I usually stop, but it's a special family party tonight, and now you've torn my dress *and* made me late...'

She didn't often fall out with her admirers. 'Some of 'em overdo it a bit,' she declared, but mostly she accepted it as part of her work. 'I'm grateful they want to see me,' she said more than once, 'but there are times...'

Another occasion was when she went dashing in at the stage door and could not get through because of a small crowd waiting there. And this was *before* the show. She knew most of their faces—they were regular followers. Fighting her way through, she grew very cross: 'You're mad,' she said, 'hanging about here this cold weather...' It was December. She apologised when she came out and saw them there again. 'I was late, and a bit edgy.' Then, in a different tone, 'I *still* think you're all crazy.'

Yet they came, and Gracie saw and spoke to as many of them as she could. Her warmth and personality drew people to her, and they adored her as much as a woman as they did as a singer.

'I'm ordinary,' she said to them, 'don't raise me too high...'

* * * *

Queen Of Hearts, the film Gracie finished in 1936 before she went to South Africa, was a great success. She did another film with Basil Dean—*The Show Goes On*—a story superficially like her own, and then in 1937 Monty Banks directed her in *We're Going To Be Rich* (in the USA this was titled *He Was Her Man).*

This was Gracie's second film with Monty

directing; she still did not care for film-making, the stage was her real forte, but she was committed to the films for a while. It seems generally agreed among the critics that Monty Banks captured Gracie on film as well as anyone ever did.

She and Monty Banks had a lot in common. Both had been poor and through sheer guts and hard work had reached the top. Monty's name was really Mario Bianchi, and he was born in Cesana, northern Italy. His first wife was Gladys Frazin, an actress with a history of mental illness. He had been a stunt man and an actor before his directing days. As well as being an exceedingly good director, he was full of fun.

'Everyone *liked* Monty,' Tommy Fields told me. 'He was easy-going and a laugh a minute. His greatest fault was the gambling. He couldn't stop, and he got through a lot of money. In the end, like most gamblers who keep on, losing more than winning.'

He and Gracie grew to like one another very much, and gradually it became a lot more than that, and Gracie knew that, if she was free, and Monty asked her, she would marry him. Archie wanted a divorce so he could marry Annie Lipman, and since 1932 he and Gracie had been unofficially separated and leading their own lives.

Gracie was doing a film a year, tours, concerts, records, appearances at charity functions where she always 'gave 'em three penn'orth not two', to use an expression of hers. Wherever she went in a private capacity, crowds gathered and persuaded her to 'Give us a song Gracie, just one.' She nearly always did; she said more than once about her fans, 'I don't know what they'll ask me to do next, but whatever it is I'll do it.'

In 1938 she made *Keep Smiling,* with Roger Livesey as her co-star, and in 1939 the film that completed the four that she was paid £50,000 each for, *Shipyard Sally,* which also had Sydney Howard in the cast.

For many months she had not been feeling well, and when that last film was in the can, she went to the doctor. He sent her to hospital where they did an exploratory operation. Afterwards they told her she had cancer and they wanted to operate again.

'They gave her less than a fifty fifty chance,' Tommy Fields said, 'but if she didn't have the operation she would be dead within the year.'

Gracie, now aged forty-one, had always wanted children. As the eldest she had mothered her two sisters and her brother, possibly more than most elder sisters because, being on the stage and away from home, she really had looked after them when Jenny sent them out to join the company on tour. When the doctor told her gently, 'I'm afraid it means a hysterectomy,' her dreams in that direction were swept swiftly away.

'The hours in which I had to tell myself—well you can't have everything—weren't all that easy,' she said later, 'but maybe I was getting a bit long in the tooth for kids anyway, yet somehow, until then I had still hoped.'

After the operation in June 1939 she was unconscious for three days, and almost without exception the nation prayed for her. In churches of all denominations prayers were offered, asking, *begging,* for her recovery. *Half a million* letters, hundreds of bunches of flowers and gifts were sent to her at the Chelsea Hospital for Women. It was an incredible demonstration of affection for this woman who had sung and clowned, but especially sung, her way into the hearts of so many people.

'Gracie gravely ill,' read the headlines, 'Miss Gracie Fields underwent an internal operation last night. Her condition is serious.'

'As I write the nation is hanging on the news from the Chelsea Hospital for Women. It is "Our Gracie" who is fighting. Readers will not desire that I should say more.'

The pavements outside the hospital were covered with straw to deaden the sounds;

bulletins were issued twice daily to cope with the overwhelming flood of enquiries, and the *Daily Express* cartoonist Strube showed his famous 'Little Man'—Mr Average, with bowler hat and umbrella standing outside the hospital with a bunch of flowers in his hand and looking upwards towards a partially opened window.

Slowly, very slowly, Gracie recovered. 'Whenever the pain was bad,' she said in her book, *Sing As We Go,* 'whenever I drifted away and came back again, I always saw Mary by my bedside. I think she could never have gone home. One of the most wonderful things I remember about that long illness was the sight of Mary there whenever I opened my eyes.'

Mary Barratt (later Davey) had come to work for Gracie in the middle thirties and remained one of her closest friends. Monty Banks, as well as Mary Barratt, was her constant companion while she was so ill, along with her mother and father and favourite cousin Margaret.

She only complained once, according to Mary—and that was when she grumbled about the bed being too low—she wanted one of the high hospital ones. They gave her one, and she settled down to concentrate on getting well again.

As soon as she could walk, she visited the

other wards, sharing her flowers with all the patients, until the hospital resembled a magnificent nursery.

She left hospital in July 1939 after six weeks there, to find a huge crowd waiting outside to greet her. She was pale and unsteady, and the sight of the people brought the tears to her eyes. For a moment it seemed they were about to cheer. Ballet dancer Anton Dolin was there.

'She saw this,' he said, 'or sensed it, and raised her hand to stop them. There was not a sound, and then all the men in that great crowd took their hats off. It was an incredible moment—as though she were a queen and they were paying homage.'

At that time the public were not told that Gracie had been operated on for cancer of the cervix. In 1939 the word cancer was avoided if possible, but Gracie was a wonderful example of recovery from this disease, for she lived and worked at a pretty full pace for another forty years. She had to have check-ups afterwards, but in 1954 she was told she need not come again—she was clear.

On 22 July 1939 her divorce petition came up. One newspaper reported the following day: 'The marriage was in 1923 at The Register Office, Wandsworth, and there are no children. Petitioner's case was that because of unhappiness she was compelled to leave her husband in 1932, and since then had had no communication from him. It was alleged that respondent committed adultery with Miss Annie Lipman, his secretary, at a Hastings hotel, and they had lived together at Hampstead.

'Petitioner, who gave evidence from a seat in the witness box, asked for the discretion of the court in her favour, and put in a statement which the judge read.

'The judge said he was satisfied it was a proper case for a decree, and he exercised discretion in petitioner's favour. The proceedings lasted half an hour. Mr Norman Birkett KC, and Mr Aitken Watson were her counsel, and Mr Pitt was represented by Mr P.M. Cloutman.

'Miss Fields arrived at the law courts in a private car, accompanied by a relative and a nurse. It was raining heavily and few people had assembled. When the case was over her two companions, holding an arm each, assisted her from the court to the adjoining lift. They went to the ground floor and out through the judge's exit to the quadrangle, where her car was waiting.

'The small crowd which had by this time assembled raised a cheer and Gracie waved her hand in response. She was looking pale and rather drawn. Immediately she and her companions were seated the car drove away on the return journey to Peace-haven.'

From there, a few days later, Gracie left for Capri for two years' rest as the doctors prescribed. Before she left, she broadcast to the nation, and that broadcast made history, for in the House of Commons that evening Sir Samuel Hoare said, 'Gracie Fields is on the air tonight. It is obvious that the debate must end at an early hour.'

Gracie thanked all the people who had helped her over what she described as 'the most dreadful ordeal of my forty-one years.' She thanked her surgeon, New Zealand born Mr Searle, the doctors and nurses at the hospital, and the Bishop of Blackburn who said prayers with her. Her voice almost broke as she thanked people from all over the world for their love and gifts. Then she sang 'I Love The Moon', a song written by Paul Rubens during the First World War, and to which is attached a most moving story.

Paul Rubens wrote many musical plays* and composed scores for several Gaiety hits. He fell in love with Phyllis Dare ** and followed her around the country. Suffering

* Among the most famous were *Florodora, The Toreador, Betty* and *Tonight's the Night.*
**Actress, singer, leading lady and sister of Zena Dare.

157

from consumption, he knew he had not long to live when he wrote 'I Love The Moon' and dedicated it to Phyllis.

Gracie told her listeners when she sang it in 1939, 'The words express all I'm trying to say to you now,' and in homes throughout the country people wept to hear that golden voice again.

I love the moon, I love the sun,
I love the forests, the flowers, the fun,
I love the wild birds—the dawn and the
    dew,
But best of all I love you—I love you...

CHAPTER 10

Gracie and Monty

Six weeks later war broke out. Gracie was in love with Monty Banks, and they had planned to be married once she was well again. Now Gracie's one thought was to get back from Capri to Britain and do her bit for the war effort.

They left the following day, and when Monty and Mary remonstrated with her that she was not yet fit to work, she said, 'I must. Work will be the best tonic I could have. In some small way it will be a thank you to all the folk who've helped me through this illness.'

Basil Dean was organising ENSA (Entertainments National Service Association, which comedian Tommy Trinder laughingly changed to 'Every Night Something Awful'), and he said later that the most requested stars for ENSA concerts were Will Fyffe, Gracie Fields and George Formby.

Gracie said she would entertain troops anywhere, and in November she was on her way to France; Mary Barratt and Monty

Banks were with her. The first two concerts were planned for Douai and Arras, but before they reached their destination the car broke down, and Mary and Monty had to get out and push it from the mud. They made Gracie sit still—in any case she would not have had the strength then to do anything else.

The vehicle broke down repeatedly, and on one of these occasions, near Metz, an army convoy caught them up. They recognised Gracie, who was standing by the car while the others wrestled with it, and with help from the British Army they got it going again, and Gracie gave her first concert there and then.

'How those lads sang and shouted for more,' she said later. 'I was still weak, but on that road in France, leaning against the car door for some support, and surrounded by the paraphernalia of war, I knew I was back in the fray.'

The boys in that convoy also remembered, as John Graven Hughes recalls in *The Greasepaint War*. When the leading three-ton truck pulled up, he says a corporal shouted, 'It's our Gracie.'

'And it *was* Gracie Fields, with her gaiety and humour in the broad down-to-earth idiom of Rochdale; that voice of startling clarity and irresistible quality. They crowded round to give her a welcome, and a soldier said, as they always did, "Give us a song, Gracie". She threw her hat to Monty Banks, stood on the running board and sang Sally, unaccompanied, to soldiers perched on top of tanks and on the sides of Bren-gun carriers.'

Gracie recalls, 'Most of the boys were like old friends. They'd seen me on the halls or heard me on the radio, and I suppose I was part of the life they left behind. The songs I sang—When I Grow Too Old To Dream and The Isle of Capri, and Little Old Lady, were the ones they'd whistled on the way to work, and when they heard them again in France they were back home for a little while.'

They went on to their planned venues, Arras and Douai, and Gracie admitted long afterwards that she was shaking with nerves she felt so weak.

The late Godfrey Winn described the scene as told to him by the compère, who said he never wished to meet a greater trouper: 'In front of the footlights she suddenly came back to life, but backstage she hardly seemed to know what she was doing. She was in a complete daze—a very sick woman still....'

The little party went on through France, and Gracie spent Christmas singing to the troops at Rheims. The weather was atrocious.

Mary Hemingway, who was there as a reporter for a Fleet Street newspaper, wrote later in *McCalls:*

'Some units were tented down in the empty harvested beet fields, and although with hearty cockney humour they had named the rows between tent rows after Piccadilly and The Strand, their tents were pitched open to the prevailing west wind.

'Their kitchen and mess area were set up in a mudprovoking hollow. When I wondered aloud to an officer about the setup he answered jovially, "No matter, they're not getting killed."

'Nobody was looking forward to the Christmas "holidays" until word got around that Gracie Fields was coming to Rheims to give a concert. Officers not invited. Only petty officers, tommies, and aircraft-maintenance crews could come.

'Spirits ballooned; Rheims was in the centre of the champagne country and the most uncomfortable British encampments. The Christmas Day weather wasn't too bad, and the army cooks managed to roast sides of beef for dinner. But a murderous storm whirled up that night, coating roads with ice, and camouflaging ditches with snowbanks.

' "She'll never make it", people muttered. But she did, and so did the others of her cast and the small orchestra that accompanied

162

her. (Her chauffeur told me the drive from Paris was "a horror", but Gracie said, "It was nothing, ducks.")

'The Rheims Opera House, its cup running over with tommies, must have quaked the town with the racket of the audience's welcome when Gracie hurried on stage. After the nasty drive she looked fresh as a fresh peach, cheerful as Father Christmas, bright as a tulip, with her blonde hair shining, and loving, loving. She was the happy essence of Home.

'When the uproar subsided she sang her signature tune, Sally, and at its end the old roof lifted an inch or two off its pinnings. She sang all their favourites, and for the finale Gracie and her troupe onstage joined hands, advanced to the proscenium, and clasped hands with the soldiers from the front row seats, leaning out over the orchestra pit, and the whole house sang, "Should auld acquaintance be forgot..."

'Outside in the freezing air soldiers climbed into the open backs of lorries squeezing themselves together, for a twenty or thirty mile ride, like upended planks. One after another of the lorryfuls of young men picked up the tune and sang, "Roll Out The Barrel, we'll have a barrel of fun..." and some lorries changed it to, "We've *had* a barrel of fun", their voices echoing diminuendo in the frosty night.

'Gracie Fields that Christmas was one to whom I am ever grateful.'

Listeners to the BBC after the nine o'clock news heard a NAAFI Variety Concert organised by ENSA, 'Gracie with Jack Payne and his band from Somewhere in France...'

On a couple of occasions Jack Payne and his band had transport difficulties and were delayed *en route,* so Gracie and Monty turned out an old sketch from her theatrical basket, according to Basil Dean in *A Theatre At War.* They rehearsed, and all went well, but when they came to the performance, which included Harry Parr-Davies (composer and Gracie's accompanist) and Mary Barrett, Basil Dean says that, 'Monty's startling improvisations, verbal and gymnastic, delighted the troops but reduced Gracie to such helpless laughter that she forgot to "feed" him with the correct lines, and the so-called dramatic sketch ended in Marx Brothers confusion.'

Gracie sang her way through France, then went back to Capri for a couple of weeks to recover a little. Everyone I spoke to who worked with or saw Gracie Fields during the war gave me the same picture. She went wherever was suggested as long as there were troops who needed entertainment.

Richard Murdoch and Arthur Askey

worked with her in Lille and Amiens and said, 'She was a tonic—did a marvellous show, and the receptions those soldiers gave her—absolutely fantastic.'

And Arthur Askey said, 'My God, she worked. Often when I'd had enough and they said, "There's a bit of an isolated camp down the road," she'd go. Twenty, thirty miles, she could be tired out, but she'd climb into the lorry, or jeep or whatever transport was taking her, and when she got on the stage, no matter how rough and improvised it might be, she seemed to shed that tiredness and become a different person.'

Gracie and Monty acquired a mobile tea-van, and at the next stop she had great fun when the boys crowded round to find it was 'Our Gracie' dishing out the tea.

In January 1940 they returned to Britain, and Gracie went to Greenock, singing to the Navy. She toured camps all over the British Isles, then went back to Capri to collect some clothes.

Her parents were in America with her sister and some of the grandchildren, in the block of flats she had bought when she was over there in 1936, and although she *wanted* to be married in Britain, her mother's general health wasn't good, and she was going blind, so Gracie and Monty decided to marry in California where her family could be present.

They wed in March 1940. Gracie wore a blue costume, white blouse and white shoes, and a smart pillbox hat for the ceremony, which was conducted by Judge Joseph Marchetti in her parents' home. Gracie clung to the hope that they could have a further ceremony in the church at Telscombe in Sussex where they lived and where her orphanage was. This needed permission from the Bishop of Chichester because Monty was a Roman Catholic, and both parties had been through a divorce.

It never happened, largely because events of the outside world caught them rapidly.

They both knew it might be difficult if Italy went in with Germany because Monty was still Italian. Years before, he had taken out naturalisation papers to become an American citizen but had never filled them in. He had land in Italy, several farms which his sister managed, but he had spent most of his adult life in the USA.

Tommy Fields told me, 'Monty's sister was told by the Italian government, "You won't be allowed food for your cattle unless you become a Fascist." '

All this Gracie and Monty knew, and so anxiety was an additional burden to the worries on Monty's part about his wife's health, and another stress for Gracie to cope with in her weakened state.

Two days after their wedding Gracie did a show with Maurice Chevalier at Drury Lane in London, and another in the Opera House, Paris, 'to promote goodwill between France and England'.

She and Monty both entertained the troops in France until nearly the end of May 1940, when most of the ENSA people were brought home before the German occupation. Back in Britain they toured the military camps and the factories. They returned to London, and Gracie was alone in their hotel when the legendary *Sunday Express* columnist Lord Castlerosse telephoned to urge Monty to go to America or Eire. 'It's most important,' he said, 'to do with his folks at home.' When Monty returned, Gracie took a deep-breath and told him, and together they faced the knowledge that, because he had never finished and filed those papers to make him a United States citizen, he would be an enemy, in technical terms, if not in thought and desire, of his wife's country.

Gracie said later, 'I loved my country and I loved my husband, and in the end I reached what seemed to me to be a fair compromise.'

On 11 June 1940 Italy entered the war on the German side, and Monty Banks immediately became 'an enemy alien'.

Gracie had managed to get a meeting with

Winston Churchill and two or three other ministers, and Churchill told her the best thing she could do was to earn some dollars for Britain.

'We need all the American dollars we can get,' he said. 'You, as an Englishwoman, can travel almost anywhere, but if you want to work for Britain it's no good earning English pounds, Gracie, but if you can earn American dollars for Britain you will be doing her the greatest service you can.'

If Monty had stayed in Britain, he would have been interned because he was Italian. No wife worth her salt was going to see that happen if she could prevent it. Gracie's parents, nieces and nephews were already in America. This had torn her in two as well. 'I thought, if that ship goes down with my family—I've influenced them and the children to go away,' she said.

On Thursday 30 May, wearing a red, white and blue rosette on her coat, Gracie and Monty sailed for the USA and Canada. In Canada they met more trouble. Monty, said the officials, would have to be interned.

'What about me?' Gracie asked. 'I'm his wife.'

She was there to give concerts for the Navy League, and Monty's plans were to go on to America and become a US citizen. Arguments ensued, but eventually they allowed him to travel on, and Gracie stayed in Canada with her pianist, Harry Parr-Davies, and did thirty-two concerts across the land.

That tour resulted in £170,000 for the Navy League. Gracie took no fee during the war. (The only money that actually passed through her hands was a cheque for $1,000 given her by a Frenchman after she had sung 'There'll Always Be An England' at a private party. Gracie sent the cheque to Rochdale's MP, Dr Morgan, 'for the most needy causes of our hometown'.) Her accommodation, meals and transport were provided, but that was all. When the concerts were finished, she went to California for a week to see her husband and family.

She wasn't a fit woman, and anyone who has ever undertaken journeyings of far less than the thousands of miles she did then will realise some of the strain she was experiencing. After that strenuous Canadian tour she desperately needed a rest. But that was when the hounding gathered momentum.

Headlines screamed from some of the newspapers that Gracie Fields had *deserted* her country, had taken *all* her money and jewellery abroad. 'Traitor' and 'cheat' are strong words—both were used against her, and the wounds went deep.

Monty wanted her to give up everything and live in America, but Gracie knew she could never do that.

'My conscience is clear,' she said when she returned to Canada for her second Navy League tour the following week, and the reporters rattled their questions at her. 'If I have done anything I shouldn't have done, I will go and put it right. I'm going back to England when I've finished this tour anyway; but what have I done wrong?'

In her heart she knew it was because she was married to an Italian. 'Monty was practically the cause of the war according to the papers, she said bitterly afterwards.

Mr J.J. Davidson, the MP for Maryhill, Glasgow, tabled a question in the House of Commons asking why Miss Gracie Fields was allowed to take £8,000 out of the country in October 1939, and Monty Banks, her husband, to take £20,000. The reply was that permission to take out the money had been applied for the previous October.

'The application was supported by a strong medical recommendation. It was decided that the sum asked for was excessive, but permission was given for the sum of £8,000. This *was* a large amount, but the circumstances were unusual and it was expected that Miss Fields, after her recovery, would earn dollars in America which would be surrendered to the state. Miss Fields was also granted a sum for the support of her parents in the United States, and a further sum to meet life insurance premiums payable under prewar contracts. These allocations were in accordance with normal practice.'

The answer continued, 'The restriction on taking out jewellery imposed on July 1st 1940, did not exist when Miss Fields left the country.'

Monty Banks, angry at what he saw as grossly unfair, and anxious about Gracie's poor health, said in an interview with Associated Press, '*I* am not a British Citizen and it is my own money. Anyway we followed the usual procedure, making regular application for permission to take our money with us. It is just because I am Italian that they are trying to make things disagreeable for Miss Fields. I wish they would cease. She has been giving very generously of her time and her talents. If they bother us any more I am going to telephone to her to come home and live like a normal person.'

And Gracie, hurt and bewildered, said in a telephone interview with a Canadian newspaper, 'All my assets are in England. I don't see why I should be persecuted like this. Let the government look up their files—they will soon find out I *haven't* taken everything out of the country. I have been working harder in the past few months than I have ever done before, and it has not been for myself. I am getting sick and tired of it all—it's all so unpleasant. My home is in England and I intend going back. I can't understand it—everything I have, and the same applies to my husband—is the government's whenever they want it. My husband didn't do anything wrong and neither did I. I haven't earned a penny for myself since the war started—I'm disgusted with the whole thing.'

Then she got on with the business of entertaining and raising money for the war effort, while at home the arguments went on.

Her accountants in London issued a statement saying, 'It is within our knowledge that she *has* left substantial assets here.' Dr H.B.W. Morgan, Rochdale's MP at that time, asked for the question to be withdrawn, suggesting that the information required could have been obtained 'with less publicity and without a parliamentary reference to a great native'. It wasn't withdrawn, and part of Dr Morgan's reply went, 'Her patriotism and loyalty are unchallengeable' —'an unfair reflection on a very good and fine lady beloved by numerous democrats in Gt. Britain.'

From America, where she had moved on to raise money for British War Relief, Gracie answered the Scottish MP thus:

'At this grave hour of crisis which our country is going through, when all our thoughts and efforts are united in the common cause, I feel that your investigations of financial matters are most praiseworthy. But I am sure that in my case you have been misinformed. Can easily comprehend that, as since Italy declared war we have suffered numerous other embarrassments. Appreciate if you ask manager Clydesdale Bank Lombard Street, London for copy of my husband's letter to him dated May 22nd. Also statement from Bank of England showing amounts allowed me by them since war started. I hope this information will clear the position. Before Monty Banks left England he paid his income tax in full.'

Mr Davidson said, 'I see no reason to follow Miss Fields' suggestion that I should consult her banker. The Home Secretary's reply will be sufficient. There is plenty of work for all stage artistes who want to do their bit in this country.'

Gracie also wrote to Dr Morgan, thanking him for championing her:

'Dear Dr Morgan, I do thank you for your very great kindness in standing by me during the Glasgow MP's nasty business. I guess there's always somebody trying to make trouble, as if there isn't enough in the world already. If some folks would work as hard as other folks maybe we'd be getting this awful war over much quicker.

'There has been nothing taken out of England without permission of the banks, and what I was allowed is being spent in expenses doing my job, I have used my own money for all expenses since the war began, and I haven't received one penny from anyone.

'I'm very happy to tell you that my Canadian tour up to now is a great success, and it looks like we shall attain our desire of making over £50,000—a quarter of a million dollars, for our Navy League and Red Cross etc. Anything I can attend that will help our country I have done, and I might add that I've never worked overtime so much in all my life. I only hope I can keep well and fit to continue my job. My very kindest regards to you, and again I thank you.'

In February 1941 Gracie acknowledged the Mayor and Mayoress of Rochdale's Christmas and New Year greetings with a letter which included the following passage:

'I had hoped to return to England at the conclusion of my Canadian tour, but I was advised by the British officials here that I should continue to do the same charitable concert tour through America, because as well as raising a large amount of money for our needy ones at home, it would also help tremendously in creating international goodwill between ourselves and the Americans.

I am very happy to say that both these endeavours have exceeded my expectations, and I am enclosing a few clippings which I thought might be of interest to you.

'It means a great deal to me personally to feel that I am doing my little bit to help my country, and no matter how strenuous my job may be I shall continue until the time comes when peace and sanity are again restored.'

In a letter to a friend, May Snowden, in March 1941 she says, 'I've been going steadily for a couple of months doing the whole show myself, one hour and three quarters singing. My sisters and their children are in Hollywood, and Mother and Dad....Please God this dreadful war will soon be over, so we can all go back to our normal way of living. Forgive the scribble and pencil, pens go funny on planes—get kind of temperamental, and that's what I'm writing to you on now, keep safe and well....'

The cuttings she enclosed are worth reprinting here in part. The *Portland Oregonian* said:

'Gracie Fields of the honey-colored voice virtually paralysed a capacity audience in the public auditorium at her benefit performance for British Civilian Relief. The pert English comedienne, whose performance here netted approximately 5,000 dollars for her countrymen, alternately stilled the jammed house with a voice whose quality was the texture of living satin, or brought gales of laughter that swept from the gallery to the main floor with ballads delivered in the several English dialects.

'Her ability to turn from sublime singing to the raucous rendering of a cockney ballad in the tenor of a fishwife was little short of amazing to an audience that arrived totally unprepared for the chameleon-like repertoire of the talented singer.'

Virginia Boren in the *Seattle Times* said:

'I've never been a hero worshipper. But I'm a fanatical, fervent, feverish one right now. I'm crazy about Gracie. The program said, "Gracie Fields, the toast of the army and navy, the idol of the RAF, and Commander of the Order of the British Empire." And that's not half enough! Call it brotherly love. Call it the love of one democratic nation for another democratic nation. Call it international goodwill. Call it "Hands across the sea". But whatever it was it swept up with Homeric grandeur across the footlights to Gracie Fields, the lass of Lancashire who knows how to make broad humor buy food for bombed children.... It made England and America one. It made the sponsors give Gracie 1,000 dollars *extra* for the fund she's raising for the children in Britain's bombed areas.'

Gracie travelled across America under the banner of 'The British War Relief Society'— through Canada under the auspices of the Navy League of Canada War Fund, everywhere singing and talking to thousands upon thousands of people, many of whom had heard her on records only until that time.

These concert tours made $1½ million (almost £500,000) for Britain. But *that* wasn't widely reported in the British Press; yet it earned Gracie the Navy League's highest decoration, the Award of Service Medal.

Writing in 1952, the late Godfrey Winn said about that time, 'Now in the calm and comparative peace of the aftermath let us be fair. The blitz had not yet commenced when Gracie put her duty as a wife first and went with her husband to America. But a year later when the bombing was still at its height she returned to Europe and spent three months touring the camps and factories of England. That return is now conveniently forgotten by her critics with such long memories, but it should not be so. Nor the certainty too that whatever money she was allowed to take out of the country she paid back *a thousand times over* by the performances she gave throughout America and Canada to raise money for British Relief Funds.

'How the men in the fighting zone welcomed her. There was no criticism in their hearts as they listened to the old familiar songs reminding them of home. And what must have been in her own heart as she heard their applause coming back in great waves towards her, isolated under a spotlight on the stage?'

'They want to crucify me,' she said to Anton Dolin. 'Oh God, they don't know what they've done—they've given me hell. I'll get over it—I shall come back. Back to my dear London, my beloved England some day. I'm working every minute I can, as you are, yet still it's not enough—they don't know what they've done.'

Many years afterwards, questioned about this period Gracie answered, 'I think that's life. Just the way people are. It's the sort of jealousies of a family. It *is* a shock—but you still love your family though, don't you?'

CHAPTER 11

Gracie's War

In 1941 Gracie came home to tour the camps and factories in Britain. Basil Dean, who organised the tour, received *anonymous* letters about what would happen should she set foot in this country again.

To show the other side, I quote here from a private letter sent to May Snowden on 19 May 1941, from Mr W.H. (Bill) Mooring, of Oldhams Press:

'Take it from me Gracie did nothing wrong, unless it could be called "wrong" on her part to have stuck by her husband in spite of the fact that he happened to be born an Italian.

'Personally I admire that, and having known Monty and Gracie very well long before they knew each other I was infuriated by unfair, and often untruthful stories printed in the British press about them.

'One point has never been made clear in the British press, and Gracie herself is not in a position to stress it. London newspaper editors, however, could, if they chose, secure

179

confirmation from the Ministry of Information concerning the national value of the work Gracie has been doing, and still is doing, on this side (the USA).

'Those of us who have experienced the gradual change in American public sentiment since the beginning of the war, realise fully how strong was the feeling in USA against granting Britain any kind of aid. This attitude was quite understandable because many millions of Americans desired above all other things that their country should not become involved in, what at the time seemed to be, a foreign political squabble.

'It is my belief, based on my observations over a long period, that no one individual has done as much as Gracie to help cultivate amongst Americans interest in the British character and sympathy for the British cause. That is something quite apart from the enormous amount of work she has done on concert tours across Canada and USA, which still continue.

'Last Sunday she flew in from nine concerts, the audiences of which varied from American university students to 7,000 munition workers now building planes for *us*.

'She had hoped, during May and June, to make a flying goodwill tour back home, and she tried to secure the necessary preferential travelling permit, so that she would not be held up in Lisbon. In fact she asked me to accompany her to manage the tour, and she was bringing her accompanist also. But official information this week indicated a long delay in Lisbon to be unavoidable, and this would mean Gracie would have to let down the organisers of another giant tour of Canada which she is due to start soon, and which is to be followed immediately by another cross country tour of USA—all of course for war charities.

'I explain this in case you should see reports to the contrary in the British press. These are facts beyond dispute, and if you should see printed anything to the contrary, you might perhaps like to write the editors correcting them, also get as many of your friends to do likewise. Unless the loyal Fields public rallies to her defense I am afraid it would be sometime before the British press shows her genuine fair play.'

Gracie arrived in England on 8 July, after difficulties with her air passage and a long wait in Lisbon, where her money ran out. Lisbon was in a neutral country, and during the war many people passed through. Anna Neagle and Herbert Wilcox were also at the airport waiting and were able to lend Gracie some money.

The tour was to begin in Rochdale—a wise decision in view of the happenings of the previous years. They drove up and were met at the boundary by the Chief Constable and the Town Clerk, then continued their journey to the town hall. Basil Dean said that people stood at the gates of their houses to see her go by, this time because she had been at the centre of such a controversy.

They reached the town hall—the square was packed, and, as Gracie came out onto the balcony, not yet knowing what sort of reception she would have, a roar of welcome went up and the factory whistles sounded a salute.

The tour, which took in the north of England, Greenock, Rosyth, Orkney, Inverness, Ipswich, Harwich, Chatham, Folkestone and London, lasted thirty-nine days, and she gave concerts on thirty-four of them, sometimes twice and three times a day. Eighty-six full concerts were given, and the audience figures were in excess of 410,000.

Monty of course hadn't been allowed into Britain, and this caused a fair amount of trouble and embarrassment. He insisted that Gracie must have two days rest out of the seven—he was very concerned for her health —she said herself some time later that it was a full three years before she began to feel right again. She refused to rest, however, wanting to do as much as she could, so they compromised and she had one day off a week, which was usually spent in travelling.

Gracie journeyed from Folkestone to Tunbridge Wells in an army lorry, arriving around three o'clock in the morning, and from her hotel rang Clarkson Rose, whose show *Twinkle* was at the Opera House there.

'Ee, I'm sorry to fetch you out of bed, luv,' she said. 'I'm at The Wellington Hotel. I've no idea where Tommy lives (Tommy Fields was at that time in *Twinkle*, and I'd like to get hold of him. I'm only here for a few hours, on my way to do some more troop concerts. Can you help me?'

'Clarkie', as he was known to all his friends in the business, collected Tommy Fields and took him round to Gracie's hotel.

Gracie Fields wrote me a lovely letter,' he said, 'and took one of Conrad Leonard and my songs back with her. Later she took the trouble to cable me about its success when she sang it.'

The last stop on the tour was a big concert in aid of Red Cross and St John's War Organisation at the Albert Hall, London, on 17 August. The *Manchester Guardian* critic wrote afterwards:

'There has probably been nothing quite like the peculiar enthusiasm she evokes since the days of Charles Dickens' public readings. And indeed this artiste in her own line has many of Dickens' personal characteristics—

183

the immense vitality, the rich theatrical exuberance, the sheer fun, and a popular sentiment which we are about to call unabashed, when she suddenly abashes it by turning round and mocking her own seriousness. That is a peculiar art of which even Dickens had not the trick.'

Her manager, Bert Aza, and theatre historian W. MacQueen Pope helped to arrange the tour, working closely with Basil Dean so she could cover as much ground as possible all over the country. The BBC tried, unsuccessfully to get her for a broadcast, but she only did the ENSA shows, then back to the USA because she was committed to an American radio show in aid of British air-raid victims. This was called *Carnival For Britain*. It was organised by the British War Relief Society and the American Theatre and featured Gracie, Gertrude Lawrence, George Burns and Gracie Allen in New York; Nöel Coward, Sir Cedric Hardwicke and Robert Montgomery in Hollywood; Vivien Leigh, Laurence Olivier, Beatrice Lillie and Leslie Howard in London.

In July 1942 Gracie accepted an engagement in an all-star show in New York to be called *Top Notchers,* for one month. She 'needed some cash', she explained to reporters who questioned her, as she had 'a lot of commitments, and I haven't earned anything for myself since the war began.' After the furore of her financial arrangements in 1940, she was careful to give her reasons to the papers. It was the line of least resistance, and it was the truth.

However, she became ill and had to give up her part and go to her Santa Monica home for a rest. The doctors advised several months, but Gracie said she would 'see how it went' and was in fact back on her war relief work within two months.

In 1943 she returned to Britain to do another factory and camp tour. Her husband, Monty Banks, was managing her affairs by this time under the title of 'Star Entertainments Ltd'.*

The bombing of Pearl Harbour in 1941 brought America into the war, and Gracie said she would now divide her earnings between the two countries.

The 1943 tour also began in Rochdale, where she had a rapturous welcome. 'Well,' she told her closest friends, 'I belong there—it would be terrible if they weren't pleased to see me.'

But she was welcomed elsewhere too—by the soldiers, sailors and airmen in the camps she visited, and by the factory workers all

* The William Morris Agency managed her in the USA.

around the British Isles. 'Good old Gracie, we're winning, you know,' they shouted. In spite of all the troubles, she still identified with the people.

She did broadcast during the 1943 tour, and the Central Overseas Audience Research Department reported the following: 'There is no doubt at all about the popularity of Gracie Fields at home, with both civilian and forces listeners. Her recent live programme attained a peak audience, and whenever her records are included in a programme the figures show a leap up.'

No matter what they read about her, when they saw and heard her again, vast numbers of people knew beyond any doubt that she was still 'their Gracie'—the woman who could make them laugh and cry and *feel*. Without any explanations the women knew they too would have gone with their husbands, and the men knew that, if the situation was reversed, they would have behaved in the same way. Inevitably of course some of the mud that was thrown stuck, and years afterwards there were people who said, 'I liked her until she married Monty Banks during the war.' Those who championed her said, 'What about the others—the ones who have left and are sitting out the war in a safe place? She's not doing that.'

She had property in the USA which she had bought in the early thirties when she was over there to discuss the films she was to make, in Britain, for 20th Century Fox. Her family were living there, and she returned to the USA between her wartime tours, but she was working for Britain almost exclusively. The only money she earned for herself was on two of the three films she made then—*Holy Matrimony* in 1943, and *Molly and Me* in 1945, both of which were already contracted. For the rest the dollars came back to Britain. The money from her brief appearance in *Stage Door Canteen* (1943) went to the Ladies' Guild and Orphanage.

In 1943 she also went to Sicily. Ex-signalman Cecil Gilmore saw her there:

'My Div, the 50th (N) Division were waiting for a ship to take us home to prepare for the invasion of France,' he said. 'We'd had a pretty hectic time, but then we were stationed in a luxury hotel in what is now a well-known holiday resort. Every day we used to go down and swim in the bay. There was an old ship there, and most of us used to climb up onto the rigging, swing out and drop into the sea. We never wore any clothes. One day a group of us were swimming around when a broad Lancashire voice called out, "Hi lads, enjoying yourselves?" Yes, it was Our Gracie, and that evening she gave us a wonderful show—I'll never forget it.'

Ivor Newton was her pianist on that tour, and he said, 'I wouldn't have missed it for the world. It was exciting to accompany her and impossible to be indifferent to the genuine love and affection she commanded. Her energy was incredible, and unlike singers I normally worked with, the idea of saving or nursing her voice never occurred to her. ENSA had so many requests for Gracie, and her only regret was that it was physically impossible to do more than she already was.'

In *The Greasepaint War,* J. Graven Hughes tells the story of an impromptu show put together when Georgie Wood met Gracie in Tunis. He suggested they get together with Al Jolson and Jack Benny and put on a show at an airbase in Algiers. 'Although ENSA didn't allow artistes to appear in USO shows, the ADC in Algiers explained matters to General Eisenhower and it was authorised; it really was a terrific show.'

Gracie travelled thousands of miles during the war, by jeep, lorry and plane. She didn't like flying and had several hazardous landings. During the six years of hostilities she went to Singapore and Manila, the Cocos Islands, Borneo, Bougainville, North Africa, Australia, New Zealand, New Guinea, Christmas Island, Rangoon, India, Okinawa, Balikpapan, Egypt, Italy...

Mr Fred Shepherd of Sudden has a memory of when she sang in the hospital wards in Rome: 'The Medical Officer stopped at the beds of the men who wouldn't recover,' he said. 'She sang very quietly and most compassionately for them, and left some of her flowers near them. To a South African she sang "The Rand Song", to a delirious infantry sergeant "The Lord's Prayer", and to a Polish soldier "Ave Maria". There was absolute silence, broken only by those who could not help being overcome by emotion.'

In Rangoon Gracie gave two concerts one day, and the next she kicked off at a football match and also sang from the football stand. Just after the Battle of Tunis she was there. In Singapore she visited the hospital, and in Athens she appeared twice on the day she arrived (she reached there at 2 p.m.), twice on the Sunday and twice on the Monday before moving on to Salonica, Patras and Araxes (in the Peloponnese). Wherever she went, she simply wanted to get on with the job. There were many stars and many not so well-known actors, actresses and entertainers who also did a grand job during the war, but, as this is simply one chapter in Gracie's book, it must concentrate on her efforts.

Bob Watts, who was in Australia after the war, confirmed for me a story which I know also applied to one or two other stars—who said it first I don't know, but certainly Gracie was one who did say it. Her occasion was in the Pacific Islands, when, confronted with an audience of 'brass hats', she said to the base major, 'Where are the lads? I've come to sing to lads.' As he prevaricated, she turned to her jeep driver, 'Come on, if he won't shift, run over him.' She had her way, and a little further on nearer the front line she sang to 'the lads'.

Illusionist Will Ayling was Major W. Ayling, Officer Commanding ENSA Services and Entertainments, in 1945 when Gracie arrived at Dum Dum Airport.

'It was the first time I had met her,' he said. 'She stepped from the plane clad in bush jacket and drill trousers, her hair tus-sled and packed beneath a wide-brimmed service hat, the band surrounding the crown stitched with the badges of the units and divs she had visited *en route*

'She was to be in Calcutta for a few days, and the only place large enough for her concerts was the race-course. A floodlit, wood portable structure, built as a small theatre stage, stood isolated before a packed stand, the illumination spilling onto the olive-green uniformed troops. I sat beside her on the improvised steps at the rear of the staging, whilst her husband, Monty Banks, did his stuff as a compère before introducing her.

' "Listen to my old man," she whispered, grinning at me, "gets more like a ruddy ham each day."

'It was affectionately said, and during the next three days I witnessed their happy relationship, although I did see him sulk in a corner for a short time after a mild disagreement. It didn't last long; she soon won him over.

'For that concert she wore a long black dress, over which was a beautiful ivory crochet cotton over-garment. Really two items, the top being in the form of a short coatee, the other a reversed skirt, open at the front. It was ingeniously designed in fairly large circular patterns which, although of considerable open work, served to camouflage the dress proper. Gracie confided that it was easily carried in a holdall bag and could, on removal, be shaken out and worn over a normal dress which might have been badly creased... "a bit of instant glamour", she said, laughing.

'She gladly toured hospital wards, stopped at each bed greeting the occupant either boisterously, with a joke or two, or quietly as the circumstances required. Before leaving she would sing, often in answer to a request, without accompaniment, just so naturally. It was a great experience.'

Before she left, Will Ayling threw a little party for her in his flat high in the Chowringhee. Gracie had mentioned earlier that she would like to see some real Hindu dancing, and 'through the good offices of a friendly impresario, Harnan Gosh, I had some young Temple dancers and half a dozen musicians there.

'Harnan Gosh gave a commentary, explaining the vocabulary of the gestures; the movement of the eyes, arms, hands and feet, all precisely synchronised, which unfolded a traditional tale of Rama, reincarnation of Vishnu and his courtship with the young Princess Sita and combat what Ravana, the Evil King of the Underworld who had kidnapped the fair maiden.

'Gracie took a lively interest and enjoyed it; then the impresario asked if she would like to hear Hindu drumming.

' "Yes please." How could she have known that, typical of the East, the rhythmic beating would go on and on and on...until the vibrations beat round and round in one's head...

'At last Gracie leaned towards me and, almost shouting above the sound, said, "Tell me, Will, what is Urdu for shut that b....y row?" '

She sang on the football field in Singapore too, as Donald Sinden recalls:

'I had to fight to get in, and I was sitting

high up in one of the stands. All the stands were packed, and the pitch was covered with the wounded and the POWs. It was only four days after Singapore was ours again. Down in the middle, on a tiny stage like a boxing ring, Gracie sang her heart out. I reckon it was one of the best performances of her life. She gave us everything, and when she started the first few notes of "Sally" I looked at all the faces around me. Tough men who had seen a lot of war were crying....'

As Gracie said, 'I represented home...'

She tells in her book, *Sing As We Go,* how they reached Balikpapan, Indonesia, six weeks after the first Allied troops landed: 'The Japs were still holding part of the island, and had filled the trenches with oil to burn our boys as they landed. Yet even here the lads had cleared a patch to use for the concert.'

It was here that Gracie asked them all to strike a match. 'I've been singing to you for an hour,' she said, 'and I haven't *seen* any of you yet. I'll count three and you all strike together and let me look at you for a moment.' 'It was so magical,' she said afterwards, that she asked them to do it again, but this time for those in front to turn round and 'see what I saw.' Later they heard that many of the Japanese troops had also listened to the concert.

On VJ Day, in August 1945, she was at Bougainville in the South Pacific. There, deep in the jungle, General Blamey announced the end of the war.

'The Japs have surrendered,' he said, and, leading Gracie forward, he asked her to sing 'The Lord's Prayer'. She stood on a wooden box, facing twenty-five thousand soldiers. 'Every man took off his cap,' she said, 'and there was no sound except my voice. It was one of the most cherished moments of my life.'

Before that, though, there had been more carping. The *Crusader,* one of the Eighth Army newspapers, carried an article slating Gracie for not staying long in North Africa.

Naomi Jacob, who was with ENSA on the organising side, also wrote a piece for the *Union Jack.* She tells about it in her book, *Me and the Mediterranean:* 'I wrote a column for the Union Jack when I was in hospital in Catania. I called it, "Mind Your Own Business". We had a storm stirred up—I used that word "stirred", advisedly—concerning Gracie Fields. Gracie crammed every hour of the day with work. No place, no audience was too small, no gathering of men in some vast amphitheatre too large....'

Georgie Wood says in his autobiography, *I Had To Be Wee:* 'We arrived at Maison Blanche Airport outside Algiers. We were all hungry, dusk was falling rapidly, and there was no transport. We wandered off to the Toc H canteen—they implored us to give a show. Now here is one of the many occasions when Gracie showed not only her real wish to work, but her willingness to work under any conditions. Two tables were pushed together, and between us we did a show of over two hours.'

The next day they played to over six thousand servicemen at the Base Open Theatre at Maison Blanche, and the following one gave four more shows before moving on.

In November 1945, on Armistice Day, Gracie was back in Capri and was asked to go over to Naples to do two concerts, one at the San Carlo Opera House and one at the Bellini Theatre. For three days the sea between Capri and Naples had been too rough for the boats to run, and it didn't seem as if she would be able to get over. She was also still recovering from 'flu, but, when the Royal Navy came to the rescue with a motor launch at twenty past six that evening, she wrapped herself in the oilskins they provided and made the crossing in one of the worst seas in the area for many years.

Isadore Green wrote in the Tunis edition of the *Union Jack*: 'I watched her dragging herself up the stairs; she looked ill, white, haggard, in a state of utter exhaustion.' 'I'm not a good sailor,' Gracie said. Monty Banks had made the journey too, and he helped her to the dressing-room. Ten minutes later she went out onto the stage and sang 'Land of Hope and Glory' to a packed Opera House. The audience clapped and cheered, then she sang again before departing for the Bellini. Isadore Green said: 'The drive took a minute and a half. Gracie was in a state of collapse. She could speak only in gasps—she was blowing like a boxer who has gone through fifteen rounds of tough fighting....'

At the Bellini she walked on, whistled to the audience and cried, 'Hullo, lads, I've made it.' Then she gave a full show, cracking jokes and ending with 'Sally'.

Gracie herself always said that, when she walked onto a stage, something happened to her. She became a different person. It is not unknown—Marie Lloyd and George Robey are two more who, when their music played, seemed reborn and able to rise above their sickness and soar to the heights, no matter how ill or tired they seemed offstage.

Monty Banks toured with his wife in most theatres of war, and although he did not receive the sort of recognition Gracie did, he contributed wholeheartedly in every possible way. He shared the hardships and he was very proud of Gracie. 'Isn't she marvellous?' he said to more than one serviceman backstage.

J.W. Swallow recalls an occasion when Gracie was appearing at a big reinforcement camp called Kalyan, sixty or so miles from Bombay:

'My section's duties on this occasion were confined to the security of the dressing-rooms and the area in the rear of the stage. Gracie's act was in progress, and she was doing the number where she does a cartwheel or two on stage. I was viewing her performance from the wings, and Gracie, always a firm favourite with the troops, finished to tumultuous applause.

'A fussy, ebullient little man grabbed my arm and, in broken English, very excitably indeed, said, "What do you think of her? Isn't she great?"

'I agreed enthusiastically and said that I had first seen her twenty years or so before in a touring revue called *Mr Tower of London,* with Archie Pitt.

'The man looked almost disbelievingly at me, and then moved away somewhat crestfallen, and I realised it was Monty Banks.'

Although Monty could, and did, look at other women, he never liked the thought of Gracie being interested in other men, even a long while before.

After the war, with the traumas of nationality and loyalties behind them, Monty went with Gracie to the White House, at the invitation of the President, happy to see this acknowledgement of the way she had worked.

The President thanked her for what she had done for the morale of all the forces she had visited, 'your own and ours. My boys have come back from the Pacific Islands and said how wonderful you've been. They love you as much as their own—in fact they only wish you were their own. Now,' he went on, 'I, being an American, you realise I can't create a title for you or anything like that— we just don't have those over here; but I'm going to present you with twenty-five gold pieces. Each piece is worth twenty-five dollars. These are now extinct—there are possibly about 150 of these only in the world, and so you see they are rare; I shall be pleased and happy to give you these in recognition of what you have done for our boys.'

During the war many of the American boys had been among the twenty-thousand-odd troops in Gracie's audience in Algiers when a wind storm blew up.

'The piano only had about half a dozen playable notes,' Gracie recalled later. 'Tonight you'll just have to sing popular songs, comedy ones, and those that have a story line—you can't possibly sing any of the good ballads or religious songs,' her pianist said, 'the notes simply aren't there.'

Gracie had been on stage only a few minutes when the storm blew up.

'The few copies of music we had on the piano were blown all through the audience,' she said, 'so I began a community singsong to try and drown out the noise of the windstorm, which was really frightful while it lasted.

'Those lads joined in with enthusiasm, but 20,000 voices singing as loudly as they could with me only just beat the noise of the wind. It lasted about twenty minutes, then stopped as suddenly as it had started.

'We finished singing, and for a moment or two there was an almost unearthly silence. Suddenly a voice called out, "Gounod's Ave Maria". My poor pianist was beside himself worrying about the music, the noteless piano, and the sand in his eyes, so I sang Ave Maria without musical accompaniment, alone, in the utter stillness that came over everything. Never, I think, has a prayer been so sincerely and thankfully felt as by all those twenty thousand boys. It was one of the most thrilling moments I have known.'

Gracie was proud of every genuine award and certificate she was given, and after the war many associations honoured her. She also treasured the souvenirs given to her by the boys and girls she had entertained; a brooch made from a bit of captured Japanese aeroplane and inscribed, 'To Gracie, from the boys in Tarragan'—the symbolic key to a camp of a Lancashire regiment—her brooch in the shape of the flag of *her* ship which went down at Dunkirk—and her bush hat covered with the badges given to her by regiments she had visited on her tours. She had worn that hat for months and months, and it grew heavier and heavier and was a constant reminder of 'the lads' love, bless 'em'.

CHAPTER 12

Working Party

After the war Gracie talked about retiring. She had these plans to retire all her life but often admitted, at that time anyway: 'After a few months I might find myself itching to go again—I'm still full of vitality.'

She was forty-nine years old when she toured Britain with a series of concerts called *Gracie's Working Party*. The BBC were 'extremely enthusiastic' about it. They had done their research well and said in a letter to her manager in 1947: 'From all the indications, her reputation stands very high in this country.' There were, however, problems to overcome, not least being Gracie's reluctance to lay herself open to criticism again. Another letter suggested, 'She would probably respond to an appeal made on grounds of national emergency in a way no other artiste would.' And again, 'In view of her unique position she is the only artiste suitable for this series of programmes.'

Although the war had been over for two years, many conditions were still warlike.

Food rationing, for instance, went on (although it eased) until 1954, and men and women who worked in the factories had to stay until they were given their 'release'. 1947 produced one of the coldest winters and hottest summers for several decades. Austerity was still rife, there was an acute coal shortage, and the initial euphoria of victory was two years in the past.

Gracie was paid £2,000 for the twelve programmes into which the idea of the *Working Party* eventually developed; originally six were designed, and the payment to her was to be £1,000. She gave all her fees, including reproduction ones, to the Variety Artistes' Federation Benevolent Fund.

The tour began in Rochdale in July 1947 and went on to Liverpool, Middlesbrough, Newcastle, Huddersfield, Sheffield, Glasgow, Belfast, Coventry, the Potteries, South Wales and London.

It started with a lot of unwelcome publicity from her point of view, because the Variety Artistes' Federation argued with the BBC about whether to charge an entrance fee to the concerts, and naturally enough the newspapers used Gracie as the headline.

Theatre managers sent a deputation to the then Postmaster General (Mr W.T. Paling) protesting against free admission. 'It is one thing for the BBC to admit the public free to its own studios, but quite another for it to take a cinema or hall and set up in direct competition with us,' they said. And the BBC answered, 'It is our normal practice to admit audiences to variety shows. Their numbers are negligible compared with the millions who listen to the broadcasts.'

Reporters asked Gracie to comment. 'I should have stuck to my instinct,' she said. 'I don't want to be involved in another scrap.'

'It's not *you* personally the protests are over,' said the BBC. In any case there wasn't much she could do about it at that stage becuse the contracts were signed. 'Except to go to it with my chin out and my thumbs up,' she said to her friends, 'but I wish there didn't have to be such a fuss.'

The dispute was settled, and J.B. Priestley wrote 'A Pen Portrait', in the 18 July *Radio Times,* which was much more than a publicity feature to herald the start of the series, rather an in-depth look from an artiste as supreme in his field as she was in hers:

'Her colossal reputation, unique in its period, puzzles many persons who do not understand popular entertainment. There are, broadly, two reasons for it, and one is technical and the other psychological.

'The technical explanation is that while she fused two different kinds of appeal, one sentimental and the other comic, into one unique style of performance, she was also compelled to dominate her audience more thoroughly than any other variety artiste.

'It is easy to see why she had to do this. To combine sentiment and broad comedy, to alternate them as she does, so that at one minute the monster audience wants to cry and the next minute finds itself laughing uproariously, demands complete domination or it will be a ghastly failure.

'Notice how Gracie can slide from an almost naïve but powerful sincerity, which turns some Tin Pan Alley ballad into something like a folk song, into burlesque that, before you know where you are, is gloriously funny. And to do this a performer must have the audience completely subjugated, eager to obey the slightest gesture of command. And an audience so dominated has its response raised to a higher level. It enjoys an *experience*. And for such an experience it is instantly and profoundly grateful.

'Again the Gracie Fields who thus became a great Variety star also became a symbolic figure. She expressed far more than herself. Just as Marie Lloyd had been the symbolic figure of the London of the nineties and the Edwardian era, so now Gracie became symbolic of the industrial North.

'She was the Lancashire or Yorkshire mill girl immensely enlarged and intensified by talent and art. She sang her head off, as they do or would like to do. She was independent, saucy, sharply humorous, bossy, maternal, blunt in manner but deeply feminine in her rapid alternations of sentiment and derisive laughter. She was the people in all the little back streets, now with a full orchestra and the lid off. And in the years just before the war, when she was often ailing and desperately tired, she was compelled to maintain this character, off as well as on the stage, to be both candid and high spirited, generous with her time and attention, often at a very severe cost to herself. It is no joke to be an uncrowned and unguarded queen....'

Gracie's Working Party was produced by Mr Bowker Andrews. It involved a lot of organisation, travelling and working together. It sparked off criticism among those who harboured resentment against Gracie for the war years, and it gave the BBC 'the *only* series which is earning anything like a peak listening figure', according to one BBC memo which described her as 'this truly astonishing woman'. It featured local amateur artistes in the towns they played, and boosted the morale of Britain's workers, even if it almost ran the whole *Working Party* team, from star to office boy, into the ground.

When she was asked to do another series in 1948, Gracie cabled succinctly from her home in Capri, 'Thanks very much. Impossible to do another Working Party. Imperative take rest.' She was at that time suffering from severe sinus trouble and exhaustion.

Reginald Jordan, BBC man and old friend, said after a concert where the crowds almost mobbed her, 'Surely she is the only woman in the world who can start her own riot, and with one piercing whistle, stop it!'

In 1948 she came to the Palladium for a fortnight.

'She was nervous,' Lillian Aza told me. 'Well, we all were.' She asked them—Monty, Lillian, Bert, Mary—all those closest to her—not to go to her rehearsals because she didn't want conflicting suggestions. She said she would work out her own programme.

'Gracie had an instinct for choosing the right song for the right occasion,' Lillian said. 'She did it in 1939 with "I Love The Moon", and she did it again in 1948 when she came out to face four thousand people.'

It was nearly ten years since she had appeared on that stage and heard the 'Palladium roar'. Some of them were dramatic, heart-breaking years for her. She sang, 'Take Me To Your Heart Again', simply, honestly

—not throbbing sobstuff but with a moving sincerity.

She and her audience—for they were *her* audience especially on that night—were one. As she came to the end of the song, tears were running down the faces of most of them, and Gracie was crying too.

Recovering quickly, without further ado she went into the next song, and the next, and the next. Hers was always a truly music hall approach—no wasted time, no messing about, but a quickfire *attack*.

She turned cartwheels across the Palladium stage that night and ended the evening singing with that great crowd—*or were they singing with her?*—'I'll Always Love You.'

I'll always love you.
Promise that you'll love me.
I'll always love you
Thro' all eternity,
So long as the world goes on,
Whatever the future be,
I'll always love you,
Knowing that you love me.

It was an emotional first night—almost like a reunion between lovers, the one in the glaring spotlight and the multitude in the softness of the shadows.

After that she appeared again every year,

topping the bill for two weeks at one of the meccas of variety—the London Palladium.

In 1949, under the management of Claude Langdon, she gave eight concerts at the Empress Hall, then toured Britain and Canada, meeting with success after success and knowing, after her years in the wilderness, that she was still loved where it mattered most to her.

CHAPTER 13

Widow and Bride

After the war Monty Banks played the Mayor in *A Bell for Adano*. He had good notices. He also began work on the swimming-pool and restaurant they planned below the villa.

The building of the pool caused a lot of bad feeling in Capri. People protested when the blasting of the cliffs and terraces surrounding the villa went on. 'It turned the sea into a filthy yellow mess for a time,' Gracie said, 'but everything settled down again when it was finished.'

They spent the Christmas of 1949 in Britain with Jenny and Fred. (The Stansfields had moved back after the war and settled in Brighton.) Christmas was always a crowded, happy time. Gracie loved to have her family around her, and she blossomed in the atmosphere. They were all very talented, Betty, Edith and Tommy, and had singsongs round the piano, all joining in, the older and younger generation too. Gracie was a competent pianist, and they took it in turns to play for the party.

Gracie and Monty left Britain in January 1950 to go back to Italy for her birthday celebrations on the 9th. They travelled on the overnight Simplon-Orient Express, and on the Saturday afternoon, soon after the train had gone through the Simplon tunnel, Monty Banks collapsed with a heart attack.

Gracie had the train stopped at Arona, and an ambulance waiting, but nothing could be done. Monty died in her arms. Heartbroken, Gracie accompanied his body to his birthplace, Cesana, for the funeral.

Monty, whom she usually called by his Italian name of Mario when they were together, was only fifty. They had been married for ten drama-packed years and had been looking forward to settling in Capri, where Monty would run the restaurant and she could relax between concert tours. Instead, at fifty-two, Gracie had to face life as a widow.

She returned to Capri with Mary Davey, her secretary and companion, who had flown out to be with her. Her fans wrote; many of the letters suggested work to help her over the loneliness, and she knew they were right. She could not have stayed at home doing nothing, especially after all their planning.

Most of the people who knew Gracie during the time she was married to Monty Banks regard it as a happy marriage. They loved each other, had their work as a common bond, and a similar sense of humour. Monty's biggest fault was gambling. According to Tommy Fields, he played with the big boys in America, which he could not really afford to do. On the other hand he wasn't without money, for he was a successful director in his own right and had before the war owned many farms in Italy. He liked the ladies, but he gave Gracie a good time, and he managed her business affairs abroad.

It isn't easy to be married to a big star, and she certainly was that. No matter how much she might play it down, Gracie was the one the people wanted to see and hear. She and Monty had a great companionship in their marriage. There were quarrels, sometimes explosive ones, for Monty had an ex-citable nature, but there was also a lot of love and warmth and laughter.

After Monty's death she fulfilled her existing contracts, and accepted touring en-gagements in Canada, America and Great Britain. Whenever she returned from touring, some of her family or friends went to stay.

'I was never alone, and I was terribly lonely,' she said of that time. 'I knew I'd have to get used to it, plenty of others did, and so should I. It doesn't do to start feeling sorry for yourself,' she told her friends, 'Of course I miss Mario. It was so sudden too, it's hard to believe; but we had ten years; I knew him for twelve, and that's longer than a lot of people had during the war. Now I shall have to get used to being alone again.'

One of the things she dreaded was being alone. 'Maybe some of us are meant to be loners,' she said. 'Perhaps the good Lord planned it so, but I don't like it.'

Two months after Monty's death Gracie came to Britain to record some programmes for radio impresario Harry Alan Towers. Godfrey Winn went along to interview her afterwards. He sat quietly through the recordings, as he tells here:

' "All set to go Gracie?" She went. First into one of those Lancashire stories that don't sound funny when anyone else tells them. Then into a number entitled, *I'm One Of The Little Orphans Of The Storm.*

'It was the old familiar line, and she was codding with her voice in the old cartwheeling style. Then suddenly the surprise came.

' "Now I will sing for you *Oh My Beloved Father,* by Puccini." The impact was startling. I told myself it was because I hadn't heard this lovely thing in English before. But it wasn't that. She sang the final words, "Father, I pray...Father, I pray..." in a way that you don't expect, even from a great artiste, in a broadcasting studio.

'Later, when I congratulated her Gracie smiled her old, wide, brimming smile. "I'll tell you the secret, luv. I've had the Puccini put down a tone. Gives me more of a chance. Don't have to do any screeching. My, but I want a cup of tea. Coming?" '

She didn't want any fuss—there had been enough of that when she and Monty were married. In the autumn of that year, 1950, Gracie returned to the Palladium, her first appearance there since her husband's death. The theatre had had a succession of American acts, and the critics awaited eagerly the return of a star who almost always stole the notices whether it was a simple concert or a Command Performance.

'Palladium audiences, however enthusiastically they may cheer, scream, or sigh for the Kayes and the Sinatras, always hold in reserve a special kind of reception for Gracie Fields,' wrote critic Elizabeth Frank. 'Last night, on the occasion of her first return after the death of her husband, it was possible to feel the waves of warmth and affection sweeping from the auditorium to the stage, where a Gracie who seemed just the same as ever, held them all in the palm of her hand. But there was something different. The closely cropped curly hair was grey, the approach to the audience quieter and more intimate, and there was a new dignity and graciousness about her whole demeanour.

'She has, of course, still that bland audacity which is all her own, of sandwiching a prayer, sung with nunlike demureness— between the sad story of "Our Nellie", and that everlasting giant aspidistra; of being yearningly sentimental at one moment and completely outrageous the next....'

'Gracie Fields was in tears at the end of her act,' reviewer John Barber wrote. "You've made me cry," she sobbed into heart-moving applause. "Stop it. Stop it." It is her first appearance here since her husband, Monty Banks died in January this year. Gracie is a bit sadder, her tight curls are a bit greyer. But at 52 she is triumphantly handsome. She wears a white tulle dress, girlish as her high, clear voice. Some of her serious songs are new, but they drench the house in the old emotion....'

Gracie's white tulle dress had a leaf design of green sequins across the bodice. 'I paid £40 for it in Capri,' she said, 'cheapest stage dress I ever bought, but it made me feel like the girl on top of the birthday cake.'

At the end of that first night, when the audience was still crying, applauding and shouting for 'Sally'—while the stage was rapidly filling up round her with bouquets of flowers, Gracie brushed the tears from her own eyes to sing it for them. 'Come on, everybody,' she called, the power once more returning, and nearly three thousand people *stood* and sang 'Sally' with her.

The heart she always put into her singing, and the audience's reaction on this occasion, drained her, but their love also renewed her courage; and that year, 1950, she was voted one of the people of the year in a *Daily Express* ballot. Readers were asked to name one person only, under various headings.

'Man of 1950—Britain' was Winston Churchill. 'Woman of 1950—Britain' was Princess Elizabeth (our present Queen). 'Man of 1950—World' was General MacArthur. 'Man of 1950—Leisure' was Ted Ray. 'Woman of 1950—Leisure'—Gracie Fields.

There were thousands of entries, and the *Express* commented when announcing the results, 'It was never a question of twenty, ten, or even five people in any group competing closely for the winning vote. Every one of the five names shown here had a runaway win—the voting was overwhelmingly for them.'

In January 1951 Kenneth Adams, then Controller of the Light Programme of the BBC wrote to Gracie to invite her to 'take part, and in fact to occupy your proper place at the top of the bill for the Festival of

Variety. May I press you to make yourself available to us for this programme which could not be truly representative without you,' the letter continued.

Gracie accepted and wound up the Festival of Variety which the BBC organised to celebrate the Festival of Britain. The concert took place on 6 May 1951, and she was introduced by Wilfred Pickles, who said, 'I'm going to say very little indeed about the next artiste. I welcome, on your behalf, and with all my heart, the greatest lady of the variety stage. 'I need only say two words more, "Our Gracie".'

She came on to the kind of ovation which had caused her to say in the past, 'They clap too long and too soon...'

Nevertheless, this was one of her favourite broadcasts. She included 'Sing As We Go', 'Mocking Bird Hill', 'I Never Cried So Much In All My Life', 'So In Love', 'The Biggest Aspidistra' and 'At The End Of The Day' (the first performance of this.) She sang them all in quick succession, finishing with 'Land of Hope and Glory'—'Come on, everybody,' she said halfway through, and the voices of that huge audience joined hers to a glorious and stirring finish.

The rehearsal in the afternoon was another example of the great contrast between the inner and outer woman. She walked in, wearing a smart but ordinary coat, a scarf over her grey curls, and her glasses on; and when a BBC official questioned what she was doing there, she answered quietly, 'Well, I was asked to come, luv, my name's Gracie Fields.'

Mr Alfred Richman, who was at the rehearsal, said in his report, 'Gracie bobbed and weaved and clowned on the stage—she said "By Goom", lost her music, kicked the microphone, and sang *Land of Hope and Glory* so beautifully that hardbitten professionals applauded, and Wilfred Pickles blew his nose.'

Kenneth Adams wrote to thank her on 7 May, and in his letter he said, 'Ever since, as a *Manchester Guardian* reporter, I stood by your side on the balcony of the Town Hall at Rochdale for your "homecoming" in 1931, I have dreamed dreams of your some time or other appearing for *me* on my show. Well, last night it happened, and the Festival of Variety came to its only fitting climax with you. Thank you for being the same as ever— and so unique. I don't know what your plans are, and I don't want to bother you. But please remember that, if you do feel you would like to broadcast, the Light Programme is at your disposal, any time, any place. Its audience is the people, the great mass of the people, and it is in their hearts 'you are enthroned.'

The Festival of Britain in 1951 had something of the grandeur of the old Empire building days about it. Gracie toured the exhibition while it was on, and went down the river to Battersea and sang with the band which played for the dancers at the great funfair at Battersea Park.

In November she appeared in *The Cavalcade of Variety* at the Palladium. The show, sponsored by the *News of the World*, was put on by the Grand Order of Water Rats and Lady Ratlings, an organisation which raises thousands of pounds every year for charity. The occasion was graced by a galaxy of glittering stars. Comedian Ted Ray, who was King Rat (Chairman) that year, sat on the stage wearing his chain of office and surrounded by fellow artistes and representatives of the Variety world; Bud Flanagan, Leonard Jones, Sir Noel Curtis-Bennett, Georgie Wood, Albert Whelan, G.H. Elliott, Tom Moss, Nat Mills, Bunny Doyle, Alf Pearson, Barry Lupino, Fred Russell (at eighty-eight he was the eldest amongst them), Sir Louis Sterling, Talbot O'Farrell, Cyril Smith, Dave Carter, Lupino Lane, Ben Warriss, Serge Canjou, Jimmy Jewel, Vera Lynn, Max Miller, Arthur English, Jimmy Baily...

Gracie seemed completely back in favour

with the Press and public, but she always had at the back of her mind the thought that she was getting older and would not be able to go on singing forever. Not on the concert platform anyway.

'I have to be sure I can give the same slap bang-up performance,' she said more than once; yet there was a part of her that could not say no. Her voice was still good and she could get people to 'raise the roof' in a manner few others could.

Gracie had built small bungalows in the grounds and on the terraces of the Canzone del Mare (Song of the Sea), her Capri villa, and after Monty died they were filled with friends and relatives. She had lived on Capri intermittently since 1936, and Boris Alperovici had lived there almost permanently (apart from the war years) since 1927.

It seems incredible on an island as small as Capri, but, although they had seen each other, they had never *met* properly. 'In fact Boris was among those who wrote to the authorities complaining about the mess Monty and I were making of the Mediterranean sea when we built the pool,' Gracie recalled later with humour in her voice.

Boris, originally from Bessarabia, a country which no longer exists separately but is part of Russia, went to Capri as Gracie once had, to see an island he had read about. He was on holiday at the time and simply went over from Naples for the day.

Boris was brought up by his two sisters, his mother having died when he was three years old, and his father when he was seven. He was a student of architecture in Rome when he first visited Capri but became more interested in what was then a new invention —'wireless'. He became expert at building sets and experimenting with many branches of communication through the medium of electricity, and through his work in this area he met Prince Colonna, who introduced him to Dr George Cerio and his brother Edwin Cerio.

The Cerio brothers lived on Capri and had a marvellously equipped workroom and laboratory where they experimented with sounds and pictures. Boris left university without finishing the course and went to work in Capri with them. He became like one of their own family and immersed himself in the work he loved, inventing and experimenting. He and Edwin Cerio built a television set as early as the beginning of the thirties, and in 1934, when Gracie Fields appeared on those first wavery pictures from Crystal Palace, Boris and Edwin Cerio saw her on their screen in Capri and wrote to tell the BBC.

During the war Boris had to leave Capri, which became a military zone. Like Monty, who had to leave Britain, he had nationality trouble. He held a Romanian passport, for although he had lived in Italy for so long, he had not then become an Italian citizen. He moved to a small village near Naples but could not continue with his radio work because 'It would have caused suspicion that I was spying,' he said.

In 1943 Boris became attached to the Eighth Army through both his linguistic and engineering abilities. They needed an interpreter who also knew the technical terms involved, and he fitted the bill perfectly. He spent the rest of the war as a sergeant in the Royal Engineers.

In 1945 he was one of the troops packed into the Opera House in Naples when Gracie gave her concert there. 'Land of Hope and Glory' was magnificent,' he said. 'Then she sang two comic songs which I didn't like.'

In the summer of 1951 Gracie's nephew Tony Parry (Betty's son), his wife and children were living with Gracie when her record-player broke. Tony suggested asking 'Mr Boris' to have a look at it. 'He's a wizard with electrical things,' he said.

Boris did come and mend the record player, which is probably where the story started that he was a radio-repairer. *He never was*—Boris is an engineer and inventor—as Tony Parry said on that first occasion, 'a wizard with electrical things'.

Because she thought he didn't speak English, Gracie simply smiled at him while he was working on her machine and left it at that.

She immersed herself in work after Monty's death, and it was after a tour of Canada that she returned to find that the children had been playing with her tape-recorder and it wasn't working properly. This time when 'Mr Boris'—Boris Abraham Alperovici to give him his full name—came to look at it, Gracie discovered that he *did* speak English, and several other languages too. In the ensuing weeks they came to know each other better, and they fell in love.

Gracie was fifty-four and Boris forty-eight. She had left behind her two marriages, one disastrous and one reasonably happy—he was a bachelor. They kept their romance as secret as possible to begin with—Gracie knew only too well the traumas and dangers of publicity.

She was due to come back to Britain in the autumn of 1951 to appear at the Palladium for a month, and she said in her book, *Sing As We Go:* 'I've had many crazy weeks in my life, but none quite as crazy as those. Everything seemed absurdly wonderful. The

London buses, the faces of people in the street, the thought of the journey back to Capri, the songs I sang. And all the time I kept thinking of Boris.'

The Palladium season was another great success. Then she returned to Capri. She defined the difference of emotions in her feelings as 'loving someone and being in love'. 'I loved Monty and he loved me,' she said. 'If he had lived it would have bound us together contentedly. Boris and I were "in love" with each other.'

They thought well about the difficulties that could ensue. 'I was very severe with myself,' Gracie said. 'I realised my loneliness *could* lead me to read more into my feelings than I should.' She admitted she had never liked living alone, and, although she liked *being* alone sometimes, she enjoyed having someone 'belonging' about.

Their lifestyles were very different—as were their backgrounds and quite often their tastes. Gracie's were particularly catholic: she found beauty in many areas; Boris had led a quiet life, she, in comparison, a very noisy one, but they were in love and ready to take a chance.

Boris had his first taste of what it could be like when they announced their engagement on Christmas Eve 1951. Reporters converged on the island during the next few weeks, and Gracie and Boris eventually went to Rome for a few days to get some peace and do some shopping. What the papers didn't know, they guessed, and Gracie's previous marriages were looked up and discussed—even her religion. Articles headed 'Will Gracie Fields become a Catholic?' 'Gracie will take Boris's religion when she marries.' In fact, *none of this happened.* Gracie did not embrace the Catholic religion.

She was booked for a tour of Germany, parts of which were to be recorded for commercial radio. In Hamburg and Berlin troops protested at being charged admission to hear these commercial broadcasts recorded. Gracie herself was not paid for the shows she did in Germany but was to receive a fee for the radio broadcasts of them. Before going on stage at a Berlin cinema, she said, 'I think the lads *should* get in free,' and after the recording she went to Wavell Barracks and sang to the troops there for another hour—free.

That wasn't the end of the storms, for when Mr Gordon Crier, Gracie's producer, left Berlin with Radio Luxembourg man Peter Wilson and a British Army driver, for Minden, they took a wrong turning, ending up in the Russian zone, where they were detained because they had no permits.

Gracie, who had flown from Berlin to

Minden for her next concert, said angrily, 'It's ridiculous—Mr Crier is working for *commercial radio,* not the BBC. It's a political issue,' adding, for good measure, 'I'm mad at everybody—I wish I could get hold of the chap that did it and bang him round the ear. Why don't we grab any of their people?' Then she went on to give her concert.

Meanwhile Lillian Aza flew out to Germany to ask her not to rush into marriage with Boris, who, while he might be a very nice man, was the unknown quantity as far as everyone in Britain was concerned. 'Wait twelve months to make sure you're doing the right thing,' she suggested.

But Gracie was in no mood to listen. She was in love and wanted more than anything else at that time to be married quietly in church, in a ceremony that would be, to use her own words, 'quiet enough for me to really listen to the words of the service.'

On 6 February King George died, and Princess Elizabeth and her husband the Duke of Edinburgh returned from Kenya, where they were on tour, to a country saddened by the loss of a good and well-beloved monarch.

Gracie and Boris, besieged by newspaper men in Capri, escaped to Rome again. Reporters followed them, and Gracie turned on them angrily. 'Let's get it straight,' she said, after reports in the papers that they had parted. 'Boris and I haven't quarrelled—we shall get married quietly and without fuss.'

'They're turning our wedding into a peep-show,' she said tearfully a little later.

To dodge reporters they got married two days later than originally planned, and some of their family and friends missed the service, which was upsetting for them all.

The ceremony took place in the church of San Stefano in Capri on 18 February 1952. Gracie was dressed in mauve and wore a mauve-and-white check scarf over her hair. Some of her friends said afterwards that she wore mauve as a gesture of mourning for King George VI.

She made her responses in a low voice, almost a whisper, but Boris spoke out loudly. The ceremony took about seven minutes, and, when they came from the church to the cheers and good wishes of several hundred people who were waiting outside, it was too much for Gracie and she burst into tears. She recovered quickly—her public self coming to the fore again when someone gave her a bunch of red carnations. Turning to her new husband, she said, 'Red for passion. That's us, eh?'

They had a simple reception at her home afterwards and gave the money a huge 'do' would have cost to the poorer people on the

(*Above*) Gracie's birthplace, in the bedroom above the fish and chip shop in Molesworth Street, Rochdale

(*Below*) Poster for Rochdale Hippodrome announcing twelve-year-old Gracie, August 1910

Gracie aged two

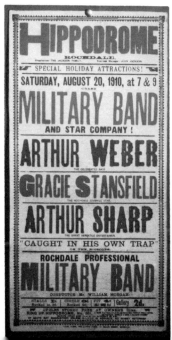

Aged eighteen

Gracie as comedienne and
actress at twenty-three

Flanked by sisters Edith and
Betty during the run of
Mr Tower of London

At the Holborn Empire —
with the kiss curl Noël
Coward disliked

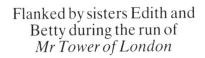

Archie Pitt, impresario, and
Gracie's first husband

Gracie in *Walk This Way* (1931)

racie in *The Show's The Thing*
(1929)

With Duggie Wakefield
and his son Michael
(Gracie's nephew)

(*Left*) Making a 'cuppa' in Bertha Schofield's kitchen in the early 1930s

(*Below*) At a BBC microphone, October 193

(*Right*) 'He's made me quite nice-looking' Gracie said when she saw James Gunn's portrait of her (1938), now in Rochdale Art Gallery

(*Left*) Gracie at the time of the release of her first film, *Sally in Our Alley* (1931)

(*Below*) In *Look Up and Laugh* (1933), with (*left to right*) Tommy Fields, Billy Nelson and Duggie Wakefield

(*Bottom*) Relaxing with director (later second husband) Monty Banks on set of *Queen of Hearts* (1936)

(*Right*) In *The Show Goes On* (1937)

The paddle steamer *Gracie Fields*, launched in April 1936,
sunk at Dunkirk, 1940

The rose 'Gracie Fields' was a medal-winner for the grower
George Frederick Letts (from Lett's Autumn Catalogue 1938)

Gracie with Mum and Dad, Jenny and Fred Stansfield, 1937

In Capri, 1939. *Left*: teaching a nephew to swim.
Right: wearing a favourite Italian straw hat

On stage at Rochdale.
Left: a comedy number.
Below: a Lancashire Lass

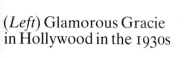

(*Left*) Glamorous Gracie
in Hollywood in the 1930s

Singing from the town hall balcony at Rochdale after a show,
and *below*, the crowd she sang to

The hat Gracie treasured –
sporting cap badges of
regiments she entertained

Hon. Captain of the Women's
Volunteer Reserve Corps,
Montreal in 1940

With the RAF

Arriving at Dum Dum
Airport with Monty Banks
– carrying the famous
bush hat

At Trincomalee, Ceylon
in 1945 with the Navy

In post-war Berlin to record for *The Gracie Fields Show*

With a sad-looking Beniamino Gigli
who has just presented her with
an enormous basket of roses

'Shall we sing?'

(*Left*) Gracie at fifty-two
by Baron

(*Right*) Having a go at an
'Elvis' number with
some of the children
from her orphanage

(*Right*) With third
husband Boris Alperovici
at Canzone del Mare,
Capri

(*Below*) Dancing and
singing in the TV
programme 'Welcome
Home to the Queen',
1954

Left: Portrait by Baron, early 1950s

At Canzone del Mare, 1975

Above: seventy-seven years young – 'I'll come round this bush and when I whistle you shoot!'

Left: hair by Hazel Provost

Below: with Norman Jackson

Below: with former secretary and lifelong friend Mary Davey

Presented to Queen Elizabeth the Queen Mother after a final Royal Command performance, 1978. Looking on (*Left to right*): Danny La Rue, Frankie Howerd and Lord Delfont

Greeting lifelong friend
Nell Whitwell, 1978

Dame of the British Empire
February 1979

island. As an extra wedding present Boris fixed the underwater lighting in the swimming-pool on the first morning of his honeymoon. This was something that had been planned before Monty died, and afterwards never completed.

They didn't 'live happily ever after' straight away, although they did eventually. Sometimes they quarrelled—there was a great deal of adjusting to do on both sides. 'The first two or three years were often stormy,' Gracie said later, 'Boris wanted to keep me all to himself, and I sometimes was very restless for the theatre.'

Archie and Monty had both been actively involved in the theatre themselves, and in Gracie's career—which was established and pretty much unalterable by the time she met Boris.

Because his knowledge of electrical equipment and its effects was so good, Boris often interfered during recording sessions, and this caused ructions all round. Gracie had a reputation for being an easy person to work with professionally—she *was* a perfectionist, but not a finicky one. She wanted everyone to do their best, and she would go to infinite trouble to get it right, but, 'I'm not a fusser, luv. If it doesn't work, we'll do a different song that does.'

But Boris and Gracie made each other

happy too. Mary Whipp, a Rochdale friend of Gracie's, recalls going to the cinema with them when she was on holiday there. It was an Ethel Barrymore film, *The Spiral Staircase,* and Gracie was very keen to see it because someone said they looked alike. Mary told me, 'During the film I glanced across to Gracie and she and Boris were holding hands.'

Teddy Holmes too remembers seeing them with hands clasped in the taxi on the way to a recording session.

Their 'romance' caught Gracie's public's imagination, and they clamoured for Boris when she appeared anywhere on stage. She seemed to encourage this attitude, bringing him on and beaming at him as he acknowledged the applause. In her public life she had always found it easy to take the lead, but in private less so.

'She was often afraid,' Lillian Aza said.

'She lacked judgement,' Irene Bevan said.

In her singing, Boris agrees that he wasn't keen on the comedy and wished she would concentrate on the serious numbers. Their humour was quite different. Gracie found a chuckle in many, many things—she *looked* for the lighter side, sought the sunshine because she knew the tears came anyway.

'I want my private life—Boris too wants this,' she said, 'but I try to explain to him that I also belong, and always will, to my dying day, to the people who have given me everything I possess.'

When famous people fall out, the world knows about it—when ordinary folk do, it is between themselves only.

Gracie's religion was very deep, very much a part of her everyday living, and when she died she left Boris her prayerbook, with a personal message for him alone inside. It shows, more than anything which can be said here, that, in spite of the darker days they experienced in their marriage—and there were some—love triumphed over their problems.

CHAPTER 14

Royal Shows

Gracie was a deeply religious woman. She didn't go to church regularly, but she said her prayers. They were the first ones she learnt as a child in Rochdale, and were followed by others she gathered as she grew older. She had to remember them all before she could rest.

'If I happen to fall asleep and then wake up I know it's because I haven't finished my prayers...'

'I believe in religion,' she said. 'I believe in it terribly strongly.'

She talked about God as a friend. 'The Good Lord always seems to be there, watching over me,' she would say, or, 'The Good Lord put all the notes there.'

She always said a prayer before going on stage, and Neva Hecker, her American secretary, said that, no matter how late it was or how tired she felt, Gracie said her prayers before going to sleep: 'Often when we've been on tour I'd sleep for a while, wake up and there she was kneeling by the bed deep in prayer.'

Sometimes she went to church with Boris,' but I find I get nothing out of it, but in the prayers I say every night of my life I find comfort, a wonderful comfort.'

In an interview for the BBC she talked about a scripture lesson she remembered from her schooldays: 'It was about Jesus dying, and by the tomb his clothes were left in a tidy heap.' After that she used to pick up her own clothes, and her two sisters', even if it made them late for school.

'I wanted to please,' she said, 'I tried to please.' And, although during her long career Gracie often made fun of and sent up all kinds of songs, she always sang the sacred ones straight.

'Her religion was inside her,' one of her friends said, 'and it was always there.'

She gave her time for churches of all denominations. If there was a job she could do, she did it, from opening a garden party to helping raise funds for the roof of a Roman Catholic, Anglican, Jewish or any other faith's church.

'Live and let live' was one of her beliefs; another which she occasionally quoted was, 'Do unto other as you would be done by.'

In 1960, when Father Borelli from Naples asked her to sing to the *'scugnizzi'*— the homeless children of the area, she went. The

231

concert took place in an old, crumbling church in Naples which Father Borelli had turned into a home. It was known as 'The House of the Urchins.'

'What could I sing to a bunch of boys and youths hardened to a ruthless fight for existence before they were ten?' she said. 'Not love songs; not sad songs; gay ones then. And she did, beginning with a bright Neapolitan song which she sang in Italian. She sang loudly, as she had in her own childhood when Jenny was urging her on. 'Come on,' she shouted to them, *'Canta.'* And they did sing. She stopped them in her own style with her errand-boy whistle... And although she did not change their way of life, she undoubtedly brightened it for some of them.

In November 1970 Gracie appeared on her first *Stars on Sunday* programme. Jess Yates, whose idea the programme was, and who was its first presenter and producer, went over to Capri specially to ask her because there had been so many requests from viewers. At first she would not agree. 'My voice isn't what it once was—I'm not sure I could *give* as I should. I haven't got the breath control I used to have.' Eventually she did agree to do it, and it was the first of many appearances Gracie would make: singing her 'Sunday Songs' was how she phrased it.

Of course she was right—by 1970 her voice

wasn't what it once had been, but it was still a remarkable voice, and, if it was lower and gentler than before, the people she was singing to were also older and mellower.

When she came over to record the programme, tying it in with the Christmas Day one she was doing, she also sang other songs for inclusion in future *Stars on Sunday* programmes.

It happened to be Boris's birthday, and Yorkshire Television canteen staff made a special birthday cake for him. When it was brought in during a break in recording, he and Gracie were sitting together talking. Jess Yates played 'Happy Birthday', everyone present sang, then Boris blew out the candles on his birthday cake and shared it round.

By then Boris had seen Gracie work many times and had toured with her ('He's better at washing the smalls than I am,' Gracie often joked), but the first time he came to London with her was in 1952, the year they were married, when she was one of the artistes in a Midnight Matinée at the Coliseum for the Lynmouth Flood Disaster Fund. He sat in a box with Bert and Lillian Aza and slipped down to the dressing-room in time to greet her as she came off.

'Gracie, you are a very great artiste,' he said. That was probably the first time Boris saw and felt her magic working on the stage.

That concert raised nearly £10,000 for the fund for the relatives of the victims of the floods, and to help people salvage what was left of their homes. The cast included many famous names—Vera Lynn, Mary Martin, Billie Worth, Kay Hammond, John Clements, Jimmy Jewel and Ben Warriss, and the Sadlers Wells Ballet Company.

Gracie was always one of the first artistes to offer her services in cases like this. She was at the King's Theatre in Southsea in 1951 in a concert raising money for relatives of HMS *Affray* which sank in the Channel south of the Isle of Wight.

During that evening she was given various articles to auction, and, when she ran out, someone called to her, 'Your stole Gracie—auction your stole.' Without hesitation she whipped it from her shoulders—it was palest pink, very delicate, with hand-painted butterflies all over it, and, amid laughter her 'auctioneering manner', she sold it for £15.

She often sold her hats. In South Africa she appeared as a guest at a charity show in a packed hall: 'Whew, it's hot,' she said to the audience, taking off her hat and ruffling her hair. Then, 'Here you are, anyone can have it if they pay for it,' she said, and a few more pounds went to the St Dunstan's Aftercare Fund. The following day Gracie bought another hat for 4s 11d.

Gracie could not bear to see suffering she could do nothing about. If she could help in any way, she was the first one there, but if she couldn't, she got out of the way as quickly as possible. Her compassion took a practical form—her sympathy for anyone in pain or trouble was so tremendous it sapped her. If she did a show for very sick or unfortunate people, she always told the management she had another engagement immediately afterwards, even when she hadn't, because, unless she could do something to ease their pain or to make their lives a little brighter, she wouldn't stay and watch. Gracie was never an accident gloater; she helped if she could, cheered where she could, then quietly went on to the next thing.

She found it hard to do shows which put such a strain on her, but she never demurred —she went on and gave everything she had to give. Her concerts often left her emotional: 'You have to control it,' she said, 'otherwise you can't do your work properly.' She put herself so completely into the role of the song that, when it was finished, the tears often came.

Mrs Wood, of Blackpool, was one of the waitresses for a reception in 1957 at Rochdale: 'Gracie sang "Three Green Bonnets" from the Town Hall balcony,' she said, 'and when she turned to come in, tears were running down her cheeks, and the crowd in the square were still cheering and clapping.' And Mary Whipp remembers a time when she was standing nearby and saw the trouble Gracie was having not to break down. 'Every muscle in her face and neck was working,' she observed.

She had heart, humanity, and a great ordinariness which was so natural that it elevated her.

Mr Bowker Andrews, who was with Gracie on her 1947 *Working Party* broadcasts, said that in the twelve weeks she covered over 2,000 miles and did six direct broadcasts and six recorded shows. He said the tour was 'a period packed with unforgettable memories' and that wherever they went they had receptions filled with so much affection for her that over and over again she remarked to him that the responsibility of repaying so much was quite beyond her, but that she was determined to do her best.

There is a little song that Max Miller wrote and sang years ago. He called it 'Be Sincere', and the words, while they possibly could apply to many different people, do fit 'Our Gracie' so much:

Be sincere, in everything you do,
Be sincere is all I ask of you.
If you break a promise,

236

A heart is broken too.
Be sincere, and as through life you go.
There's one golden rule I know,
Do the same to others
As you would have them do,
And the world will be sincere with you.

The first Royal Command Performance, and in fact the only true Royal Command—they are now called Royal Variety Shows—was held on 1 July 1912, at the Palace Theatre, Shaftesbury Avenue.

King George V and Queen Mary attended. Queen Mary was dressed in lavender silk, and King George wore a flower in the buttonhole of his dress suit. The theatre was filled with roses; from the stage to the royal box, over the proscenium arch, there were pink, red and golden roses. In the foyer were more flowers—banks of lilies and pink hyd-rangeas forming an avenue of beauty to welcome the royal guests. One hundred and forty-two artists took part, many only walking on for the finale which was called 'Varieties Garden Party', and then to sing the National Anthem.

Gracie was fourteen then—an unknown, with most of the triumphs and tragedies still before her: a tall young girl—one of 'Charburn's Young Stars', full of bounce and energy and that enormous talent which was eventually to take her to the top of variety's highest tree of stars.

Gracie appeared in ten Royal Variety Shows. The first was in 1928 and the last in 1978, when she closed the show at the Palladium as the surprise of the evening.

Royal Variety Shows are usually nerve-racking experiences, as the late Clarkson Rose remembered: he was in the 1928 one, his first as well as Gracie's.

'Ee, Clarkie luv, how do you feel?' she asked him at the final rehearsal. He told her he was nervous.

'How about you?' he said.

'I feel as if I know nowt about owt,' was the reply.

That show was also before King George V and Queen Mary, and afterwards, when she was presented to Their Majesties, Queen Mary told Gracie she preferred the serious songs to the comedy ones.

Anton Dolin was also in that 1928 show. 'It was the first time I had met Gracie,' he told me, 'and it was a first Royal Variety Show for us both. We had adjoining dressing-rooms at the Coliseum; we both arrived about six o'clock, terribly nervous, and we tried to console each other. We peeped through the curtains together to watch the King and Queen arrive, which was rather naughty and gave us a thrill, but made us even more nervous!'

Most of the reviews for Command Perfor-
maces she was in mentioned her in glowing
terms: 'Biggest cheers were for Gracie'—'A
Stardust night of triumph for Our Gracie'—
'Hits of the Royal Show were Gracie Fields
and the Crazy Gang.'

But in 1957 John Lambert interviewed
Gracie the morning after the performance in
which she flopped.

'Frankly,' she told him, 'I wonder if I'm
finished. I wonder if anybody does want me
any more.'

She had sung modern songs, presented an
altogether more up-to-date image, and in a
show where people have paid tremendously
high prices for their seats, where they are
acknowledged to be among the hardest
audiences to win...

'I know,' she said, 'I made a mistake. But
it is making that sort of mistake that makes
me wonder if I'm finished. If I'm out of
touch with what the public wants now.'

Later in the interview she said, 'I know I'm
an old woman now,' (she was two months
away from her sixtieth birthday) 'old in years
anyway, if not in the way I feel. And perhaps
my voice may be going a bit.'

She had a little grumble about the short
time—nine minutes—which she had.

'All the time I was worrying about whether

I was going on too long. Nine minutes and that's your lot. I've been singing songs like Walter, and The Biggest Aspidistra for years—do people *really* want to hear the same old things all the time?'

This was an aspect she often could not fathom. 'Over five hundred songs in my repertoire,' she used to say, 'and they always want those few.'

'I still think it's the greatest honour an artiste can have,' she told John Lambert quietly, 'to be chosen for the Royal Variety Show, so I just do as the producer tells me.'

He asked her if she was serious about giving up.

'I have three television appearances lined up for December,' she said. 'The way I feel at the moment I wish I could get out of them —I don't want to go on just as a bit of nostalgia...'

Seven years later Gracie did another Royal Show, and critic James Green wrote: 'It was a confrontation of Queens. One Queen had been driven from Buckingham Palace and was in the Royal Box. The other Queen was on stage, showing why she has won the honorary title Queen of the Music Hall. Be as cynical as you like about Gracie Fields. What is beyond dispute is that all her life she has been a marvel, and now, almost 67, she is a ruddy marvel....'

This time she took no chances—she sang 'Sally' as she came on, 'Getting To Know You', 'Glocca Morra', 'Scarlet Ribbons', 'September Song' and 'The Ugly Duckling' and went off to 'Wish Me Luck As You Wave Me Goodbye'.

Afterwards, at the presentations, the Queen said to Gracie, 'It is so nice to see you back once again,' and Gracie replied, 'It's nice to be back, ma'am—it's like the horse that's been let out of the stable once more.'

One Royal Show, when 'Cheeky Chappie' Max Miller was told to do eight minutes and overran to the extent of doing eighteen, caused consternation for everyone connected with it. Max felt that the American acts were getting a better deal than the British ones, and he did a different and much longer turn than the one he had rehearsed that morning. As something timed to the second as the Royal Variety Show is, it was embarrassing and upsetting for management, artistes and backstage staff. American singer Dinah Shore, already worked up to tension pitch and waiting in the wings, began to cry. It was Gracie who walked over, cuddled her and told her to dry her tears for it would all work out. Which it did, and Dinah was a big hit that night.

In 1952 after Gracie and Gigli had both done their single acts, they sang 'Come Back

To Sorrento' together. 'Theatre history was made last night when Our Gracie and Beniamino Gigli sang together for the Queen,' wrote the critics.

Gracie's stage dresses were elegant: sometimes rich-looking, sometimes simple, but always right for the occasion. One Royal Variety Show frock was covered with several thousand sequins which she and her secretary, Mary Davey, helped to sew on. 'Every spare minute we had we were stitching like mad,' she said when complimented on the dress after the show. Over the years she wore black velvet, pink tulle, gold lamé, white satin and in 1978 a blue and gold kaftan.

The 1978 show was Lord Delfont's last one as organiser and, with an all-British cast, was a special tribute to Queen Elizabeth the Queen Mother. Gracie was thrilled and nervous and practised and exercised her voice thoroughly, working on it every day from the time she knew she had been chosen again.

Irrepressible Gracie gave her family a big laugh on this occasion. Annette called on her one morning, and, over the inevitable cup of tea, Gracie said, 'I'm going on the Royal Command Performance. It's a surprise, you mustn't tell anyone—you mustn't tell our Tom, because, if he goes round the pub and has a few drinks, he'll tell everybody—then *I* shall be in trouble.'

'So I promised not to tell him,' Annette said. 'Our brother-in-law Roy (Betty's husband) gave us the tickets. We arrived at the Palladium—in the second row we were, and just before the curtain rose Tom turned to me and said, "Our Gracie is on this bill."

' "Pardon."

' "Our Grace is on this bill."

'Amazed, because I hadn't thought he'd suspected, I said, "Tom, how do you know?"

' "Well, she told me," he said, "but she asked me not to tell *anyone*, not even you".'

Gracie loved setting up something like this, and both Annette and Tom had kept the confidence from each other.

The long and excellent show drew near to the finish; and then, what a finish!

Compère David Jacobs introduced her, as the orchestra went into her signature tune and she stepped forward. That final 'Sally', when her voice seemed to have gathered in all the richness of her eighty years' experience —when, halfway through she broke off to say to us, 'I've been singing a man's song all me life,' and artiste Danny La Rue's deep, throaty chuckle came clearly through the mike to mingle with our own laughter and tears as everyone joined in.

In that one chorus it was as though Gracie was giving the people a glimpse of all her voice had achieved in days gone by—the essence of her personality was there in all its richness in that last Command Performance.

She had a standing ovation, and as the applause echoed through the theatre, she gave her errand-boy whistle to stop. 'Cease, cease,' she said, then, turning towards the Royal Box, 'Our Gracie' led everyone in singing 'God Save Our Queen'.

CHAPTER 15

Two Gracies or One?

We all have more than one character, although often one aspect is dominant, and people sometimes wrongly assume that this is all there is.

To succeed as she did, Gracie *had* to be a powerful person on several levels. She was. As she said more than once, 'I'm a strong, hardy daughter of the north, and folk expect certain qualities.' She also had a tender side—so much so that she turned it into her 'don't let us be sloppy' side, when she would suddenly switch from the romantic to the ridiculous, the sad to the silly, the grand to the gauche. It was a way of getting over the emotional part of her nature in public.

In the world of theatre there is sometimes much falseness—often beneath the gloss is a different person. Gracie was two people: Gracie Fields, the superstar and great professional, and Grace Stansfield, the woman. Both were genuine; only she could adequately separate them, and over the years the two merged closer together, held strongly by that golden cord of true sincerity and genuineness that was the heart of both Gracies.

Myths grew up around her. Often she wanted people to know what she was like, yet she could not show them 'the ordinary person I am outside of my voice'. She was naturally forthright and intelligent, and the two forces, the honest-to-goodness Gracie who *wanted* to believe in fairy tales, and the blunt and sharp one who realised she was often being used, clashed and made her a very lonely person. Because she understood this and disliked being alone for too long, she tried to come to terms with it, but her innate honesty with herself prevented her from accepting less than she gave.

In her audiences she found the devotion she sought. It is one thing to love an audience while you are in the theatre and together, quite another to do when they have scattered and gone their separate ways. Gracie needed individual love as well, at times desperately. The outgoing, exuberant personality the public knew, was also the shy, retiring lady who wanted peace and quiet and above all, loving companionship.

She would often not ask for a cup of tea, her favourite beverage, in case it put someone out, and when she visited her agent, she seldom let her know—just turned up, having already eaten either a sandwich or a pork pie in a café along the road. She didn't always see that this could be hurtful.

Quite often she forgot appointments, being utterly engrossed in something else at the time. At a prearranged dinner party once, everyone was assembled except Gracie. All these people hoping to meet her, and she had gone out to dinner with Norman Wisdom!

She had been to the ice show, *London Melody*, at the Empress Hall, and when impresario Claude Langdon saw her sitting in a box with bandleader Henry hall, he asked her to come onto the arena to greet the artistes.

'The microphone was switched on,' he said, 'but not caring two hoot, Gracie threw her arms round the little (then almost unknown) comic of the show, hugged him and said, "In two or three years lad, tha'll be the biggest comedian in Britain." She thought he was terrific. When he asked her to go out to dinner with him, she said everything else went from her mind until the following morning. In her professional life she was always punctual and reliable, but she loved to do things on the spur of the moment at other times. The following day she telehoned to apologise, and, being Gracie, she not only did so to her manager who had tried to organise it but also rang each guest individually.

'It was always difficult to arrange any kind of a "do" for her', Lillian Aza told me, 'because on her way to it she was likely to notice a film she hadn't seen and slip into the cinema instead.'

Exasperating as this was, part of the reason could have been that she knew there were going to be other people there, and she thought one less would not make much difference. She never deliberately didn't turn up anywhere because she could not bear to let people down. She was often afraid they would find her less exciting than they expected. 'I'm very ordinary,' she said, while admitting that on stage she *was* a different person. She knew she changed, vibrated a power over the audience which she suspected came from outside herself, and it often worried her.

Her brother Tommy says she was a shy, modest person in private life, but he agreed she was incredibly noisy. 'She was deaf in one ear most of her life (due to an ear infection as a child), and I think she shouted because she couldn't hear herself.'

She did have a magnetism of which he thought she was completely unconscious. 'Winston Churchill had this, even Adolf Hitler had it—they don't know at the time, but they literally hypnotise the people, and you can hear a pin drop when they're talking, *any* of them. When Grace came into a room, she needn't say anything at all yet people's heads would automatically turn to her. If she was in a room for about an hour, by the time she left, although she'd hardly done anything, you were *exhausted*. She would possibly be exhausted herself, and she'd go and lie down to recharge her batteries, then come back and exhaust everyone again. I think these people *are* aware of their importance—she never emphasised it, but you felt the power of the person.'

She was one of the most approachable of stars, and the formality of a special evening for people to meet her she deemed unnecessary. She gave most people who wanted to talk to her a quarter of an hour so that as many as possible could do so, and maybe also because she was unsure of herself. 'They might rumble me—I'm nothing like the paragon they think I am.'

In Capri, though, when a fresh coachload of visitors arrived to see her, she used to go down to the pool (there were nearly one hundred steps from Gracie's villa to her swimming-pool), and sometimes she did this three or four times a day during the summer.

'It must be a thrill for your fans,' someone said to her once, 'but it's a long way down—don't you get tired of it?'

Gracie smiled. 'They come all this way and

look up at my terrace, hoping to catch a glimpse. If they still think that much of me, why shouldn't I go down to see them. I wouldn't go looking for them—I'm too shy to do that, but if they've asked for me—that's different.'

She was on home ground here and probably felt more secure. She knew from the letters she received that many came hoping she would be there, and she understood their sentiments so well. Basically hers had been a Cinderella story—poverty to riches, mill to Mediterranean island—she knew that many of them ignored or were oblivious of the bits in between, but she was happy to share with them that glimpse of what it was possible to achieve.

When a holidaymaker asked if he could dip his feet in the swimming-pool, 'because I've come two thousand miles to do just that,' she knew what he meant. 'Go on, lad, have a bash,' she told him. Nevertheless she was embarrassed when crowds having tea shouted, 'Hullo, Gracie,' as she came into sight. She never knew what to do then. On stage there was no problem—she commanded and they obeyed. The shy side of her was uppermost when faced with outside situations. At a loss she usually joked and became the loud, noisy woman who was only a tiny part of the real Gracie.

When she had anyone to tea in the villa, she walked to the gate with them. 'I'll come and see you off—must let you see I've been brought up proper,' and she would laugh and maybe even pull a face at them, but she would be there with a smile and a wave when you turned round.

In 1973-4, when Sir Anton Dolin was living in Capri for six months, he gave a party and invited Gracie. She wasn't a great party-goer, but she attended a few. The party was spread out over two rooms, and Gracie sat in a huge armchair while people milled around her talking, and eventually someone said, 'Will you sing for us, Gracie?'

She looked across to her host, who added his voice to the others.

'Got a piano?'

'No.'

'A guitar?'

'No.'

'Never mind.'

She smiled and started to sing unaccompanied, very quietly at first, and people were silent, listening—while those from the other room heard the pure notes gather volume and expression, and crept along the hallway to crowd into that room and hear her. She sang for twenty minutes—all new songs, and they gave her a wonderful ovation, which she loved.

Afterwards Anton said to her, 'Gracie, come over and do a concert. You could fill the Palladium for two weeks.'

'I'd love to,' she said, 'if I can do new songs. I'm not going to sing those old ones any more. If they'll let me do new ones...but they won't. And there's the microphone, that's another thing. They'll *think* they can't hear if I don't use it, and I don't like the b.....thing. It's fine for a small voice, but I can send mine all over the theatre—we always had to. No, luv, if I came, I'd have to use the mike and sing only oldies. I'm happy enough here, but I would love to do a programme of modern songs...'

Gracie always thanked people—she had natural good manners without any of the affected words or gestures that seem so false. 'Thank you for asking me,' she said to Michael Parkinson when she was a guest on his show with Sir John Betjeman in 1977.

She never presumed folk would be glad to see her. She *thought* they would, *hoped* they would, yet never took them for granted; and if they took her for granted, or took what she considered liberties, she showed her disapproval.

Once, when some fans were helping her to stow china into a new cabinet which had arrived, and she climbed onto a chair to fix something at the top, one of them playfully smacked her bottom. She was furious and well and truly ticked her off.

Gracie loved bright colours and mixed them freely. Annette Stansfield (Tom's wife) told me about the second time she met Gracie in 1966, when she called unexpectedly at Annette and Tom's house.

'I was the only one in,' Annette said, 'and when I opened the door, Gracie was standing there dressed in an orange blouse and a red and purple skirt—all of the brightest hue.

'I said, "Just a minute, Gracie, I'll go and get my sunglasses," and she laughed and laughed.

' "Mmm," she said, 'it is a bit dazzling, isn't it—I'm in one of me bright moods this morning." '

Perhaps it was bravado to wear such brilliant colours all together, for she was always nervous meeting new people. On stage she was completely at home and could put them at ease, but offstage her personality was such that she often hid the shyness beneath the loudness.

She loved pastel shades too: again there was the contrast—the loud and the soft, the harsh and the delicate. Gracie loved pretty things, exquisite china, lovely pictures, fine glass and porcelain; she adored pink—and liked pretty underwear.

Although she developed a sound dress

sense in her later years, when she was young this was lacking. George Black, manager of the Palladium from 1928 until his death in 1945, said about this in 1935: 'Either she has no sense of dress or she is not interested in it...the latter I think, for she has a natural love of beauty in pictures and music. But she goes about in any sort of clothes without the slightest regard for her appearance.'

Monty Banks' influence showed in her clothes for they were far more sophisticated and right for her during the period of their marriage (1940-50) than they had been when she was with Archie Pitt. But her own natural instinct was good when she chose to exercise it.

'Gracie was never vain,' Hazel Provost, another friend, said, 'but she knew when she looked all right, and she could, when she desired, look the picture of elegance.'

Of course, in the early days she could not afford very much, and she was working flat out for the show, not having the time or the energy to spend on her own wardrobe.

In 1928 she made her Command Performance dress, and when the Cotton Textile Exhibition was on in London, she attended in a dress made from Lancashire cotton which had been a gift to her from the mill girls.

Often she referred to herself in letters and

talk as 'GF'. As Gracie Fields, people *expected* her to be funny, break into song and entertain them—it was natural to her, and she had done it all her life, but it wasn't everything. There were all the other parts which went to make the whole person. GF *had* to be the most dominant—she had a strong personality, and it took over whether her audience was one person or a thousand.

Another aspect was her quiet moods, when it was necessary for her to be alone for a while. She gave out so much that she needed to catch up from time to time. She didn't want long but simply to stride out (and she did stride, even in her seventies), usually a couple of dogs with her, to 'be quiet and peaceful' she used to say. She could cope with the crowds and the noise—part of *her* was noisy and she revelled in it, but the quiet bits needed expression too.

Tom and Annette Stansfield tell a story which illustrates her understanding for this need in others *and* her rapport with children. It concerns their youngest daughter, Marisa, when she was quite small.

They were at Gracie's house, and there were a lot of people there, mostly family, but a lot of them. Marisa went up to Gracie after a while and said plaintively, 'Auntie Gracie, *I'd* rather see you on my own.'

Gracie said, 'Would you? Well, we'll

make a date. Shall we have tea together tomorrow?'

Marisa smiled at her. 'Yes, please.'

'Right, what time do you finish school?'

'Three thirty.'

'Well, you walk down the road after school tomorrow, and I'll have the kettle on.'

The following day Marisa and Gracie had tea together, and *nobody* else was there.

Sometimes she embarrassed the children. 'When she burst into song on top of a bus, or something like that,' Annette said.

They all loved her socks. 'Come on, Auntie,' they used to say when they were small, 'let's have a look at your socks. Which colour have you got on today?' Gracie used to show them and laugh. 'Well, they keep me warm when I'm in England.' They were always eyecatching—purple, orange, red, yellow...

Gracie admired Annette's trousers one day. 'I wish I could get some like that,' she said. So Annette took her to the shop where she had bought hers, and Gracie promptly bought a pair in every colour they had in stock.

'She was lazy about clothes,' Lillian Aza said. 'She often used mine.' When Gracie went to collect her CBE in 1938, she borrowed Lillian's hat, and on another occasion it was her pink dressing-gown. 'I like this.

It's right, it's comfortable,' she said. But when she used the same tactics over a coat with fur round the collar, Lillian refused to give it to her. Gracie was married to Boris by that time, and he too said it suited her.

'It suits me too,' Lillian said. 'You go and look for one of your own.'

Shopping was, of course, a bit of a hazard because Gracie was usually recognised. She seldom actively disguised herself—dark glasses sometimes, but that was all. She liked to wander round the shops if she felt in the mood to. In Brighton one day, when she went in to buy a leather jacket, the assistant said, 'Has anyone ever told you how much like Gracie Fields you are?'

'I *am* Gracie Fields,' she told him.

He glanced towards her uncertainly, then grinned. 'You're not.'

'I am,' Gracie said, enjoying the encounter now.

He nudged her, 'Go on with you, you're not—but you do look like her.'

Gracie began to sing 'Sally', and the man nearly dropped the tape measure he was about to put round her.

'You are,' he whispered. 'Oh my goodness, you really are.'

She had spells of 'having it in' for different people, according to those who lived closest to her. Lillian said she would sit at her dressing-table with her hand on her cheek and keep moving her jaw—moving her tongue round her jaw. When she was like this with someone, they could not do anything right for her. She went all round, her manager, the conductor, her friends.

'I usually kept out of her way when I noticed her doing it while I was there,' Lillian said, 'and sometimes, after a while, when I looked in, she'd say—"Where have you been—haven't seen you for days!"'

She didn't often talk about her inner feelings. Lillian said, 'She was easily squashed. If you told her she was good, she gained confidence, but she didn't have a lot without this encouragement.'

'I don't like a fuss,' she said all through her life, but her personality and standing were such that it was impossible to avoid it. When she sang to prisoners in Pentonville in the thirties, the street was packed solid with her fans when she came out, and extra police had to be drafted into the area; if she went shopping or for a walk and was recognised, not simply a few dozen folk gathered round her but hundreds.

When she visited a youth centre run by the Reverend Jimmy Butterworth, a few hours before her last night at the Palladium in May 1953, to unveil a plate named after her in honour of Variety, a crowd of over two thousand jammed the pavements as she emerged, and when they called for a song, she said, 'It's such a long time since I was down here, I did not think you would know me with my white hair.' She sang 'Sally', unaccompanied except for the huge throng who joined in, bringing traffic to a standstill as hundreds more rushed across the road to see her when they heard that voice, as one man said, 'could only be our darling Gracie's.'

She had a tremendous rapport with the ordinary people, if there is such a person as an 'ordinary' one. She was interested in them, in their lives and circumstances. 'Everyone's so different, yet most of us have similar sorts of dreams for ourselves and our families,' she said.

CHAPTER 16

Beyond the Mask

The woman was often hidden beneath the artiste. The performer was so dominant that the woman sometimes became swamped, but she was there, and many found her. She was in the letters Gracie wrote—in the hugs and handclasps, and in the thoughts and prayers she generated.

When she allowed a boys' club to camp in the grounds of Canzone del Mare in 1954, one of the lads fell ill. Gracie nursed him for ten days, until he could rejoin the others in the outings.

Hazel Provost, who first became an admirer of Gracie's in 1958 after hearing a record at her grandmother's farm, corresponded with her for a year before meeting her at the Wood Green Empire, when she did a TV show from there. In 1965 she went to Capri for the first time and visited Gracie at Canzone del Mare. They had tea, and Gracie posed for snapshots, as she usually did with her fans.

In 1966, 1967 and 1969, Hazel returned to

Capri. On the latter visit she visited her every afternoon, and each day as she left Gracie said, 'You can come tomorrow.' In 1972 Gracie offered her a job. But let Hazel tell her story as she did to me:

'It was a marvellous life there in Capri with her, and she seemed so happy to have me around the place, and kept telling me so. She must have told half of Capri that I was her daughter, and even to this day many people are surprised when I tell them I am no relation.

'We would spend the day in a variety of ways, starting by washing up her and Boris's breakfast things, when she would potter around in the sunshine collecting flowers and arranging them in the many vases she kept about the place. To her dying day she loved "playing flowers" as she called it.

'Then there was always someone calling to see her—it could be a little old lady from Manchester or an Italian Count or Countess, but everyone was the same to Gracie, and they were all treated with warmth and generosity.

'Lunchtimes were always spent with Boris, and sometimes they ate in the house and sometimes in the restaurant of Canzone del Mare which Boris looked after. If they ate in the house, I always ate with them, and after lunch Gracie would come into the big,

261

yellow, sunny kitchen, grab herself a teatowel and join in with the drying-up.

'Maria, the maid, always said, "Signora, no," and I would say, "No, Gracie—go and have a rest. We'll do it," and she'd say, 'Aw go on—let me be your friend,' and she'd help to the end, especially if there had been guests and there was lots to do.

'She always thanked Maria, often almost picking her up in the air with a *"Grazie,* Maria—*multo buono,* Maria," and Maria would giggle and say, *"Prego,* Signora."

'In the evenings, we would eat in the house, Gracie, Boris, the housekeeper and myself, then Gracie would usually play patience, getting us all at it. But often Gracie, Boris and myself would eat out, then go to the cinema—taking our own cushions as the wooden seats were so hard. The films were always in Italian, the English words being dubbed. Poor Boris was our translator, which he did with great patience.'

The woman in Gracie was to the fore too when Tom and Annette's daughter was ill. Marisa Grace was born on 21 June 1968; she was a beautiful baby, but, as she grew and eventually tried to walk, she couldn't. She fell over all the time and obviously had tremendous difficulty in getting any balance at all. The doctor referred her to the hospital—it was congenital dislocation of the hip. She

262

would need extensive treatment and possibly surgery.

Marisa was in hospital a long time without any success at all, and Gracie telephoned regularly and kept a close and loving watch. One day Annette went to the hospital and found Marisa strung up on weights on a traction frame. She took it on herself to discharge her, and that evening, after they had put her to bed, Gracie telephoned again to see how she was. Annette told her.

'What are you going to do?' Gracie said.

'I don't know, we've got to work something out.'

'Well, just a minute—let me have a think.'

The following day she telephoned again, and 'How many calls she made in between I don't know,' Annette told me.

'Can you take her to see Frank Foster?' she said. 'He's an osteopath, and he's done a lot of work for me with the orphanage children. If he can't do anything for Marisa, he'll tell you who can and put you in touch with them.'

Annette said, 'But however much is this going to cost?'

'Oh that doesn't matter,' said Gracie, 'as long as the child's all right. Don't worry about the cost.'

Tom and Annette took Marisa to see Frank Foster, who, after examining her and checking her X-rays, told them, 'I can't do anything for her. She requires surgery.'

He sent them to the leading hip surgeon at the Royal National Orthopaedic Hospital —David Trevor, who said she needed extensive surgery on her hip. He operated, and Marisa came home ten days later in plaster from her chest down to her feet. She was two years old. A year later she had the pin taken out of her hip, and today she walks, runs, rides, dances, swims...

When Marisa was better, they all went to Capri for a holiday. 'Gracie was fantastic with the children,' they told me. She was seventy-three then, but she loved having them around.

One day while they were there, she and Boris had friends coming over from Naples.

'You and Tom are invited out for the day on their yacht,' Gracie said. 'I'll look after the children.'

'They weren't very old,' Annette said. 'Marisa was three, Vicky six, William nine and Joanna eleven.'

'Oh Gracie, you don't really want to look after all those kids, do you?'

'Yes,' she said. 'Yes, of course I do. You and Tom go and have a good time.'

'When we came back,' Annette said, 'the children had had a lovely day. They were all in bed, scrubbed and fed, and had been read and sung to.'

It was the same at the orphanage Gracie founded and supported in Peacehaven. She loved to go there and be with them all. Whenever she was in Britain, she visted them if she possibly could—talking to them, playing with them and joining in with gusto whatever activity was on the go.

Lillian Aza says she didn't think Gracie took all that much interest in children: 'She never took any of the kids from the orphanage under her wing. She could have done, educated them and looked after them, but although she was always happy to see them when they contacted her, and to go there when she was in England, she never took up with any of them.'

Talking to Florence Desmond one day in the thirties, Gracie said, 'You know Florrie it's a funny thing—if I have anything I love it's taken from me. If I'd had a child I think I'd be afraid—even my dog got run over.' Later she said, 'I know I could have adopted a baby, but at the time I was so involved in my career that it would have meant leaving the child for another woman to take care of. And I didn't believe in having a baby for someone else to look after.'

She spent a lot of time with her nieces and nephews when they were small, and Greentrees, the house she bought after she and

Archie parted, was often filled with laughter and noise of children. The garden was equipped with a swing, slide, fairycycles...and indoors were children's books, puzzles, bricks, everything a child could want. At Christmas-time she would dress up in a Santa Claus outfit, complete with flowing white beard, and invite the neighbourhood children as well as her own numerous nieces and nephews, in to share the fun.

It was the woman and not the artiste who wrote all the letters and cards. There was no need to do it for the sake of her career. She did it because she wanted to keep in touch with people, because of her very deep concern for individuals.

Sometimes, especially when she had been away, she would go to her office and work with her secretary on what she often referred to in her letters as 'this mountain of mail'. She loved these letters, and she kept faith with the people who wrote to her by answering them. When they were typed by someone else, Gracie always wrote a few extra words before signing them.

Margaret Hazell, who worked at Ealing Studios in the days when Gracie was making films there, recalls a later time when she helped Gracie to write her Christmas cards. Gracie was in London, staying at the Westbury Hotel. They worked through the alphabet in her book—Gracie writing the cards, Margaret addressing the envelopes, and Irana, her housekeeper from Capri, sticking on the stamps. At the end of the evening, very late, Margaret said, 'We've got to L—.' Quick as lightning came Gracie's answer, 'And there's an 'ell of a lot still to do.'

But she always did them, personal cards signed by herself and often with a special message applicable only to that person. She did have printed cards too, but if she used these for friends or fans, she crossed out the printed words and wrote them in herself, so Mr and Mrs Alperovici became Gracie and Boris, and very often she left the space for Boris to write his name, so it was *absolutely* from them both. Sometimes the card was sent out before he had done this—the space for his name was empty, and you could picture her saying, 'There's a pile of cards there for you to sign, luv...' but before he did so they were whipped up and posted.

It was the woman not the star who invited Gertie Sammon into her dressing-room at the London Palladium before her show because it was such a beastly night. Let Gertie tell the story herself:

'It was a wintry night, and I was outside the stage door of the Palladium. Gracie came along, looked at me and said, "Come on in, luv, you looked perished—Margaret's just brewing up."

'We all had a cup of tea and chatted. How many would have taken a young fan into the star dressing-room and treated her like that? She was lovely.'

George Black, the Palladium manager for so many years, said of her:

'Most stars, and especially the smaller ones, are a great trial to managers. They complain about lighting, scenery, the orchestra, and everything else. But not Gracie. When anything goes wrong she puts it right by making it part of her performance. Her brain acts like lightning. If all the lights went out she would sing in the dark as if nothing had happened. If all the scenery were moved off she would perform in front of the brick wall.

'Once, *not* at the Palladium, when a lights man missed a cue, I saw her deliberately pause in the middle of a song and *wink* at him. The stage manager might tick him off, but not Gracie.'

I wonder if she was singing *to* him for a moment, knowing it might make him miss his cue. The little devil dancing in her laughing bright blue eyes, slightly to alter the words of a song she used to sing ('Laughing Irish Eyes'). It is quite possible.

One time when Bert Waller was accompanying her and she was singing to pensioners, she realised halfway through 'Swanee' that it wasn't what they wanted to hear, and as she reached a high note she swung into 'Walter, Walter, Lead Me To The Altar', to their great delight and his amazement.

However, Bert Waller followed her, and after the programme he said, 'Look, lass,' (Bert Waller also came from north) 'if you ever do that again, send me a telegram first.'

Gracie replied, 'Bert, if you couldn't have done it, I wouldn't have done it either.'

George Black wrote in an article for the *Sunday Chronicle* in 1935:

'Backstage staff, programme sellers, chorus girls, and all the other theatre people loved her. She knows the stagedoor keepers' troubles, and just when the fireman's wife is expecting a baby, *and* the baby gets a birthday present.

'One day the manager of the Palladium came to me and said, "Here's a pretty mess. Gracie Fields is coming into the Crazy Gang show next week, and the star dressing-room is taken. If I turn anybody out there will be a big row, but what am I going to do with Gracie?"

' "If I know Gracie," I said, "you needn't worry."

'His problem was solved before she arrived.

Two members of the Crazy Gang went to the manager and said that they would turn out of dressing room number one to let Gracie have it.

' "Give us a screen and we'll dress in the corridor," they said.

'But when Gracie arrived she would not hear of this arrangement. "Put me in with the other girls", she said, "it will be like old times." '

Australian-born Vola Young, who toured as Vola Vandere, recalled a time in Scotland when she was given the star dressing-room by mistake:

'It was a luxurious suite,' she said, 'and when I had dressed for my part of the programme, I found Gracie Fields changing in the "prop" room, among all the dust and cobwebs. She had come into the suite, borrowed something, but said nothing.

'Horrified, I said to her later, "You should have *told* me."

'And Gracie smiled and said, "You were settled in there. I didn't want to disturb you." '

In that Palladium Crazy Week Gracie borrowed a pair of Jimmy Nervo's trousers and Bud Flanagan's battered straw hat and twice nightly joined in the fun with as much relish as any of the comics. She did everything— took part in any gag, and even stood against a board while the knife-throwing Carsons outlined her figure with daggers.

Bud Flanagan found her in the theatre one afternoon when he had come to fix up a trick. Surprised, he asked her what she was doing there so early. 'I'm enjoying myself so much,' she said, 'that the show can't start too soon for me.'

It was the woman not the performer who boarded the liner in which Georg Black was a passenger on a Mediterranean cruise in the late thirties.

'We called at Naples,' he said, 'and Gracie came over from Capri to see me. She had a great welcome from the passengers, and a special luncheon was given in her honour. When the time came for her to leave she was asked if there was anything she wanted.

' "If you don't mind," she said, "I'd like a nice piece of bacon. It's hard to get nice bacon in this country."

'I shall never forget the picture she made as she sat in the boat which was to take her back to Capri. She was surrounded with flowers, but clasped in her arms was a large piece of bacon from the ship's pantry.

'Everybody on board crowded to the rails to wave farewell to her, and as the boat glided away Gracie began to sing. She sang song after song until gradually her voice died away in the distance.'

When a friend who had been with her asked her afterwards, 'Gracie, did you have it in mind to sing to them?' she replied, 'No. I just felt like it. They were so kind to us.'

Often she would ask people she knew were coming out, to bring items she had difficulty in obtaining in Italy. 'When you come, bring me some Boots cold cream please,' was one request, and Norman Jackson from London went every year and took English teabags and Scottish Shortbread.

She was a very precise housewife. Written on the back of a photograph she sent to one of her fans was the following list, which acknowledged receipt of the items sent out on her return to England: 'Paper table napkins (pink, blue, yellow), Sponges, 4 Calendars, Kitchen floor cloth, 2 dusters, 2 diaries, 2 kettle pot/pan holders, 2 dish washing rags. 2—I think face cloths, yellow and blue. Fancy blue bath sponge, yellow and white bath sponge.' Underneath the list she had written, 'I always like to check 'em all off—so you can be sure all arrived safe and well. Thank you again, luv, Gracie.' A simple list which speaks volumes.

It was the woman who said, when confronted with a mass of letters on her return to Capri after a holiday, 'These b.....letters—I get more now than when I was working for me living,' but she said it with a laugh, and she gathered them to her and took them off to the office to read and answer.

And it was certainly the woman, the insecure woman, who wrote to her friend Mary Whipp, 'Don't put me too high on a pedestal luv, I'm sure to slip.'

CHAPTER 17

Magic Moments

Most lives have some magic moments. In this chapter are a few which do not fit easily into the text of a life story but which are part of, and show, Gracie the woman and the artiste in moments which, for those who witnessed or were part of them, have left a picture which will never be forgotten.

Gracie was a great clown, so, to begin with, here are some recollections of a song she wanted very much to record but alas never did.

Mr Norman Yates recalls a sales award trip to Capri with his firm when Gracie and Boris were invited to an evening meal at the hotel. Many of the salesmen did a turn, and one of the waiters sang with Gracie 'in a rich, golden voice'.

'Then Gracie sang again, on her own, and one of the songs was "Send In The Clowns." When she reached, "making my entrance again with my usual flair...", Gracie twirled her hand over her head and turned round with the grace of a young girl—she was

274

nearly eighty and so full of charm and personality it was difficult to believe this, even when she eventually said, "It's time the old girl was off to bed now," and made an emotional exit through the group who were clapping and singing "For She's A Jolly Good Fellow".'

Hilda Harris also has a 'Send In The Clowns' memory:

'It was in May 1979, and Gracie took Hazel (Provost) and me to a cinema in Anacapri. Boris met us afterwards and we all went to a pizza café for a meal. We wandered along, happily discussing the film and later went into a taverna for a drink. We were the only customers at the time, and Gracie suddenly did a little waltz around the tables, singing all the while "Send in the Clowns".

'The proprietor, unaware of who she was, wanted to book her on the spot to entertain and draw customers in.'

Hilda has another magic moment which happened in the early 1960s. She spent Christmas with Gracie and her family in Peacehaven:

'There were about two dozen family and friends relaxing after a real festive lunch, and Gracie and I sneaked into the kitchen and tackled the mountain of washing-up. She was happy and sang away quietly, and I was in seventh heaven. Then she began 'Summertime' and 'Bess' from *Porgy and Bess,* in a much higher key than usual. I was up to my elbows in soapsuds and holding my breath for the top notes, which came out as clear as a bell, when I felt her hand on my shoulder and she said, "Are you listening, luv?" She was nearly seventy, and as thrilled as I was that she had reached them so easily.'

Bernard Braden has a moment too:

'After a long recording session in 1949 she took me to lunch, and on our way back to the studio kept stopping in Bond Street to window-shop. Dressed in a mink coat, with a matching fur hat, she looked remarkably genteel, and I overheard another well-dressed lady say to a friend, "Isn't that Lady Churchill?"'

'At that moment Gracie glanced at her watch and realised it was time to get back to rehearsal. She stepped off the pavement with her arm raised towards an approaching taxi and, putting the fingers of her other hand to her mouth, produced a piercing whistle, followed by a shouted "Oi!"'

'I really thought that the other two ladies were going to faint!'

Bernard had another story: 'It was four years after the taxi episode—we met again in Edinburgh where I was playing to half-empty houses in a theatre and she was filling the Usher Hall. We bumped into each other in the lobby of the hotel in which we were both staying, and agreed to have a late supper in the hotel restaurant that night.

'At two in the morning she was recounting hilarious anecdotes to me and nine waiters because there were no other customers left. None of the waiters seemed anxious to go home, and Gracie realised that, if anyone was going to bring the soirée to an end, it had to be her. She had a good look around the room, eyed each of the waiters separately then looked at me and said loudly, 'Well, as you haven't asked me to sleep with you, I'm going to my bed now...' '

Nell Whitwell's greatest moment was in 1978 when Gracie returned to Rochdale to open her theatre. In the morning she went to Broadfield School, and Nell, who hadn't been well and could not walk much, had been taken by car and was sitting in a corner at the front, but away from the crush.

'Suddeny it all went quiet—the children stopped chattering and listened as sounds were heard coming along the corridor, then I heard her voice outside saying very distinctly, "Where's Nell Whitell?"

'As she came through the door, Cyril Smith (MP for Rochdale), who was leading, said, "She's here, see," and Gracie walked straight across the hall, and as she came, I stood up.

'She took me in her arms and kissed me, there in front of everybody, and she talked and chatted away so naturally until Boris came and told her they were all waiting for her in the corridor—the Mayor and dignitaries, all waiting to come into the front row which had been reserved for them.

'Gracie and I had been friends for sixty-five years, and I felt very, very proud at that moment.

Nell had another memory in her heart, one from years back when she had been in hospital for a serious operation. Gracie was working in Manchester, and she came over one afternoon to visit Nell.

'After she left for the theatre, my mother noticed something under the settee, and when she pulled it out, it was a bag of fruit. As she went around the room, she discovered more of these bags of different kinds of fruit—under a chair, the sideboard—Gracie had bought all this and dotted it around the room, yet I'd not noticed. She always was restless, wandering about, and she must have done it under cover of that. In those days you didn't often see so much fruit outside of a greengrocer's shop.'

While we are in Rochdale, there are the football moments. On several occasions Gracie kicked off for the Hornets, and there was usually a little impromptu fun. In 1934, arriving in football boots, a borrowed international cap and a fur coat, she walked out onto the field and was introduced to the captains and players of both teams: 'Right lads,' she said, removing her coat, 'I've come prepared, see'—beneath the mink she was wearing the red, white and blue jersey and white pants of her team. Stepping back, she took a run and a great kick at the ball, then joined in until she was ordered off the field by a laughing referee.

In November 1931, when Rochdale Football Club were in financial difficulties, not having the fare to go to their next match, she sent a telegram to the Mayor, 'Have just seen report in *London Daily Mail* re Football Club. Am quite willing to defray travelling expenses of club to Barrow and wish them luck.' The outcome was that the team went to Barrow, and Gracie paid not only their expenses but also the players' salaries for that week, and a short while afterwards gave a concert in aid of club funds.

Sir Anton Dolin remembers 'a joint signing session' with Gracie in Capri: 'I had been to lunch, and immediately afterwards someone came in to say there were hundreds of tourists down by the pool, several coaches with daytrippers, all hoping Gracie would be there.

' "Come on luv," she said. "You're

coming with me.''

'I protested a little. ''Nonsense, they'll love to meet you, come on''. And together we went down, and for an hour sat there signing autographs, talking to fans and smiling for ther cameras. She was so natural and seemed to have the right word for them all.'

Another time, when Sir Anton and the dancer John Gilpin were there for lunch, Gracie said: 'What would you like to drink?'

'Campari and soda, please.'

'You're a b.....nuisance,' she said. 'We haven't got any soda, and I'm not going all the way down to the restaurant for it. Choose something else.'

So they had Campari and orange juice. Gracie had some too. 'It's good,' she said, 'best drink I've had in years.'

Some time later, when she was in London and Sir Anton enquired what *she* would like to drink, she replied unhesitatingly, and with a twinkle in her eye, 'Campari and *orange,* please.'

In 1932 there was a sixteen-year-old blind boy in her audience. His dream was simple —to shake hands with the star who so often brightened his dark hours on radio or gramophone.

He came to her dressing-room, shook her hand and touched her face, and they talked together for a while. Gracie asked him if he would like to stay for the second house. Eagerly he told her he would, so she arranged for a chair to be placed for him behind the scenes where he could hear the programme through. Then she had a word or two with her pianist and changed several of her songs so he should hear something new, the second time around. He never forgot that.

One day, back in the thirties, when Gracie caught the last bus after her show, the conductor recognised her, had a word with the driver, then turned to his passengers and said, 'We're turning off at the next corner and taking Gracie right home. Anyone object?'

No one did, and at one o'clock in the morning the twenty passengers, driver and conductor were drinking tea and having 'a bit of a singsong' in Gracie's house. Thirty minutes later the bus returned to its route and finished its scheduled run for the night.

On a visit to Rochdale in 1964, to open a new hospital extension, Gracie demonstrated in public an emotional exuberance that was so natural it was a joy to see.

With crowds watching, she was handed a velvet-covered box containing a silver key— she moved forward—there was a great burst of song from that outdoor audience, and, as their voices swelled towards the top. Gracie ran over to the barrier and conducted them.

'You sing it better than me now,' she said,

laughing and crying together, and a chorus of voices contradicted her: 'No one sings "Sally" like you Gracie. Come on, luv, sing it with us.'

She did, and before the emotion on both sides could turn the occasion maudlin, Gracie remembered the Mayor and official party and holding up the box in her hand she said, 'I've got to go, loves; nobody can get in because I've got the key.' She smiled her apologies to those she had kept waiting. 'It was such a magnificent welcome—I could *never* have ignored it,' she told them.

Gracie had many magic moments of her own, funny, moving, sad, and she often regaled her friends with the funnier ones. Like the time she was singing to soldiers, and after her first song a very Scottish voice called out, ' "The Holy City," Gracie.'

'I said—all right, luv, I'll sing it for you later on, but not right now.

'I finished my next song, and again it came "The Holy City".

' "I've promised you I'll sing it, but a little later on in the programme."

'OK Gracie.'

'After the third song. "The Holy City".

'This time I didn't take any notice, but went right on to my next number. When I'd finished he yelled once more—"The Holy City".

'This time some of the boys, feeling they'd had enough of these interruptions, bashed the poor lad on the head. Right then and there, long before I had intended to, I sang the song. I was afraid if I didn't do it straight away he'd be *seeing* the Holy City instead of hearing it.'

One time when she was visiting a poor district in Birmingham, she accidentally brushed against some washing on a line, and a woman shouted at her, ' 'ere, where are you going. You've dirtied my Albert's shirt an' I've used up all me soap.'

Before Gracie had time to apologise, the woman's neighbour said, 'Shurrup, that's Gracie Fields.'

'I don't care if it's Joan of Arc, she can't come 'ere dirtying my man's clothes,' was the cross reply.

Another story she used to tell against herself was of something that happened in the thirties in London.

'I was very lonely,' she said, 'everything seemed so different to working on tour. This will show you how green I was in those days.

'I went into a teashop by myself and asked for a pot of tea.

' "Indian or China—or would you prefer Orange Pekoe", the rather pert waitress asked me.

' "I don't know anything about oranges",

I said, "but bring me a pot of tea."

'When it came there was a little bag inside the teapot, tied up with a piece of string. I didn't like the look of that so I chucked it out. Then I found I'd thrown away the tea!'

One story she relished from the other end of her career comes from a tour of Australia and New Zealand when she was sixty-seven. She and Marlene Dietrich were staying in the same hotel, and Gracie saw her on the stairs one morning. Later she said to her secretary, 'I've just seen Marlene Dietrich and she looks marvellous.'

The little maid who was also there, cleaning the room, looked across and said stoutly, 'Don't you worry—I clean her room as well as yours, and first thing in the morning she looks just as bad as you.'

Just before she went on stage for the 1964 Royal Variety Show, she received a cable from Capri to say that her dog Lady had given birth to seven pups. Excitedly she turned to her fellow artistes waiting near, 'First time she's been a mum', she told them, her blue eyes gentle with happiness.

And from 1952. A merry reveller on New Year's Eve boarded the packed Victoria to Brighton train at midnight and as he wandered through the carriages looking for a seat, greeted everyone cheerfully with, 'A happy New Year to you all'. The great

British travelling public read their books or papers and maintained an aloof silence against this well-wined person. Then suddenly from one carriage where he gave his greeting came a reply, 'And a reet happy New Year to you an' all, luv.' It was Gracie, travelling back to Brighton after a show, who answered him.

The orchestral conductor Geoff Love recalled a magical moment when they were at a dinner party in a restaurant in St Martin's Lane, London:

'Gracie and Boris were among the party, and for some reason Joy and I had to leave first, and as we were just deciding that we should make a move, Gracie started to sing, very quietly, "Arrivederci—Roma".

'She would not stop to say goodbye to us, and as we moved away from the table she followed us, her voice getting louder and louder, until she was in full flight when we reached the door. You can imagine all the other customers in the place were tickled to death with her serenade. We always had a great deal of fun working with Gracie—she was a great lady to both work and be with.'

Florence Desmond recalled working with Gracie in *Sally In Our Alley* in 1931. During the break for lunch most of the cast took off their shoes and put on a pair of slippers. They were often standing from 6 a.m. to, sometimes, 11 p.m., but Gracie never changed into slippers. 'She had a pair of clogs, very beautiful they were, tan leather with rough studs round them. She told me they had been made for her by a fan. One day I said to her, "Wouldn't you be more comfortable in a pair of slippers?" "No, luv," was Gracie's reply, "I'm more comfortable in clogs than anything else." '

In 1948 Val Parnell, then manager of the London Palladium, said to Florence Desmond, who was closing the first half of the bill that week, 'Gracie Fields is in the box. I want her to come back to the Palladium but she won't risk it—she thinks the people don't want her any more.' Florence said to her pianist, 'As soon as I've finished—while I'm taking a bow, run as fast as you can to the orchestra pit and ask them to be ready to play "Sally". Then she said to the audience, 'There's somebody here tonight that you know and love, and she's never stopped working for this country. As a tribute I'd like to sing a verse of "Sally".'

She did, and the spotlight found Gracie as she finished and 'the house went wild. They clapped and cheered, and Graice stood up while they all took up the second chorus, which she sang with them. Afterwards Val Parnell brought her round to my dressing-room. I'll never forget it—tears were running down herface as she said to me, "Florrie, you little bugger...." ' '

One of Norman Jackson's magical moments occurred when he was taking a photograph of her in 1977. Incredibly, for she really did look years younger then, she was seventy-nine. 'Seventy-nine years young', as she used to say. They were on the terrace, and Gracie did a bit of organising.

'Right,' she said, 'I'll come round this bush—you have the camera ready, and when I whistle—shoot.'

'We won't get a good one like that.'

'Yes, we will—you just have the camera poised and as soon as I whistle—you snap.'

With many misgivings Norman did as she said. The result is a lovely picture, which is reproduced in this book. When he sent her a copy to autograph for him, she wrote on it, 'Hi there Norman, *you* sure take a jolly good photograph.'

CHAPTER 18

Fans and Friends

Gracie's mother died in 1953, and her father in 1956. Jenny was seventy-eight and Fred eighty-two. They were both very proud of all their children.

For Jenny, Gracie's achievements in the theatre were worth all the hardships of the earlier years. She was interested in achievement more than in money, although she was a sensible woman who never underestimated its value. She also relished the acclaim given to her eldest daughter, but the deepest satisfaction was in her own heart.

Fred, amazed at first by his daughter's fame, warned her not to 'get above yourself lass—never get stuck up', then settled down to enjoy the comfort and privileges that came with her career.

They both travelled with her a great deal in the earlier days, sitting proudly in the audience at shows, launches and openings of fêtes, and applauding heartily in public, saving their criticism for private hearings.

Jenny never lost her love for the theatre

and stagefolk, and Gracie took her on to the London Palladium stage on matinée afternoons, and they sang together.

On Jenny and Fred's golden wedding day she said, just before the end of her turn, 'Shall we ask them to come up?' As always, Gracie made it a family occasion, a meeting of friends, a party—and with an arm around each of them they sang 'Just A Song At Twilight', to that audience's great delight.

Once Gracie began making money, she was generous to all her family. 'I'd rather they had it now while we can all enjoy it,' she said once. 'Silly to wait until I'm dead.'

Jenny especially shared Gracie's love of children: eventually she had many grandchildren of her own because Edith, Betty and Tommy all married and produced families.

When, in 1952, Gracie married Boris, Jenny commented pithily, 'Can't understand our Grace—she always marries the enemy.' When she met Boris, she liked him. 'Happen you'll be all right now,' she said to her daughter.

Both Jenny and Fred were buried at Peacehaven, in the little church where they had worshipped for so many years.

Gracie worried deeply about her family. After her mother died she more or less became head of the clan. The Stansfield family were very matriarchal. Gracie was afraid of their growing too far apart and felt she had to keep everyone together.

Although she could not always be there with them, if they were in one place she could keep her eyes on them all more. With this in mind she built three bungalows in the garden of her Peacehaven home, one for Edie, one for Betty and one for Tommy. It worked for a while, but eventually they all moved out—as their families grew, they needed to spread.

All her life she loved and worried about her family. At different times she had them all over to Capri for holidays—her own generation, their children and their children's children. Even ex-wives and their new men —all were made welcome, but especially the children.

She loved to go to their concerts and open-days at school if she was home, but it wasn't easy to do this because word usually got out that Gracie Fields was in the audience, and it became a celebrity occasion. This made her reticent because she could see what was happening—the effect it had on the others; she overshadowed them, and although on these occasions she tried not to, she could not help it because of her name. She could never be someone's auntie in the audience, and no matter how she tried, others outside the family and close friends would not treat her naturally.

She had a power over the rest of the family. They didn't fear her, but they wanted to please her and did exactly as she told them. When she was in hospital during that last illness, they telephoned and spoke to her and even suggested going over.

'No,' she told them, 'No, I'm perfectly all right and don't want a fuss.' So they didn't go.

She had a very strong personality: her aura, magnetism, whatever you like to call it, was so compelling that sometimes it frightened her. 'It's a gift,' she said, 'a terrific gift. I don't ask for it, but since it's there I can't deny it.'

Her sister-in-law Annette said, 'If she asked Tom to do something, he would never *not* have done it.'

It helped to make her lonely. She realised people did extra things if she was there. 'I don't want them to feel they've got to run around after me,' she often said.

Gracie had a marvellous brain—was quick at picking things up and absorbing them—from dance routines to problems. She was nervous about educational subjects though, because she had not had much formal schooling. She could do it but lacked confidence. On the stage, where she had been most of her life, she had the confidence of her ability, and, although often filled with nerves before a performance, she went ahead. It was what life had trained her to do. She said that when she went to school she could not keep up with everything. She was moving around with the juvenile troupes, singing, dancing and never staying long enough in one place to have any continuity of schooling, and when she *was* back home she was only 'a halftimer'.

'I wanted to learn,' she said, 'I wanted to know everything. I *wanted* so hard, but I had nobody to help me at home. Mother, who was very ambitious, couldn't, and father wasn't all that interested in education.'

She said that in one of the juvenile troupes the matron was teaching one of the girls to write, and, 'I knew I wasn't good at it. I couldn't write properly at all and I was ashamed.' She loitered by the girl's shoulder all the while the lesson was in progress, then dashed back into the bedroom and practised all she had been watching.

When she was slightly older, she read everything she could lay her hands on. 'I used to read Dickens in bed by the light of a candle,' she said. 'I couldn't get enough education. I had such a lot of catching up to do.'

The fact that she did catch up didn't compensate in her eyes—she still thought she was uneducated and often commented about it in a joking fashion.

When her nieces and nephews were doing homework, she always asked about their progress. She was keenly interested and listened, but then she would say, 'Well I don't understand what it's all about—you ask Boris, he knows all these things.' It was lack of confidence really, because she was an intelligent woman who absorbed details very fast. She was also keen for Boris to feel one of the family, and involving him in this way possibly helped, although he didn't really understand the British system of education as she did.

On the back of a photograph of herself she sent to one of her fans who had just passed an exam in the Open University she wrote, 'Congratulations, you're a clever lad, *you* don't have to sing for your living like lass on't front, luv, Gracie.'

When she was made an honorary MA at Manchester University, in 1939, she commented, 'I wonder what my old schoolmaster would say now?' A reporter asked him, and he said, 'I never thought little Gracie Stansfield would get a degree.' Because she was ill, she could not attend the ceremony for her MA so had to have it sent to her.

She remained nervous about educational matters for most of her life. 'I've knocked about a bit,' she said, 'so I suppose I must have picked up some scraps of knowledge along the way.'

She wrote a good letter—always reaching the point quickly and clearly, and often humorously.

'We came back from America on this little rowboat,' she wrote on the back of a post-card of the *Queen Mary*, and in a letter to May Snowden she told her about a song which was all the rage in the USA:

'It's called White Christmas, which is something no-one who has always lived here has ever seen.'

Her words were vivid. In a card to Nell Whitwell she said, 'Thank you Nell for thy letter. You sound real lonely. Cheer up, luv, Gracie.' No waste there, and in dialect, which she often wrote to her Lancashire friends.

This letter to Mary Whipp gives a good picture. It was to thank her for some carrot seeds which followed her round the world with redirections and finished up at the Palladium, where they caught up with her: 'It's a wonder the seeds didn't arrive as "cooked carrots," ' she wrote. And one to Bill and Edna Grime said, '...so much mail. I'm sure I've answered some twice—mi maid moves things around so much, so don't think I'm going "off" if I've already thanked you for your lovely cards and good wishes.'

Another example to Mary Whipp: 'Gee could I do with thee here to answer all this so and so fan mail after the life story and me ITV job. I keep on sending out thank you's'is'is all the time, and can't find time to get a swim, and it's darned 'ot 'ere I'll tell yer and a bit muggy too. I get rattling on this 'ere machine some days and could scream when I've to stop and get out the dictionary, which I have to do a plenty when writing somebody proper like, an' it teks hours.'

You could write part of Gracie's story through her letters, for, although they were often short, she *said* so much in them: 'I *do, do,* thank you....' And one where she mentioned a photograph she had enclosed—and forgot to enclose it, 'They take folks away when they get as bad as me love,' it said on the print which followed by the next post.

Touches of humour, a putting-down of herself in a way, came through in many letters and cards. She never wanted people to think she was showing off about her achievements, yet she wanted to give them the photos and the joy she knew they derived from them.

'I'm a very lucky "Old Gal",' she wrote in one letter, 'I must say too—I feel embarrassed by all this devotion—but oh so grateful. You are such kind folks. God bless you and keep you well, and a big, big thank you. Love, Gracie.'

'Glamorous Gertie' she had written across one picture of herself in a beautiful evening gown.

She never entertained illusions about her voice: 'I'm pleased you and so very many enjoyed the Batley Club BBC show. A great pity the BBC were unable to have taken it during the first three nights I was there— then my voice *was* real clean and clear—they had to come and do it the night before I fin-ished my two weeks work.'

And to writer Naomi Jacob, just after her marriage to Boris, 'You will be saying I know, what a B.....is that there GF. Well, after all the silly excitement and nonsense I'm now a *respectable* married so and so, and very, very happy indeed with a real fine fellow. I hope you will meet him one day, then you'll know what I'm a talking about.'

She always wanted to do the right thing; deeply instilled in Gracie was a need to conform if she could—and again that other exuberant aspect of her nature—the other side of the coin that said, 'What the—hell; it's my life.'

She wrote hundreds of letters and cards every year—her postbag, from the time she became famous, was huge. At the peak of her career her manager and his staff dealt with it, only giving her selected ones. As she grew older and did less professional work, she read and answered her mail herself.

Her love of colour and variety came to the fore in her choice of ink for her letters and cards—sometimes it was blue, sometimes green or red—and always that distinctive bold writing...

Often, for fun, she signed herself Uncle Charlie, Maggie Driffen, Fanny Adams, to people who knew her well and would get a laugh out of it. She was always most concerned that her fans should not be out of pocket when they sent her anything, but they were only too happy to do so, and she never failed to say 'thank you' and sometimes gently chide them for 'wasting your hard earned cash on me.'

Gracie's address books travelled with her all round the word; her friends and her fans (we shall presently look at the division, and how some crossed the line) received Christmas or birthday cards from her when she was in America, Australia, New Zealand, Hong Kong...

'The *real* fan took the rough with the smooth and realised that artistes *were* different—had to tie up two kinds of lives, and accepted them as they were,' Margaret Hazell said.

Connie Entwistle was offered a job by

Gracie once—and turned it down because at the time she was with a family, looking after their children, and her employer was expecting another baby.

'I told her what an honour it was for me, and that I thought a lot about it, but I couldn't let them down when they really needed me, both then and after the new babe was born. Gracie treated me just the same, never held the refusal against me.

' "It's because that's the way you are that I asked you," she said.'

Tommy Keen became such a fan that Gracie used to suggest that people who wanted her records should write to him. 'I've sent her records all around the world,' he told me.

Ray Rastall named a cocktail after her— 'Our Gracie—my personal tribute to a great Artiste and lady,' his Cocktail List reads.

Graham Garner's memories include her making one of his dreams come true:

'Ever since I heard her sing "Happy Ending" in a taxi in one of her films *(This Week of Grace*—1933), I cherished a hope that one day she would sing it in *my* taxi. When I drove her about when she was at Batley Variety Club in 1968—we had been to Rochdale where she visited friends and relatives, then I took her back to the railway station. I had told her about my ambition some time before, and she was the last one out of the car I said, "Oh, you never sang 'Happy Ending'," in a half joking manner, and she laughed, climbed back into the car and sang "Happy Ending" for me.'

Another time when he was driving her, she had a bag of liquorice allsorts and was passing them round. She offered him one, and, as he reached out to take it, she said quickly, 'Don't take your hands off that wheel,' and she popped the sweets into his mouth each time.

She always behaved naturally—in an interview once where this being 'one of the people' aspect of her character was mentioned, she said, 'Well I'm a homely girl. I guess I *am* one of the folks—I like everything matey. I like to think we're all one big family. They belong to me and I belong to them.' Which she did, but only to a certain point—beyond that point was a very, very private woman whom few people knew well. She wasn't basically different from the public one—more relaxed, more serious, more worried by things written and said about her and her family—more introspective.

Among the fans who did cross that line, to become part of her private life, was John Taylor, who met her in 1947, although he had been fascinated since the early thirties when he heard her records on his grandmother's wind-up gramophone. He waited outside a theatre in Newcastle after she had finished one of her *Working Party* broadcasts. She was there a long time signing autographs and stopped as she reached him.

'Ee love, I'll have to go—write to me,' she said.

'Feeling very let down, I went home,' he told me, 'and after thinking for a while I decided I would write. There was a quick reply and an autographed photograph. She explained that she was tired that night, and that, if I liked, I could keep in touch. True to her word, she always replied, and during the two years I spent in the Royal Navy at Portsmouth, I met her again when she came to the King's Theatre for the Affray concert. She remembered all I had written, and in the middle fifties I went to Capri on holiday for the first time and visited her there.'

When John married, he took his wife to meet Gracie and Boris, and eventually they always spent two weeks at Canzone del Mare every year.

Neva Hecker, who comes from the USA, was intrigued by the contrast in Gracie's singing styles in her films. From 'Walter, Walter lead me to the Altar' to the softest, sweetest ballad, 'It hardly seemed possible it could be the same woman,' she said. She wrote to Gracie, who replied, and for a while they corresponded. Eventually they met, and Gracie offered her a job as her 'American secretary'.

Mary Barratt met her during the thirties. She was then working as a companion to someone in Lytham St Anne's. She and Gracie wrote to each other, and when Gracie was appearing in Blackpool, they met for the first time. Gracie said she took an instant liking to this woman she already knew from her letters, and impulsively offered her a job. Mary's reply, 'I'd love to if you can wait for me. I can't leave the woman I'm working for until I'm sure she'll be all right,' made Gracie more sure than ever that this was a good omen.

Mary came to work for Gracie, as she says, 'doing anything that needed doing—I typed letters, washed the car, did the cooking on cook's day off, did Gracie's hair, anything and everything over the years really.'

Also over the years a deep friendship grew. Mary was with Gracie touring during the war—she met her husband, Leon Davey, then—and it was Mary and Lillian (Aza) who organised and protected Gracie in her stage life, as much as anyone as volatile and impulsive as Gracie *could* be organised and protected. Lillian's husband, Bert Aza, once told the BBC, 'I could *never* undertake to get Gracie to say anything which was written down.'

In another letter in 1948, when the BBC were hoping to 'talk her into doing two more live programmes', he wrote: "Gracie is certainly coming to this country, but we will not know until she comes bouncing into the office, which will be within the next ten days I should think. I cannot get Gracie to make up her mind what she is going to do, and nothing will be settled until her arrival here.'

She didn't really like long-term commitments, conforming in this respect because of her work, but what she thoroughly enjoyed was doing things on the spur of the moment —there was excitement in that for her.

In 1955, when the *Daily Express* asked her whom she would invite if she were giving a party in her hometown, and only twelve people could be included, she asked for time to think. The following week they published the list she sent them, and here it is printed in full because it shows the serious Gracie who was always only just below the surface of the comical one.

'The strangest Christmas party of them all was being planned in detail at Rochdale yesterday. Strange because hostess and guests know it will *not be held*. Gracie Fields, spending her first Christmas in Lancashire since before the war was asked to name twelve guests she would like to have at a party in her home town. Here is her list:—

Mrs Bertha Schofield and her daughter Ada. Alderman Charles Bryning and his daughter Florence. The Chief Constable Mr S.J. Harvey and his wife. Mr and Mrs Norman Scott. Cousin Margaret Fielding and her husband John. Miss Mary Whipp and "Uncle" Tom Wolfenden.

'All are close friends and three are over 80. Said Gracie, "We'll ask Mr Bryning if we can have it at his place—he's always been my champion."

'The 88-year-old alderman, who has a red-brick detached house in the suburbs replied, "Delighted—leave it to Florrie."

'And Miss Bryning, entering into the spirit of make-believe, started to plan. The large refectory table covered with a gleaming black American cloth. For the centre piece a yule log. Instead of an ordinary Christmas tree, a branch from the garden, silvered and bearing painted eggshells and coloured handkerchiefs shaped like miniature umbrellas. The food? Traditional. And after it a singsong.

'Mrs Scott was formerly Dorothy Crewe the concert pianist. Mrs Schofield went to school with Gracie's mother. She remembers Gracie at Christmas parties in the back room at the little fish and chip shop in Molesworth Street.

'But back to the party. After the singsong they dance in the large lounge. After the dance, then? Over the log fire to count again the milestones which have led "Our Gracie" from the back streets of a Lancashire mill town, round the world to an elegant villa at Capri.

'Gracie, on her way back to Blackpool last night with Boris, smiled happily.

' "Real or make-believe", she said, "the wish is there, deep in my heart." The heart of Lancashire.

CHAPTER 19

Irrepressible Gracie

Gracie was fifty-four when she married Boris. She was rich—Monty left over £70,000 when he died, and she had been earning steadily again since the war.

She went on working because her voice was too good to waste. The people wanted her, and, as Lillian Aza said, 'What artiste doesn't feel a thrill over that?' There was also her great sense of duty. It was a duty she loved and could not fully live without: she had to sing.

'As long as the ordinary folk want to hear me sing, and want me to make them laugh,' she said, 'it's my job to go on. I was born an ordinary girl in a little Rochdale street, and I had two sisters who were prettier than me. But God gave me a gift, and I can never forget that all my life I am under an obligation. While there are hospitals to be cheered up, and crowds who come in out of the rain and pay for a seat, it's not enough for me to decide that I've made enough money out of them and they can go to blazes.'

She toured Canada, America amd Great Britain, appearing on the first Independent Television show (ITV) in Scotland, and Boris went too. He wanted her to retire, and although she didn't do that, she *did* cut down on her work.

In 1956 she was ill again, not desperately so as before, but she needed an operation for gallstones. They were in the USA at the time, and Gracie was taken by ambulance to hospital in New York. She recovered well and took it easy for a while.

Britain saw much less of Gracie in a working capacity after she married Boris, but she did many tours, Canada, Greece, our troops in Germany, and everywhere she went she drew the crowds and filled the theatres.

In 1955 she won the Silvana Award on American television for her performance in a straight play—Barrie's *The Old Lady Shows Her Medals,* repeating her success in this play in Britain the following year.

Barrie's story of the lonely old Scotswoman and the 'son' she longed for, gave Gracie an opportunity for acting which she used fully. The reviews were good and in some cases sounded surprised.

'A New Gracie,' said one. 'Armchair Theatre, produced by Denis Vance was another winner. Gracie Fields gave a moving, sensitive performance in J.M. Barrie's

"The Old Lady Shows Her Medals". Here was a Gracie never before seen on TV, an actress of deep perception, warmth, and human understanding, in the Barrie classic of the lonely spinster who longed for, and found, a son. *She must* have moved millions to tears.'

'Stripped of glamour, and dressed in a shawl, she played the lonely old Scots char who becomes a mother-on-probation to a soldier orphan. With a first-class performance from Robert Brown as the soldier, she reminded us that there is much, much more to our Gracie than just a comic song,' said another.

Neva Hecker, her American secretary, said, 'I wouldn't have said she was a great actress, but she acted from the heart and that was the important thing. I remember in *Paris Underground* (1946) there was a scene with Constance Bennett when she was let out of prison. Every time I saw that shot it made me cry. Lights, technicians, noise, it caught me every time because she did it for real.'

Gracie was in America with Boris, some time in the late 1950s, when they were locked in the dressing room. She always liked to be at a theatre with plenty of time to spare, but on this occasion they had every possible sort of delay and she rushed in, made up quickly —'Right, I'm ready.'

They went to the door; it was locked—the catch had jammed. For a few minutes they both struggled to open it, but it was well and truly stuck, so they looked up for other means of escape. There weren't any. Gracie shouted for help at the top of her enormously powerful voice.

Help arrived quickly but could not get in, and the fire brigade were sent for. They knocked the door down, and Gracie, brushing the dust from her dress, raced on stage as they were finishing her opening music, singing it as she went on. (Her theme song in the USA was 'All For One And One For All'). It was an open-air theatre and a windy evening. The breeze blew her flimsy scarf into her mouth, but she sang on, eventually managing to detach the scarf and do a bit of business with it in her hands instead of round her neck.

She had a tremendous following in America and went on a radio show when she was eighty, answering questions and singing snatches of songs with a vivacity which enchanted her audience, who seemed to appreciate her direct and blunt answers to their equally blunt questions.

Australia too always gave her a wonderful welcome, and she had many fans there. She wrote regularly to them—although she was often unpredictable about attending parties, she kept up a flow of letters and cards to people all over the world, for years.

Gracie was always a great professional. Clifford Ashton, of Rochdale, who photographed her many times, said that in the early years when flash bulbs were so expensive, all the photographers lined up and when everything was set, one person was delegated to fire the flash. 'Gracie was a natural,' he said, 'whatever she was doing, when we were ready, she held the pose for a second or two to enable us to get our pictures.'

She was quite uninhibited as to how she posed—licking a cornet, eating an apple, pulling faces—she never minded. 'It'll get a laugh,' was her response to any query.

On one occasion when a cameraman asked her to pose, she said, 'All right.'

'Would you like to comb your hair first?' he asked, as she had just come across from an aeroplane and was a bit windblown.

'It will still look just as bad,' she said. 'Snap it the way it is.'

When he asked her to pose for a second picture, looking the other way, she laughed. 'Is it to see if I've got the same teeth on the other side?' She turned round for him and posed again.

She was quick and impulsive and had a vivid sense of humour. Neva Hecker says that, walking down the street one day, when she was feeling particularly good, she started dancing and singing. She glanced at Neva, then said to her, 'All right, you can walk the other side if you like—you don't *have* to know me.'

'Gracie being Gracie' is what her fans called it. Ray Rastall returned a beautiful photograph to her once because the autograph was fading, requesting that she re-sign it. She did so and wrote, 'yesterday' against her signature, then enclosed a small, personal snapshot of herself as she was then, and wrote, 'today' against that.

In Florida, when she had laryngitis at rehearsal, to save her voice she whistled 'Now Is The Hour' instead of singing it. 'Afterwards,' she said, 'I overheard the pianist tell the rest of the band, "You may as well pack up, boys, I just heard the new act. She's a middle-aged whistler." '

She often made fun of her own status. On another occasion she was too early for a rehearsal and the only people about in the theatre were the stagehands. 'I've come for an audition,' she said. A *just* long enough pause, then, 'Me name's Gracie Fields, and I sing,' with an extra emphasis on the g at the end of the word.

On stage at a concert for the Royal Navy, she said, 'I'm forty-four—I have teeth that were made by a mechanic; I wear glasses, and my legs...eh lads, I'm glad I earn my money with my throat...'

Pianist Russ Conway played for Gracie several times. 'I idolised her when I was small,' he said, 'and when Teddy Holmes recommended me to her for a concert, I was thrilled. It was in Malta just after the war, and she was singing to the troops.

'She flew out, and I was to follow in another plane, but fog or something hindered the take-off, and we were delayed for hours. We finally got off the ground, but I knew I shouldn't make it in time, and I was terribly worried.

'It was a mad dash from the airport to the theatre—Gracie was already on, singing unaccompanied. We waited until she had finished the number, then someone took me on stage and introduced us, in front of two thousand troops. I had never actually *met* her until then. She took it all in her stride.

' "Hullo lad," she said. "Are you all right?" I was sweating. She smiled. Such a friendly, warm smile she had.

' "We'll arrange for some beer and sandwiches for you in a minute," she went on, steering me gently over to the piano.

'I sat down and played for her, and it was a wonderful experience. I learnt more stagecraft by playing for two artistes than from anyone else in the business. One was Dorothy Squires, and the other—Gracie Fields.'

The stories of her washing up are legion. When Mary Whipp stayed with her, she said that after the meal Gracie picked up her plate and glass and took them out to the kitchen. 'Thought I'd better do the same,' Mary told me. 'Her secretary, Neva, who was there too, took hers out, and Gracie washed up while we both wiped and the two maids put away.'

Graham Garner remembers washing up with Gracie wiping, in the kitchen in Capri, 'and we were both singing "Happy Ending",' the song she sang in his taxi some years later.

Irene Bevan, her stepdaughter, said Gracie embarrassed people by doing this. 'She wouldn't let her staff get on with their job—she had servants to wash up.' Irene said this too was a bone of contention with Archie. 'He liked to eat graciously while she preferred something on her lap in front of the fire.'

'It was the same with this business of catching a bus,' Irene said, 'she could well have afforded a taxi, but she *preferred* standing at the bus-stop, often laden with shopping, because people recognised her.'

It depended which camp you were in here. The fans loved it when they met her unexpectedly, and it was often possible to do this, but to some of the people who were close to her it was an annoying habit and showed lack of consideration for *them*.

'I remember her ringing me up once when she was in England and reasonably near where I was living,' Irene Bevan told me.

' "Can I come over and see you?"

' "Yes, of course," I said.

' "What bus do I catch? I'm at so and so."

' "Get a taxi."

'But she wouldn't—she waited for a bus, which involved a change, and reached me an hour and a half later, when she could have done the journey in forty minutes and in comfort by cab.'

She didn't cling to her background—she was rich for a longer period than she was poor, but poverty usually leaves the deeper memory, and she admitted that she really *did* enjoy talking to people. 'You can't do that in a taxi.'

At certain times, in certain moods, she delighted in being recognised. When she was no longer appearing regularly on a stage, it was gratifying when someone said, 'Excuse me, but—aren't you Gracie Fields?'

'It's easy to encourage applause,' she often said, and she usually stopped it, of course, but if she *wanted* to be recognised, talk theatre or have a singsong, she only needed to break into 'Sally' for it to happen. Some found it distasteful, while others thought it endearing.

She liked being a housewife for some of the time. 'I'm either starring or charring,' was a phrase she coined.

When her brother and his family were staying with her one time, she said, 'We've got people coming to lunch—be up from the beach at noon.'

Annette Stansfield told me, 'I took pretty dresses to the beach for the children to change into, and respectable clothes for Tom and me to appear in for lunch, and when we returned Gracie said to Tom, ' "We'd better mix some cocktails, hadn't we? I've got a fantastic recipe."

'Tom said, "Right—where's your cocktail-shaker?"

"Haven't got one," she said. 'How about using this?" and she produced an enormous glass vase.

'Tom said, "You don't really mean it, do you, Grace?"

' "Of course I mean it. Make it up in that. It's a glass vase. We can pour the cocktails out of that."

'So there was Tom with a glass vase,' Annette said, 'a beautiful cut-glass vase full of these high-powered drinks. Of course it was terrible when we came to pour—it went

314

everywhere—all over the terrace; we were awash in cocktails.'

She enjoyed improvising, sometimes with hilarious results; but there was the other side of her which liked things to be done perfectly. Mary Whipp recalls watching her with admiration as she skinned, cut and sectioned a salmon expertly. 'We've got salmon for lunch and steak and kid ney pud for dinner,' she said. And she told Cilla Black when she was there, 'I make the best Yorkshire pudding on the island—well, I'm the only one who makes Yorkshire pudding on Capri I think!'

While Gracie enjoyed elegant living, it was never at the price of comfort. Her homes were gracious, colourful and *comfortable*. She had two on Capri—Canzone del Mare at Marina Piccola and a smaller one in Ana-capri.

Derek Warman waited thirty-five years to meet her. 'We corresponded,' he said, 'and I met her for the first time only five months before she passed on.' She was waiting for the bus to take her back to Anacapri, and she drew him a little map showing him how to find the house. 'I'll leave the gate open for you,' she said, and sure enough, when he arrived at the appointed time the following day, the little brown gate was open in welcome. He had a friend with him, and after tea and talk with Gracie he asked if he might take a photograph of her.

'Wait a minute, let me put some lipstick on—got to look right,' she said. The result was an exciting picture, so full of Gracie's character that it seems alive.

All her life Gracie seemed tough and vulnerable at the same time. 'You had to be tough,' she said, 'to survive in our business, but it didn't mean you never felt anything.'

'She *was* easily hurt,' Lillian Aza said. And Gracie told Mike Sunnucks of Maidstone, 'Being a star is like being placed on a tightrope—they cheer you, but there are always people waiting to shake both ends of the rope.'

'She was often suspicious,' Irene Bevan said. 'She couldn't assess people.'

'I don't like rows,' Gracie said, 'but I'm not influenced. I make up my own mind about people.'

Frank and Joy Foster met Gracie in the mid 1950s: 'We were in a taxi on our way back to the piazza when we heard her whistle from *inside* the gates of the Canzone del Mare. The driver stopped for her to get in, and she laughingly told us all that she had an appointment with her dentist.

'Frank asked her why one of the dogs was

limping, and she said, "He jumped in the sea to follow me when I was swimming and must have hit his leg on a rock."

'Frank said he would look at the dog if she would like him to, and she said, in the broadest Lancashire, "Ee, are you one of them there bonesetters?"

'Frank, whose birthplace was Bolton, replied, "Aye, I am that." ' He put the dog's leg right, and they all became friends.

Gracie kept most of her friends all her life. She entertained her fans when they visited Capri, trying to have only a few there for tea at a time. Some tried to become part of her family, 'But I can't allow this,' Gracie said. 'I don't like to be any more to one than to another.' She was kind to them all but firmly resisted any overtures into her private life unless *she* made them herself.

Family and friends meant so much to her, and sometimes she was bossy with them. She liked to feel in control, liked to know where all her family were, and while the one side of her sometimes longed to get away from it all and not be answerable to anyone, the other was maternalistic, the Victorian matriarch. She would have been marvellous with a huge family, tending each one's special needs—in fact, this is what she did on a large scale.

Her impulsiveness is well demonstrated in

an incident that took place when she was appearing at Drury Lane back in the thirties. There was no publicity involved because no one ever knew it, except the taxi-drivers and the waiters at the Savoy.

She was leaving Drury Lane one night after the show, on her own. It was pouring with rain, and in the Strand all the taxi-drivers were huddled in their cabs.

'Haven't you got any customers?' she asked.

'No, Gracie. It's such a filthy night there's nothing doing at all.'

'Come on then, forget about it. Leave your cabs where they are and come with me. We'll all have some supper.'

(Gracie seldom ate much before a show— usually a cup of tea and piece of cake or a few biscuits, then a meal after she had finished work.) She took the cabmen across the road to the Savoy Hotel and treated them all to a slap-up meal. On her first night at a theatre anywhere in London after that, there was always a huge bouquet from 'your taxi-drivers'.

The antithesis of this story is the one Arthur Askey tells about Gracie and Boris going into a hotel in Manchester after a show. The manager sent the waiter to the fish and chip shop for a meal because the cook had gone home and he had nothing to give them. Gracie saw the waiter return, and when the meal was served, on plates, she laughed and said, 'You could have left it in the paper—it would taste just as good.'

Trumpeter and band-leader Nat Gonella told me, 'Gracie Fields started me on my career. I met her in 1925 when I was seventeen and leader of the orchestra which played for Archie Pitt's shows.

'Gracie always took such an interest in anyone connected with the show. She thought I "had a lot of talent" and encouraged me to practise; she gave me a wind-up gramophone and six dance-band records.

'Until then I had only known I wanted to play, but not which type of music, but when I listened to these records, I *knew* I had to play like this. So really it was Gracie who put me on the road to success.'

He also recalled her taking all the band out for the day on the Sunday. 'We were working in Plymouth, and she took us all over to an island for the day—there were fourteen of us. She hired bicycles and told us to go off and enjoy ourselves.'

Bernard Miles said, 'She was a wonderful artiste with a pure voice. People often spend years of time and vast amounts of money trying to achieve half the sound she managed naturally. She gave me some excellent advice. She told me to work nearer the floats (footlights), so that if I leaned over I could shake hands with the band or take a shilling out of someone's pocket in the front row. She also told me to speak up—"and that doesn't mean to shout, but to tilt your head so you can be heard in the gallery." '

Deeply interested in talent and how other folk expressed themselves, she would often watch an unknown act from the wings. She watched with great concentration and encouraged those she found good, often suggesting them for a place on a bill where she was appearing.

Mona Newman saw her at a charity concert at the Phoenix Theatre, London just before the war.

'She was the principal artiste on the bill,' she said, 'I was standing in the wings watching the various acts when someone dug me in the ribs with the remark, "He's good, isn't he?"

'We got talking, and Gracie chatted about herself, *not* in any way boasting. She said that her housekeeper had been coddling her, sending her to bed tiddly most nights to try and rid her of a cold in anticipation of this concert.

'Between talking she would suddenly do a high kick and then settle down beside me again. I found her a most warm, friendly individual, and not in the slightest degree aware of her own importance.

'One of the artistes, not by any means a well-known one, was complaining about being the next but last on the programme. Gracie, without hesitation said, "OK, luv, you take my place. I don't care where I go on."

'She did go on after the interval; and the audience was loth to let her go.'

CHAPTER 20

Indian Summer

Gracie gave many 'final tours', and every time the reporters asked, 'Is this a farewell? Are you retiring?' She even laughed about the number of them herself, but, each time she said it, she fully intended it would be so.

After concerts in America in 1965, one paper reviewed her performance like this:

'Newspaper reports from America show that Gracie Fields achieved one of her biggest triumphs on her farewell performance in New York last week. Earlier she had announced her retirement from the world of entertainment.

'Gracie sang "Now Is The Hour for me to say goodbye" as she left the stage forever and made her final bow to an audience of 8,000 at an outdoor stadium. She cajoled, enlivened and saddened her audience for an hour, but still they roared, "One more, one more."

' "What's the matter, haven't you a home", she shouted across the footlights.'

The Metropolitan Opera of New York,

which presents the summer concerts at the stadium, billed the programme *Salute to Britain*. The crowd chose to turn it into a *Salute to Gracie*. The New York critics warmly praised Gracie's performance. In the *New York Times* Harry Gilroy called it a triumph:

'She swept the audience along in a tumult of laughter and applause that suggests that Gracie Fields had better reconsider retiring,' he wrote. 'This time however, Gracie is really in earnest about her retirement. Before leaving New York to fly back to her home on the Isle of Capri she said, "Enough is enough. Now I just want to be with my husband and enjoy the rest of my life." '

But she said she could not bring herself to do a farewell tour of Britain. In 1964 she did one for impresario Harold Fielding which *some* sources said was to be her farewell to her homeland. It began on 6th September in Blackpool and finished on 4th October in Eastbourne.

'One of my first remarks to "Miss Fields", as I called her years ago at my first meeting with her,' Harold Fielding told me, 'was— what special arrangements do you want in the dressing-room?

'I said this because at the same time I was handling concert tours for people like Jeanette Macdonald and Grace Moore and Lily Pons, a few of the great ladies who came to me via America. Sometimes their demands were quite extraordinary, such as red eggs for breakfast, or a white drugget right from the point in the dressing-room where the evening's gown was put on, extending all the way to the spot on the stage where she entertained the public.

'Gracie summed it all up very simply. "Just nothing, luv—I don't even need a mirror to brush me hair in."

'My wife and I found over the years that this was true, and matched with another quirk of dear Gracie which we soon masttered. The tour would start out with four or five travel cases. As we progressed from town to town, the cases mysteriously got less and less, until it was very soon down to just one case.

'Mary Davey, the wonderful lady who looked after her on tour here, let me into the secret—almost every day Gracie would insist on diminishing the cases by posting parcels back to London.'

For the 1964 tour Harold Fielding gave a reception at his theatre, the Prince Charles, and Gracie, in tremendous form, even had the Press singing 'Hullo Dolly'.

Two days before the tour began, she switched on the Blackpool Lights before a crowd estimated at over ten thousand, who cheered, applauded and pleaded with her to sing. 'It's always been an ambition of mine to switch on the Blackpool Lights,' she confided to friends.

Organist Reginald Dixon, often called 'Mr Blackpool' because of all the years he had worked there, had played a selection of Gracie's songs before she arrived, and then the people began to chant, 'We want Gracie, we want Gracie...'

She came onto the platform wearing a short fur coat over a black dress and accompanied by her husband, Boris, and the Mayor of Blackpool. Thanking the crowd for the wonderful reception, and in response to their demands for her to sing, she said, 'I'll be glad to sing any song you want, but remember that I've not been working in the theatre for six years and on Sunday I start a concert tour so I dare not sing too much out of doors in case I harm my throat for the tour. Just one song—please be satisfied with that, and realise I'm 66 not 36, even though I may only feel 36 right now.'

She sang 'Sally', then, in spite of her words, could not resist their applause and cheers and broke into *'Volare'*, substituting words of her own to fit the occasion.

Afterwards Gracie, Boris and the civic party toured the illuminations on a decorated tram before going on to supper at the Imperial Hotel.

It brought back memories for eighty-year-old Mr William Robinson who recalled the time he had presented her with a sword which had belonged to the skipper of the *Alabama,* the first great ocean raider of modern times, which was sunk in the English Channel in 1864. On that occasion she had led a tour of the illuminations for the Blackpool Disabled Men's Association, and Mr Robinson had said as he handed her the sword at a ceremony in the Town Hall. 'A tribute from a Yorkshire lad to a great Lancashire lass,' and Gracie, her eyes twinkling with laughter, had chased him round the Mayor's Parlour with it saying, 'It's the war of the roses all over again.'

Two days after switching on the lights, she opened at the Opera House, Blackpool, the first venue of her eleven concerts in a four weeks' tour.

Some of the critics in the papers were dubious, some were scathing, a few were encouraging, when it was known that Gracie was going to embark on a concert tour of Great Britain at the age of sixty-six and after a five-year 'retirement'. 'It's the reporters who say it's a farewell tour, not me,' she often said, 'I've never committed myself to retirement.' (She once told actress Florence Desmond, *'Always* leave the door open in case you want—or need—to return.')

'A Comeback for Gracie Fields' one headline said. 'I've never been away,' she answered. But she admitted that for five years she had 'semi-retired' in her Capri island home.

The reviews after each of those concerts were immensely satisfying to an artiste who never short-changed her audiences. Even the critics who had predicted a 'nostalgic success' admitted that this was entertainment with a capital E.

'What a comeback for Gracie. On the opening night of her concert tour she had yesterday's two capacity audiences at the Opera House in frenzied applause and yelling for more. The silver-haired star, dressed in a glittering seagreen twopiece and a bronze evening coat (which she delicately placed on the piano—'nice and posh like Boris told me to') reigned on stage supremely for the entire second half. One might have expected an evening of pure nostalgia. It wasn't. Because this was no famous has-been singing a swan-song. In front of us stood an utterly dynamic performer who swept her listeners from breathless silence to laughter at the tilt of a lilt.

'She sang her "S" songs (they all begin with S and have all been lucky) September, Summertime in Venice, Scarlet Ribbons, and of course Sally. With a green scarf as her only prop she embarked on her comic range, and went Irish, Scottish, and Rochdalish in her inimitable way. She was a scream, was our Gracie.

'In contrast she went into medleys, one from The King and I, one blending old and new songs. And you could have heard a pin drop during Bless This House....'

Another said, 'Today the concert halls of Britain have been taken over by the pop groups. Everybody says that there is no audience for anything else. But our Gracie has proved them wrong. And last night four vanloads of flowers were sent by Gracie to Blackpool hospitals.'

'I suppose the youngsters will call me ''Mother Beatle'',' she said amid laughter.

Another critic wrote: 'A stoutish, handsome woman drew the crowds in Blackpool last night. She captivated two capacity houses, each of 3,000 at the Opera House, with the voice of a mischievous angel and the humour of a tough minded mill girl....'

Boris had not wanted her to do the tour. 'Sometimes it's hard for me to understand why she wants to leave the sunshine of Capri for the possible grey clouds of England,' he said at the time.

Gracie was excited and happy, yet realistic. 'It's not so much for the brass—I've never squandered my money, never even lived up to my income,' she said. 'I don't want to be forced to work when I'm old; I'm doing this tour now because I love my work and I love my audiences, and I miss the people. The old voice is working well enough, and I'm not singing every night.'

The impetus of the Blackpool welcome occurred everywhere she played. 'It's not just a northern hullo for one of their own,' Gracie commented, with relief.

In Torquay, after her two shows there, 'It's Graciemania,' shouted the headlines. 'Seafront traffic screeched to a halt when hundreds of people rushed towards the stage door of the Princess Theatre to shout their thanks to Gracie Fields. The area around the theatre was jammed, and people lined the road on both sides.

'Gracie drove along the seafront, the sunshine roof of her car down so she could stand and acknowledge their cheers and cries of "thank you Gracie". And well she deserved their thanks, for she proved to them during the show that she had retained that old magic which for so many years had people laughing and crying at the slightest change of her mood.'

Another critic wrote, 'The biggest surprise of all was her voice. It never wavered, and she struck the high notes as clearly and as definitely as of old.' In fact, as she was the first to admit, she had 'put everything down a key'.

In Portsmouth a young reviewer wrote, 'As I took my seat high in the Portsmouth Guildhall last night I felt the perfect outsider—like a communist at a moral rearmament meeting, or a teetotaller at a stag party.

'The hall was packed, many not the sort you expect to find at Sunday night concerts. It was not only age which separated us, but excitement.

'I sat curiously detached. To me, like many young people, Gracie Fields was just a name. I had heard her singing on the radio and once caught a glimpse of her on television, but my reactions at those times were uncharitable to put it mildly.

'I knew of her great reputation, but the Gracie Fields cult was a mystery to me. It is no longer. After spending an evening in the company of the ever-young Gracie, you can count me in as one of her admirers. Gracie Fields had won me over.

'She is a remarkable woman. Sixty-six, yet lively, energetic, versatile, and vital—with that spark which drives all the big show business names. Gracie ended with Now Is The Hour, which included the poignant line, "while I'm away please remember me"— How could we forget her.'

In 1964 Beatlemania was at its peak, and

reporters were quick to ask Gracie her opinion of the Liverpool four, and indeed of the general trend in the music of the day.

'I like the Beatles,' she said, 'I've got some of their records, but I wish they would get their hair cut now they're accepted. They could be such ambassadors for England among the younger generation.' And the Beatles replied, 'It's part of our image—we can't change that.'

Impresario, and organiser of that tour, Harold Fielding says, 'Until the advent of Tommy Steele and the way he can go down a street and bus-drivers and cab-drivers alike will lean out and say, 'Hullo Tommy,'' Gracie was the only artiste in world I had found who would be besieged all the way down the street by the public, not being cheeky but being loving—who would hail her one after another with ''Hullo, Gracie.''

'I well remember standing on York Station one day and wondering why the train did not take off for our next stop, when suddenly I realised that the engine-driver was down talking to Gracie.'

But Harold Fielding's most poignant memory is of Bristol:

'The Colston Hall where she was appearing was one of our happy hunting grounds, and it stood with a large facade of steps in front of it like St Paul's Cathedral,' he told me. 'Around me in 1964 were many of the stars such as Johnnie "Cry" Ray, for whose safety one sometimes worried, but Gracie got the biggest crowds of all, and that night at Bristol when she wanted to walk down the steps there were literally the whole two thousand audience standing there to greet her.

' "Leave it to me, luv," she whispered, and then to the crowd, "If I sing 'Sally' to you, will you the then let me walk down quietly?" and just as if it was a miracle, and without any encouragement from the police, the whole crowd parted and left her a safe walkway down that myriad of steps.'

The last concert of her tour was at the Congress Theatre in Eastbourne. Here it was the same story—all seats sold and an hour before her performance a queue hopefully waiting in case there were any cancellations. 'I'd have given a fortnight's holiday pay just to see her,' someone said, 'I was too late to get a ticket.'

Boris had only stayed for the Blackpool concerts. 'He had to fly back to look after the old joint,' she laughingly told reporters. They telephoned each other every day, but Boris didn't want to be away from Italy for a month—especially on such a tour, when, as he said himself, she was 'Our Gracie', 'and I should like her to be *my* Gracie.'

As the tour progressed, there were rumours

that Gracie was coming back to Britain to live. 'No,' she said, 'I shall be going to Capri when I've finished.' She stayed for almost another week after that last show, visiting her family and friends at Peacehaven and Brighton, doing some Christmas shopping, taking in some of the London shows; then, on the following Saturday, she flew back to Italy and Boris. 'To do a different kind of knitting,' she said, laughing with the reporters. (From the early days Gracie referred to her work as 'doing me knittin'.)

She still sang—to the tourists who came out in summer—

'Give us a song, Gracie.'

'Right—what d'you want to hear?' And her voice rang out clear and true still.

She sang around the house, in the bath, on top of buses when she was in Britain on a private visit. 'Come on, let's have a song,' and in a few moments an astonished driver heard his passengers warbling 'Sing As We Go And Let The World Go By', led by a voice that could only be 'Our Gracie's'.

She would have liked to come home to live—home, as she often said, 'meaning England', but Boris wasn't keen on moving; Italy *was* his home.

They usually did come to Britain for some time during the winter months in a private capacity—often for Christmas, as in 1971.

They stayed on for the New Year, and Boris had a heart attack and spent some weeks in hospital. In a letter to friends Gracie said, 'We expect him home tomorrow. We are getting older'er every year and trying to do as we did thirty years ago, so this has been a warning.'

But before that, in 1965, she followed her British tour with a return to Australia and New Zealand under the banner of J & N Tait (the concert division of J C Williamson Theatres Ltd.) It began in February in Sydney, where originally three concerts were booked, then three in Melbourne, two each in Adelaide and Brisbane, all so successful that return concerts were played in Adelaide, Melbourne and Sydney. Boris wasn't in Australia with her. He returned to Capri unwell —he was awaiting a hernia operation at the time, and they spent their thirteenth wedding anniversary apart.

The New Zealand concerts took her to both North and South Island; the tour finished in March at Dunedin in the South Island, and on 2 April, the day before she left for Capri, she gave a final concert in Melbourne. It was twenty years since her last concerts in that part of the world, when all the proceeds were given to war charities and funds for servicemen—a total of £67,000.

'I saw more in one day this trip than I did

in three months in 1945,' she said. 'I was so rushed last trip; Australia was army camps and hospitals, and wondering when I would get to bed.'

The reviews were good and affectionate. 'Gracie's art is ageless,' read one, 'whether singing a song, telling a story, or just being herself, the vital personality, irrepressible humor, and gift of mimicry which have made "Our Gracie" a household word for generations, shone through triumphantly to the end.'

'Gracie still a rich brew,' said another. 'In Brisbane in April 1945 she left her audiences cheering themselves hoarse. At the City Hall, 20 years later, the audience demanded encore after encore. With a verve and polish that any younger entertainer would envy, Miss Fields at 67 gave a stimulating two hour performance.'

'They ate out of her hand—the shortest cut to a lynching in Brisbane last night would have been to stand up in the city hall and shout boo. If ever an artiste had an audience eating out of her hand it was Gracie Fields.'

Gracie read the reviews if she had time, but mostly she took her cue from her audience and her own instinct. She made it look so *easy*. That was part of her professionalism —Gracie always did her homework. She knew what her voice was capable of. 'Not

The Holy City now—I know what I *can't* do, luv,' and when pressed, 'Numbers like that need orchestration or a choir, and I don't think it would be fair on the audience.'

In between her shows she visited, as always, homes, hospitals, the young and the old. Quietly, without fuss. 'I'm Gracie Fields —can I come and have a chat?'

After her visit to the children's ward in Christchurch Hospital, she sent them a giant Easter egg—she chatted to the nuns at the Little Sisters of the Poor Home in Randwick after she had sung and talked to the patients there; and at a blind school in Sydney, when she wasn't getting any response from the children, she suddenly sat down on the floor with them and said, 'Do you know any of the Beatles' songs?'

'Yes,' they chorused.

'So do I,' and within minutes they were all singing 'Yea, yea, yea'—and half a dozen others, swaying and rocking with Gracie on the floor.

She went to Bondi Beach hoping to watch lifesavers in action, and when someone mentioned the Freshwater Surf Carnival, she was interested. Someone else suggested hiring a car and going along, but Gracie was already talking to the crew of the North Bondi boat who had a truck with their boat on a trailer. In a short while she had an invitation for her and her friends to ride in the back of the truck with them. 'It was great,' she said when she arrived. 'They're a wonderful bunch.'

She spent two hours at the surf carnival, 'The first I've ever seen,' she admitted, 'except on the films.'

They asked her to attend the official tea. 'What will you drink?' they said.

'A cup of tea, please.'

More in fun than anything else, they said, 'Give us a song and you can have a cuppa,' and to quote one person who was actually there, 'Cor lumme—if she didn't give 'em a song with the throttle right out.'

In 1968 Gracie returned to Britain for two weeks at Batley Variety Club in the West Riding of Yorkshire. The Club started in 1966—a dream come true for James Corrigan, former fairground barker and bingo-operator. The site it was built on had once been part of a sewerage works.

It wasn't Gracie's first appearance in Batley—fifty-two years previously she had passed that way in the review *It's A Bargain* and merited three lines in the *Batley News*. 'Particularly smart is Gracie Fields, a lady mimic whose impersonations of famous comedians of the day are very amusing.'

Now she was seventy years old, only a month away from her seventy-first birthday, and she had the audience standing to cheer. ('I don't often have a standing ovation in England,' she said at the time.) James Corrigan, founder and proprietor of the Club said, 'She was fantastic...she lost forty years when she was on the stage.'

One reviewer wrote, 'There were quite a few sons and nephews in the audience, cajoled into the trip by a mother or aunt who had never crossed the threshold of a nightclub in her life before. You could pick them out in the audience.

'One of the "pressed" men said on the way in, "I'm only going to keep my mother company," and asked on the way out what he thought of the show said, "Completely converted. I never thought she'd be like that—she was magnificent. I hope she comes again." '

Gracie watched the scampi and chips being served and commented to her audience, 'I know I was born over a fish and chip shop, but I never expected to sing in one.'

'I'm doing it for the lolly,' she joked with the Press when they interviewed her. 'I plan to see all my folk right for cash before I go.' But when one reporter persisted in that line of questioning, asking how much money she was giving to her family, Gracie told him very sharply to mind his own business about that and stick to getting a story about the show.

When it was learned that Gracie was earning £10,000 for her fortnight at Batley, MP Tom Swain tabled a question in the House of Commons asking if she would be allowed to take all her earnings out of the country, and whether this salary for two weeks' work was taxable at normal rates.

Gracie split her two weeks at Batley with a week's rest in the middle, so she could be 'on form' for each, and she made a typical 'Gracie' gesture by going on an hour earlier than the usual 'star spot', so her fans from Rochdale, thirty miles away, could see her and get back home in reasonable time. 'Anyway, I think ten thirty is quite late enough,' she said.

Her outstanding success at Batley amazed many of the younger generation, and gained her hundreds more fans among them. At a time when young people were very much in evidence in the entertainment business ('and some of them are very, very good,' she said), Gracie drew headlines like, 'Gracie Fields is wowing the youngsters in the clubs.' 'Even the young ones fall under Gracie's magic spell.'

After announcing 'Little Old Lady', she said, 'I used to sing that for my mother —now I sing it for myself!' As before, she mixed the bag—the old ones for her audience, the newer ones for herself, but also for 'the customers', as she called them.

'She gave us quite a few modern numbers in a way that was a lesson to some of our microphone-hugging younger performers,' wrote one reviewer. 'Her "Those Were The Days" left no doubt that show business of years ago really were the days. Judging by her repose, breath control, and brilliant technique they're just not making artistes like her any more.'

After Batley it was Christmas in Britain, then back to Capri. Gracie enjoyed her home and over the years had made it beautiful. When she first went there she took with her many 'bargains' she had purchased in the Caledonian and Portobello Road Markets, and gradually she and Boris added paintings, china and glass from all parts of the world. Built around a tree outside is a table consisting of tiles painted by local artists with scenes from the Sistine Chapel in Rome.

The wide terrace which overlooks the swimming-pool has been the setting for hundreds of photographs, as indeed has the pool itself. Gracie was a tremendous swimmer and there are many stories about this. She taught a lot of people to swim, including children, but one person she never managed to teach was Hazel Provost, her friend and companion from 1972.

'Gracie was a very good swimmer,' Hazel said, 'and often used to say that she could live quite happily in a lighthouse. However, I am no swimmer and never will be—and this used to aggravate her and make her determined to teach me. She used to pull me into the pool and drag me along by the straps of my swimsuit, much to the amusement of the onlooking waiters and guests, in the vain hope that I would learn.'

When an Egyptian champion came to Capri to organise a special swim across the Bay of Naples, Gracie asked *him* to try to teach Hazel.

'I was his only failure,' Hazel said. 'He tied me to a huge rope and pulled me round and round the pool edge like a puppet, but all to no avail. As soon as he let go, I went under.'

Gracie enjoyed diving too—to watch her dive from the top board was a wonderful sight, so graceful, so one with the elements. She seldom stayed in the water for long, but she swam every day, usually going in early before the crowds were about. 'I stopped diving when I was eighty because it worried Boris so.'

When she was seventy-eight, she fell while posing for a photograph by a loose railing. In a card to Nell Whitwell soon afterwards, which continued a discussion about their ages from previous correspondence, she said, 'So you're 82 and I'm 78, and look it—after a bad fall I had. Four cracked ribs, mi head bashed, but now I'm OK, thank heaven, apart from a lot of backache, and it's put years on me, the shock of it—falling six feet on a concrete terrace. Having a snapshot taken and the rail behind hadn't been fixed after one of our workmen finished a job.'

Because the ambulance could not get down the steep road, firemen carried her on a stretcher to the vehicle, where she joked with them about the damage she might have done.

She had a quiet courage that sometimes hid the depth of her wounds from the unaware. In 1964 she went on for a show after a wound in her head—caused by the removal of a cyst—had been stitched. She styled her hair in a 'bang' to hide the plaster and did her full show.

When she had shingles in 1977, she bore the pain stoically. 'I think she was about the most umcomplaining person imaginable,' Hazel Provost, who wintered in Capri that year to help look after her, told me. 'Just got to grin and bear it,' said Gracie when the pain was extra bad, and later, with recurring attacks, 'Past forty shingles is harder to lose than before, and,' with a laugh, 'I'm well past that!'

Age didn't bother her—and sometimes she

reminded others that she 'wasn't twenty-one any more'.

At eighty she was receiving genuine offers of work. 'People want me to do a concert to keep their theatres open,' she said, 'but they must realise my age—they'll have to have younger, newer talent.'

She had a vitality which belied her years. Her features, always strong, became gentler as she grew older. In youth she was in turn dark-haired, golden-haired and auburn. In maturity she was grey, silver and eventually white.

In a card to Bill and Edna Grime after a holiday when they had taken snapshots of her and sent them, she wrote, 'The all three together one is very good, the one reading not so good. Now I'm back to my own normal hair colour, silver grey. I couldn't stand the dark blonde any longer, so got one of the new special hairdressing salons to get it back to (as near as dammit my own colour), so I'm very pleased indeed—they did a jolly good job, and now it's all matched and ready should I return home any time (Home being of course, England).'

Hazel Provost said, 'She had beautiful, strong, thick, easily managed hair—it was almost pure silver in colour—and in between occasional visits to the hairdresser I used to look after it for her when I was there, setting and cutting it regularly, and she was always pleased with the outcome—telling me I should have been a hairdresser.'

In 1972 Bill Grime asked Gracie if he could have a photograph of her sitting in a chair in front of the scroll and casket she received when she was given the Freedom of Rochdale in 1938. He wanted it for a lecture about the town which he was doing in the autumn.

On 6th October Gracie wrote, enclosing some beautiful snapshots of herself and showing the casket and scroll behind her:

'Dear Bill and Edna Grime, Bet you've been thinking G/F's let us down. Not being a Master photographer (among his many other accomplishments Bill was) I got into quite a mess—forgetting my camera needed a battery to work from, so wasted two twenty reels of film until I found out the trouble— and at last have got enclosed photographs for you. I may have a better'er one in the reel I've in my camera right now, but it's funny how long it seems to take to shoot 20 photographs. Anyway this will have to do, hope it's OK.'

She went to so much bother to get exactly the snap he wanted for his lecture, yet was dismissive about it. She always maintained her interest in Rochdale and what was happening there, signing the petition to keep open the Memorial Gardens opposite the

Town Hall and keenly appreciative when she was informed about various town activities.

In October 1970 she opened the Vitool factory on a site opposite her birthplace. Handed a hammer to put up the plaque, she gave an impromptu rendering of 'If I Had A Hammer', before climbing a chair to do the job. There were never any half measures for Gracie—if she was to bang a nail in, she did, pausing long enough to hold a pose for the cameras before she got on with the job in hand.

Hilda Harris recalled an evening at a concert in Birmingham Town Hall: 'My seat was level with the platform on her left. In the middle of a song she spotted me, and moved to within inches. The spotlight followed her. I was getting hot under the collar wondering what trick she was up to—then she winked—and moved away.'

Gracie's irrepressible fun shone through every performance, yet no matter how she made her audiences laugh and cry, when she came offstage she was her ordinary self again immediately. The unwinding came later. On stage she was Gracie Fields, the artiste, there to entertain the folk. She had the talent—'God gave it to me'—and she kept it fresh.

This business of changing so completely on stage worked the other way round too. May Snowden remembers an occasion when she was waiting with several others to see Gracie before a show. This was unusual anyway, because she rarely broke her own rule about not seeing folk before a performance. In fact, they were all waiting on the offchance because she was going straight on somewhere afterwards.

Her touring manager came out of the dressing-room and said, 'Don't go in yet—she's upset.' Gradually they drifted away, and May was just going herself when the door opened and Gracie appeared.

'She looked very emotional,' May said, 'and had obviously been crying. I simply took her hand and walked up the stairs with her—there were quite a lot of them. We never said a word. At the top I left her and went to my seat; as the lights dimmed, I said to Annie, my cousin who was with me—"I don't know if Gracie will be on. She's all upset, been crying."

'A few moments later she was there in front of us, looking absolutely wonderful in her white dress. She sang "If I Should Fall In Love Again", and it was perfect. She was completely composed and in control of her emotions—no one who hadn't seen her just beforehand would have believed it. She went on to sing "The Lord's Prayer"—something I shall never forget.'

Hilda Harris had another story of her pro

fessionalism: 'It was in 1977. I was her guest at Canzone del Mare when she had a telephone call from Canada asking if she would broadcast in a link-up the following day.

'We were at lunch when the call came, and with no rehearsal she sang, ad-libbed, answered questions for over half an hour. I felt very privileged and moved, and she was elated.'

Hilda first visited Capri in 1959. 'In spite of being famous and so much in demand, she always found time to help the less fortunate in very personal ways,' she told me. 'Gracie encouraged me to "save your pennies and have a holiday". Knowing my working-class background, she lifted me out of it and let me share some of the glamour and comforts of her life; she was never forgetful of her own early struggles.'

Hilda had a wonderful holiday—free access to the pool and grounds, hospitality every day and an invitation to return as Gracie's guest at a later date for a month.

She recalls with affection the old 'banger' Gracie drove all over the island. 'We rattled up to Anacpari, often getting out to give it a push, then jumping in as it moved.'

When it did finally give up, Gracie travelled by bus or taxi, as she said, 'in style'. She could have afforded a new car, but the old banger suited the island's hilly territory, and it suited her lifestyle there too. It was 'right', and she was happy and comfortable with it. She swore at it sometimes when it was being difficult, but she raced about the island in it, and it afforded her as much pleasure as any of the 'posh' cars she was used to being driven in on official dates.

She also loved walking, and strode out with her dogs. Always Gracie had dogs about her, much-loved animals who accompanied her as often as possible over the years. When in her seventies, she climbed to the top of the crag overlooking her home with the speed of a woman many years younger. 'There are 365 walks on Capri,' she was fond of telling her visitors, 'one for each day of the year'.

She was extremely knowledgeable about the island's history, and about her own property, telling the story of the house's origins to any interested party.

Wherever she went in the world, especially in her later years when she could spend longer in a country and the pace of her work was more spaced out, she found out about 'the things that make it tick'. 'Mostly the people,' she said, 'but there are other factors too, industry, natural elements, but more than anything else the people determine a country's character.'

When rheumatism caught her quite badly,

she still walked. Her advice to Norman Empire, one of her correspondents who was in the grip of it, was contained in a viewcard of the island sent in 1974: 'Sorry you're being troubled with arthritis—it's a rotten ailment. (Touch wood) I got rid of rheumatism—old ladies' and gents' complaint—I had it very badly four years ago, and the Good Lord took it away. I try to do a lot of walking.'

When she had visitors for tea, she used to go down to the restaurant, returning up all the steps, which were fairly steep, and balancing a huge gâteau on her hand. She knew this created a minor sensation and she loved it.

The islanders accepted her as one of them. 'She often helped them in difficulties,' Hilda Harris told me. 'On one occasion we were chatting to a young teenage lad who was terribly shy and self-conscious about a large, abnormal growth on his face. Gracie suggested he could have treatment to remove it, but he explained it was impossible locally, and he obviously couldn't afford specialist treatment.

'Discreetly she made enquiries, and in a short time he had a successful operation, never knowing the cost of all that was in volved.'

She did so many kindly acts in this manner, quietly, tactfully, pleased to be able to help in a practical way.

CHAPTER 21

Dame of the British Empire

In 1978 Gracie returned to Rochdale for the last time. She went to open a theatre named after her, and, as she remarked in a broadcast in America a few weeks later, 'While I was there they had me opening the market and one or two other things as well.'

At first she thought a group of students were runnng the theatre, and she agreed to come and give a concert for the opening. 'They are calling it The Gracie Fields Theatre, so naturally they want me to be there for the opening,' she wrote.

The visit turned into a royal return. Bands played, brass was polished, the red carpet and flags were out. Over two thousand people waited to see her when she arrived to unveil a statue in the new shopping centre. Before that the town band played songs from her repertoire, and the crowd sang them. As ever, she stopped to hold a baby and talk to the people, especially the older ones on this occasion. For two days Rochdale fêted its famous daughter.

Gracie visited Broadfield School and watched a pageant put on in her honour. When the children did a mime about various incidents of her childhood, she mouthed the words with them and afterwards went across and acted and danced for them, showing how she had rattled her box following the maypole and singing all those years ago. In the hall she went down amongst the children and sat crosslegged on the floor with Boris and chatted to them.

It might be a good idea now to see what some of those children, to whom she was simply a name, or a voice coming from a gramophone record (certainly none of them were old enough to have seen her on stage— only on TV as an old lady singing on *Stars on Sunday)*, thought of her when asked after the visit.

'When I told my mum that Gracie was coming to our school, she was *green* with envy'—Christopher.

'Gracie Fields to me was not really someone important. I thought of her as just an old person who used to be a singer but now had been lost in all today's music. This is what I thought *before* I saw her at Broadfield'—Jill.

'I imagined Gracie to be a high-class, well-to-do person, and because she was getting on a bit, I thought she'd be a crosspatch, bad-tempered and boring. She wasn't like that at all; she was a good old Rochdalian' —Helen.

'She was ready to join in everything, and by showing us this attitude she gave us actors confidence'—Rosemary.

'When the sketches were being performed, she watched with great interest and joined in when some of her records were played'— Elizabeth.

'She joined in and sang aloud. She also talked to us about when she was young and lived in Rochdale herself'—Belinda.

'She had us all laughing, and she enjoyed the sketches that the school put on to try to remind her of her younger days'—Susan.

'I thought the best part was when she was singing and dancing'—Neil.

'I'll tell my children and grandchildren about Gracie, and also how she sat on the floor with the children at the age of eighty'— Rachel.

'I hope that she will come to our school again very soon, and I think everyone will be glad to see her'—Julie.

'She is not just a name any more; after she came, to me she is a real person. I am *glad* that I am in the house named after her. I will remember her, and I think that the school as a whole will remember her always'— Helen.

'What had started as a fairly good morning had turned into a *fantastic* morning'—Simon.

'We should all be proud to have gone home and said, 'Gracie Fields came to school today.'' And our friends at home might say, "So what!' *But they'll never know what they missed'*—Wendy.

At eighty Gracie still had that charisma that could turn a bunch of children who could not be expected to be wildly enthusiastic about her into a cheering audience.

From the school she went on to a luncheon in the town hall, but the highlight of her visit was the concert on the second evening. The morning of the day of the concert she said, 'It has been a wonderful visit so far, and I hope and pray my voice lasts out so I give the performance I have come to give—and everybody is still speaking to me afterwards.' She did—and they were. She sang seventeen songs.

The Gracie Fields Theatre seats 670 people. Its stage is 90 feet wide and 33½ feet deep. It has six microphone positions and a film-projection facility. Council-owned and run, it is part of the Oulder Hill Complex and is three miles from the centre of Rochdale. During term time and daytime it is a school hall—in the evening a theatre. It cost £800,000 to build. The architects were the Greenhaigh

& Williams Partnership. It is moderm, with sharp corners and angles from the outside, but Gracie, for the evening she was there, did what she had done before—what she used to tell people to imagine—she turned it into everyone's front room with a piano and a group of friends (who overflowed into a hall outside, to which the concert was relayed).

Gracie said to her audience at the end of the concert, 'Tonight has been one of the most wonderful, fabulous moments of my life. It's like a dream. Thank you for making it come true. At eighty it's wonderful having a theatre named after you—as long as I don't have to come back tomorrow and clean it.'

And for many in that audience who knew her when she did in fact scrub the stage at the Rochdale Hippodrome, and for others who knew she had done so in her youth, it proved yet again how close to her roots Gracie was.

The reviews the following day were vigorous. 'She was bathed in spotlights and showered with flowers (was there a living bloom left in Rochdale that didn't end up at her feet?),' asked Jack Tinker of the *Daily Mail*.

'The Grand Lady of Rochdale, 80-year-old Gracie Fields, sang her heart out at a concert in her home town on Saturday night,' wrote

354

Ann Morrow of the *Daily Telegraph*.

'The hankies came out and the tears flowed as amazing Gracie launched into Sally with a voice which belied her 80 years,' wrote David Thomas of the *Manchester Evening News*.

Before she left Britain, Gracie attended a Variety Artistes' Luncheon in Manchester where she was given a golden disc from Warwick Records for her contribution to the growth of the record industry, and a silver heart for her work for handicapped children. Rochdale MP Cyril Smith was there:

'The luncheon was in aid of a new kidney unit for Booth Hall Children's Hospital, and as we were moving from her room to join the assembled company she pressed a cheque into my hand for £500, and said quietly, "Put that in the fund." Then we went down to meet the other guests and the Press, and she bubbled over with excitement at the idea of being given a "prize" for her contribution to the world's entertainment.'

Gertie Sammon, who had been one of the crowd during the visit and watched Gracie open the market, also went to the railway station in the hope of seeing Gracie and Boris off. She bought a platform ticket, and, because the rheumatics in her knees were playing up pretty badly, was using her stick that day. She walked along the platform, and then she saw them, and smiled at Gracie through the window.

'Gracie got up,' she said, 'and came to the door. I told her I just wanted to thank her for all the joy which had helped me through life, and to wish her and Boris a safe journey home.

'Gracie looked down at my walking-stick—"You shouldn't have come on those bad legs, my love, but thank you for coming to see us off." She shook my hand. "God bless you," she said, then the guard was closing the doors and she went back to her carriage and Boris, but she waved and smiled as the train pulled out.'

This was the real Gracie—no publicity, no photographers, the simple human warmth of one person for another. You can't turn that kind of feeling on and off. She could have sat on that train and not come along to the door to talk—there was no one to record that kindly gesture, but it happened, and it is one of many such incidents throughout the years.

Back in Capri there was an enormous mail waiting to be answered.

'Often when she was supposed to be resting for an hour during the afternoon, the door would suddenly open and there she'd be, having just remembered something or other, or someone special that should take priority in being answered,' Hazel Provost told me.

'While I was sorting the mail, sometimes the door would re-open three or four times. She often complained that she couldn't sleep as her brain was jumping all over the place! In the end she used to get up and put the kettle on.'

She had a passion for tea; in all her homes there were always lots of kettles, teapots, mugs and cups.

In November of that year, 1978, came the excitement—and it still *was* exciting to her— of an appearance at her tenth Royal Variety Show.* She practised each day from the moment she knew, keeping her voice 'easy'. 'I don't want to sound like an old lady.'

All the papers mentioned her the following day, with headlines reading, 'Gracie steals the Royal Show,' 'Pride of our Alley surprise of the evening.'

She and Boris were in America when the New Year Honours List was published.

'Dame Gracie...' said the headlines now, just one week before her eighty-first birthday.

She came over in February to receive her award from the Queen Mother. Crowds of fans were waiting outside Buckingham

* Eleven invitations—the 1956 one was cancelled due to the Suez Crisis.

Palace for her. It was a cold day, but Gracie, well wrapped up in an apricot mink, waved happily to the people outside the Palace. She was nervous—'It was like a first night,' she said, even though she had met the 'Queen Mum' before.

As her car drove through the Palace gates, the cameras clicked. Gracie wound the window of the car down so the fans could get their pictures. It was almost second nature with her to make it as easy as possible. Over the years a wonderful rapport grew up between Gracie and her fans—a tangible feeling, strong and honest; as they waved, and she waved back, you could feel the gaiety in the air; it was like a party, the fact that Gracie was going to receive the highest accolade, the official recognition at last. Many of her admirers felt that she should have had it twenty or more years earlier, but the delight in the crowds outside the Palace was evident then.

The band played, the TV cameras were adjusted, people talked, reporters roamed amongst the crowd recording interviews for their programmes later that evening; and all the while the excitement mounted.

After a time, cars began to return. Air Force, police, then, after a long while, the Queen Mother drove through, beautiful and gracious as ever. The people waved, and still the crowds stayed. The Victoria Memorial was crawling with life—people clung on and watched, waiting for the car that would bring Dame Gracie through the gold-tipped gates.

She came at last, and she waved and smiled, but it wasn't enough for everyone. On this day of days they wanted to see more of her, and suddenly, like a huge wave that had got out of control, the great crowd who had been clinging to the Victoria Memorial opposite, surged across the road and into the path of Gracie's car. The driver stopped, and people lay across the bonnet, peered into the windows, trying for a glimpse of their idol. All traffic was held up (not for the first time—as we've seen, Gracie was always a traffic-stopper). The driver daren't try to move for fear of hurting the people who were surrounding him.

Looking rather nervous, but with that courage that she had displayed so often in her life, Gracie got out of the car. And there, outside Buckingham Palace, with traffic squeezing by where it could, she talked to her fans.

There was another party that evening, and those present toasted Dame Gracie.

'I'm still the same cup of tea I've always been,' she said. 'I haven't changed colour or anything.'

But she was very proud of her Dameship.

'Dame Gracie—fancy that!' she signed a letter soon after, and on the back, 'I hope my friends will still think of me as "Our Gracie".'

She sent hundreds of photographs to her fans and friends, many with a personal message on the back, and on these, her 'Dameship snaps', she wrote, sometimes in blue, sometimes in red and sometimes in green,

'THE NEW DAME
OLD GRACIE.'

In April she went back to Capri with Boris and answered all the post that was waiting there. Derek Warman, who visited her soon after, says he will never forget the stack of letters in neat rows which covered the table and which she was working her way through.

CHAPTER 22

Our Gracie

In July 1979 Gracie fell ill. All her life she was prone to bronchitis, but this time she was taken to a Naples hospital with bronchial pneumonia. She was there for six weeks, and when she returned home, looking so frail, she set about answering the further piles of mail on her table.

'The Good Lord isn't ready for this old gal yet, so slowly each day I'm getting stronger,' she wrote to her friends.

Hazel Provost said, 'She seemed to recover well enough to enjoy the company of her gorgeous little great-nephew Guy from Australia and was soon looking after the flowers once more, and occasionally we would go "up to the big city" as she often called the town of Capri, to "see what was new"—but she tired much more easily.'

On Thursday 20 September, one week before Gracie died, she, Boris and Hazel had lunch in Anacapri. Hazel said, 'I remember the flowers on the table and the waiters fussing around—she seemed very happy and she enjoyed the meal.'

John and Ann Taylor, who always stayed with them towards the end of August and beginning of September, went out.

'Due to her illness we were prepared to put it off,' John said, 'but Gracie would not hear of this.'

'I'm looking forward to seeing you in a few days' time,' she told them over the telephone.

A short while before their departure, John injured his back.

'Gracie and Boris were just finishing lunch when we arrived,' he told me, 'and the shock I got in seeing how thin she was, rid me of the pain in my back immediately. I realised she was a sick woman.

'After our greetings she returned to bed, and we met again at teatime. We discussed the details I had taken out for Mrs Aza about plans for Gracie to appear in a film to be made about her life. She was as keen as ever to be involved and did seem to pick up a little.

'Sunday 2 September was our wedding anniversary, and Boris opened champagne, and we talked as usual and took some photographs.

'Before lunch we all went into the lounge and sat down, and Gracie walked over to the piano and sang three songs—her favourite

"September Song", and then she said, "And for you and Ann I'll sing this one," and she sang, so beautifully, "I Haven't Said Thanks For That Lovely Weekend."

'At other times when we were due to leave, we usually said goodbye the night before, as she rested in bed, rising about ten, but strangely, on the morning we were going, she was up at 8.45. She came onto the patio where we were, sat down and said, "Well, this is it, my loves."

'Then she gave Ann two miniature wall plaques. Turning to me, she said, "I've already paid you."

'As we left, I had the feeling that we would not see her again, and during the journey home my thoughts kept going back to the look on her face as we left. It was one of contentment, happiness, and at the same time appeared to be saying goodbye.'

John telephoned her when they reached home, and typicaly she was concerned for his back problem and how he had stood the journey.

'She seemed much better and surprised me by saying, "We're coming over at the weekend for a visit to Sussex. I'll talk to you from there".'

Gracie never made that visit. On Thursday 27 September she woke, commented on what a lovely day it was and said she would go for a little walk after breakfast. She went back to sleep and died holding Boris's hand.

'Gracie didn't suffer,' he said. 'It was all over in a few moments.'

Gracie was buried in Capri. Six pall-bearers dressed in white tee-shirts and black trousers, who worked in the restaurant at Canzone del Mare, attended the coffin. They paused for a moment on the terrace to salute the view she had loved. Island taxis and five of Capri's buses took the mourners to the cemetery at Anacapri.

There are always flowers on her grave, and a light burning (a candle which is replenished every four days). On the stone it says simply, 'Gracie Fields in Alperovici. 9.1.1898-27.9.1979'. By the flowers is a small plaque—'Our Gracie. 27.9.1979'.

It had been a wonderful last year: the Rochdale concert—the Dameship—and the knowledge that so many folk cared.

When she died, the flag on Rochdale Town Hall, and on many other buildings, was flown at half-mast, and a portrait of Gracie, taken on her last visit in 1978, was hung in the reception hall of the new municipal offices.

The manager of a bingo hall decided not to announce the news because he said so many elderly people who loved her were there, and the shock to many of them might be too heartbreaking.

One lady, whom a radio reporter told of Gracie's death, passed out in the street in the centre of Rochdale and was taken to a chemist's shop to recover.

The sorrow which was reflected in hundreds of hearts and homes throughout the country that day when the news broke, was reported in the *Sunday Post*. A young reporter from that paper was sitting on a bus in Glasgow at lunchtime on Thursday 27th September. He was beside a pensioner and says he could not help but notice she was distressed. When he asked her if there was anything wrong, she said, with tears in her eyes, 'Oh son, I've just heard Gracie Fields has died.'

She was much more than a star, more than a public figure in people's lives; to so many she was a *real* friend—someone who cared how they were making out—someone who was very much a part of their lives....

A few weeks afterwards there were memorial services, one in Peacehaven, one in Rochdale and one in London.

The Rochdale service took place on 20th October at the parish church where her parents had married and she and her sisters and brother were christened. The vicar, the Reverend Canon Hoyle, said:

'Friends, we meet together in this parish

church to worship God, Father, Son and Holy Spirit, and to give thanks for the life and the work of Gracie Fields. We remember especially the tremendous pleasure she has given to so many people of so many generations in our own land and beyond the shores, and her immense zest and love for people.'

The Mayor of Rochdale read the first lesson, Miss Violet Carson ('Ena Sharples' from *Coronation Street)* read the second lesson, and the Reverend Canon David Clegg of St Margaret's, Prestwich, and chaplain to the Actors' Church Union, gave the address. Over five hundred people crowded into the church, family, local dignitaries, actors, actresses and ordinary folk.

The London service was held in St Martin's-in-the Fields on 15th November. It was a beautiful service—simple, dignified, very moving. There were daisies in varying shades of pink either side of the altar, and a full congregation. The Reverend Austin Williams conducted the service, Michael Parkinson read the lesson, Roy Hudd gave the address, and Elizabeth Harwood sang 'Ave Maria'.

Afterwards, on the steps of St Martin's, with the first drops of rain beginning to fall, the congregation mingled. This was the atmosphere, a getting-together of friends on this sad occasion.

The Peacehaven service took place in the

village church where Jenny and Fred Stansfield are buried. Annette Stansfield, Gracie's sister-in-law, told me, 'You saw what Gracie really meant to the people at that service. They trudged over the downs, and it wasn't an easy journey for many of them. It was an autumnal morning, very chilly; people came on horseback, on foot, in cars, and the service was relayed into the village. It was beautiful.

'We had a telephone call from a lady called Beatrice Hockley who was in her nineties. She wanted to come very badly, but there was no transport, so Tom went for her. He brought her to the church, and during the service we asked her to get up and say something about Gracie. She had no idea we were going to do this.

'She had brought a little picture of Gracie with her, and she propped it up in front of the pew and said, "I'm a widow, and I was ever so lonely, and I've written to Gracie and she's always written back. I've got all these letters..." and she had a great wadge of letters in her hand.

'Now we had never heard of her at all until she rang up, and she was only one of hundreds.'

At that service the veterans of Dunkirk, who had kept in touch with Gracie for so many years, asked if they might come and form a guard of honour, and if they could

367

bring a poppy wreath for Gracie and put it on her mother and father's grave, which they did.

There were tributes on radio and television here and abroad. American radio put out a two-hour show about her life, and national and local newspapers printed articles and tributes. In January 1980 a limited edition of a china memorial plate was made. In white, green and gold, it shows Gracie in full song at her 1978 Rochdale concert when she was eighty years old.

A Memorial Appeal was launched in Rochdale which raised over £10,000, with money contributed from fans all over the country, and including £1,000 from Bielefeld, Rochdale's twin town in Germany. The money was spent on new equipment for the Moorland Children's Home and on a pathway being constructed leading to the home (it had been a rough track before), which is now called 'The Gracie Fields Way'.

Many people would like to see a statue of Gracie in the Memorial Gardens, and maybe one day there will be one. The face of Rochdale, as of most of our towns and villages, has changed tremendously during the last thirty years, and many of the folk who live there now know Gracie only as a name and not as a person; so many who do remember, who turned out to see and cheer her in 1978, cannot afford the amount of money a project like this would take.

Before Gracie died, I had begun a book about her which I called *The Singing Years* —changing this later to call it simply *Gracie*. Part of this she saw and checked, correcting dates and facts for me. Eventually I decided to publish it as a tribute and give the royalties to cancer research in her memory.

Most of the books were sold through the post, and it was gratifying when people wrote back for another copy, and sometimes copies, for friends. The letters were a revelation. They showed how consistent Gracie was about keeping in touch—how enormously faithful she was to her public, who had long ago become her friends. They weren't all from old people—several came from youngsters in their twenties.

'I know I'm too young to have heard her at her peak,' one lad wrote, 'but I've listened to my grandmother's 78s, and I've never heard a voice so pure and uncluttered.' One remark almost all the young people made was that could understand the words, 'which so often you can't with many modern singers'.

One man, who wrote that he was nearly blind now, told of how he sat in his chair fighting the tears when he knew she had died:

'For a bit of comfort I reached out for my pipe off the mantelpiece and my hand was gripped, really *gripped* as though someone was shaking hands. Years ago I used to be on the halls—I played the harmonica as a lad, and if ever Gracie was on the bill, she always shook my hand like that before we left the theatre.' Was Gracie comforting him then, or was it his own memory of her?

Ray Rastall, who runs a bar in Coventry, has a large frame on the wall with her photographs and cards in it. On the Saturday morning of Gracie's funeral he and his staff went into the bar to open up and found that the frame, which had been quite firm the night before, had fallen onto the floor, the glass shattered into hundreds of pieces. He picked up the photographs and cards, which were all completely undamaged, swept up the glass and has now had a new frame made. Almost as though the old life is over and a new one beginning.

Boris has stayed on in Capri—visiting his wife's grave each day when he is well enough. The 'trophy room' he set up in the Anacapri villa shows certificates and awards Gracie earned during her career. She seldom looked back and never bothered to keep scrapbooks and records of herself—'Never really had time, luv—always left it to others'—although in the last few years of her life she did 'get things together a bit' and left a bequest to Rochdale Museum of the casket containing the Freedom of Rochdale scroll, theatre posters, programmes and song sheets of some of the numbers forever associated with her.

When Norman Jackson went to Capri the year after Gracie died, he went for a cup of tea with Boris the day before leaving the island. 'Gracie always *insisted* on giving me two bottles of wine made from their own grapes before I left each year,' he said. This time Boris came to me with two bottles in a plastic bag: 'Here,' he said. 'My Gracie always liked you to have these.'

CHAPTER 23

A Woman of Quality

Gracie Fields was a star through the 1930s, 40s, 50s, 60s and 70s—five decades, and although she did much less during the last two, the mention of her name, or one of her songs, recalls memories for thousands who saw her and for many, many more who heard her on record, radio or television.

She never made a film of her life—it was suggested many times, but Gracie herself vetoed it. In 1956 when she was fifty-eight years old, they talked of doing so.

'No,' she said. 'I'm not *that* doddery yet. They want me to sit in a rocking chair and say—"Now let me see, lass, what was I doing back in 1910?" That's not for me. I hate going backwards, I like going forward. *That's* what keeps me young.'

And that was the pattern each time. 'Doing a life story is tantamount to saying you've had it—that you're going to drop down dead any minute,' she said another time, 'and I'm not ready to say or do that yet.' Various actresses did go to Capri to meet her from time to time, the idea behind the meeting being that of a life story. But nothing came of it during her lifetime.

Being Gracie Fields cost Grace Stansfield much of her private life during the first few of the famous years, when she was recognised and mobbed almost everywhere. She learned to cope with this in her usual twofold way, with dignity and fun.

She was an interpreter of moods—there were so many Gracies—elegant, sentimental, realistic, vulnerable, romantic, funny, blunt, serious. She reflected all of them through her songs, and in doing so transmuted them into golden magic.

The essence of Gracie was in her voice— all the feeling inside came out this way. She often sang the verse too—'The lyricist took the trouble to write a verse and it's part of the song—it complements the chorus, or it should do...' she used to say.

Gracie was in her natural element when she was singing—anywhere, from a stage to a street, a mountaintop to a mine—as long as she could sing, she could communicate fully. For some it's dancing, painting, writing, talking...Gracie came across to people through her voice. 'Come on, folks, I want to *tell* you something,' she'd say, and go straight into a song.

Gracie gave generously in every way,

money, time, and talent. She hated fuss, bigotry and pompousness; she admired loyalty, kindness and hard work. She loved everyone, of any creed or colour, and she judged them by what they were, or what she thought they were. As with most of us, sometimes she was caught—in her position it was easy to be conned, and it *did* make her withdraw into herself over the years; but it never stopped her from the giving which was as natural to her as breathing. Her heart was infinitely generous, and she left a legacy of kindness which stretches throughout the world.

The depths and the richness, the quality of her voice need to be recorded. Print is a poor substitute, but it is better than nothing. The records and tapes will fade, break or wear thin—some already have. The way she was as a person too—the glory of Gracie cannot be captured within the pages of a book, but if a glimpse of what she was can be gleaned from her story...

She was about all of humanity—the fun and the sorrow. She depicted it for us with her songs, but more than that in the colours of her voice because, as *The Times* said in its obituary of her:

'The excellence of her singing at one time seemed a menace to her performance, for the sentimental ditties on which she lavished so much artistry were quite unworthy of her talent. Early in her career she had an entrancing trick of indicating her real opinion of these tearful ballads by introducing into the middle of her song some ludicrous trick of voice, or by absentmindedly scratching her back between high notes.'

As an artiste she was supreme and reached millions of people. She touched their lives, but, never content to be a figure alone on the stage, she followed her own advice, which she once gave to Lord Miles—she reached down into her audience with her inner being, and she touched hearts with vast multitudes of them.

She was idolised and spurned during her career, and, to quote from Rudyard Kipling's beautiful poem. 'If'.

If you can meet with triumph and disaster,
And treat those two imposters just the same...

She did. There is much in that verse which fits, but I'll simply mention one line more: 'Or walk with Kings nor lose the common touch.' Gracie did that all her life. She never lost the common touch, and she managed it all without patronising and without sycophancy—simply by being her natural self.

Like us all—and some of her appeal was that we imagined she *was* like us all—she made mistakes and sometimes hurt people, but in all her life she never deliberately did anything mean or underhand.

Although enrapturing her audience *en masse,* she made each one love her individually too. It was a very personal feeling as well as the excitement of being part of this experience. For seeing Gracie on stage, being in the theatre with her, was a magical, uplifting experience.

During the course of research for this book I was asked, 'Was "Our Gracie" a myth? Someone created by Archie Pitt and continued by the publicity barons?' No. Definitely not. It was sometimes an embarrassment to her, for there were many, many other aspects in her character, but she did embody the traits of 'Our Gracie'. Written down, it sounds sentimental—in the flesh it wasn't, it was real and true. In any case Gracie *was* a very sentimental person, keeping treasured letters and notes in folders, and rereading many times things she loved. She was also a very down-to-earth person, outspoken and often stubborn.

When she was going to marry Boris Alperovici, Lillian Aza and Mary Davey asked her to wait a while, to be sure she was doing the right thing, but she would not listen to them. She always 'cut the cackle' and went right to the heart of the matter over anything she was involved in. Straight there in the most direct manner.

Her mother's influence in the early years was the dominant one, but her father's wit and stamina were very much in evidence too, and she always acknowledged her parents' sacrifices for her career: 'Basically I'm lazy—if it had been left to me I might have worked in the mill all me life—if I'd managed to keep my job that is.'

Her life spanned five reigns—from Queen Victoria to Queen Elizabeth II. She met three Royal generations personally—King George V and Queen Mary, King George VI and Queen Elizabeth, and Queen Elizabeth II and Prince Philip.

The Duke of Windsor, when he was Prince of Wales, attended several of Gracie's concerts, often accompanied by the then Mrs Wallis Simpson, who later became the Duchess of Windsor.

Sir Anton Dolin compared Gracie with that beloved lady Queen Elizabeth the Queen Mother: 'She had that warmth and care in her that is so much a part of the Queen Mother,' he said, 'the remembering of people's birthdays, all the little touches that came from the heart.'

Madame Tetrazzini, who all those years before had tried to persuade her into opera, would go to hear Gracie Fields when she came to Britain—no one else.

Gracie had a tremendous amount of natural energy and stamina—she *had* to have stamina to undertake the often gruelling tours she did, and in her younger days she thrived on them. Later she felt the effects—during the 1947 *Working Parties* she was often far from well.

She always wanted to be doing something, although in the latter years she did relax more. 'I drove myself hard in the early days,' she said, 'almost burnt myself out once or twice. I thought of my work as a hard job; I loved it, but it was strenuous.'

Over her work, Gracie was a perfectionist. She made it look easy, tossing off remarks at interviews about 'trying out the old voice—one or two notes—yes, it's still there luv—we'll have a go.' In fact she was ever conscious of the trust her audiences had in her, and always made sure her voice was to concert standard.

She had endless patience with everyone, 'but I can't sit still to write or paint all day—that would drive me up the wall. I need to be out and about.'

When she talked about retiring, which she did frequently, she used to say, 'Sometimes I don't know if I could do it—retire. I know I'm a restless sort of lass. Yet if I don't, there's the danger of looking like an old crock—I think maybe it's better if I pack it in.' That usually meant that the next time someone wanted her to do a tour she refused three times instead of one before she said yes.

Her talent was an all-round one. It had its heart in the music hall, but, because she was born too late for the peak of that era, she reached an even larger public. Through records, radio, television and films, millions of people saw and heard Gracie Fields.

The best of Gracie the artiste was in the theatre—there you caught the magic of the love-affair between performer and audience. In the theatre Gracie gave her heart completely *while she was on stage,* and the thousands who watched and listened gave theirs. She turned a huge theatre into everyone's front room, and she lit up that room as two people do for each other, and a very few people can do for hundreds and thousands of others. 'God gave me the wonderful gift of providing laughter,' she said.

That unique quality she had, that was as much at home being serious or comic, blended with the more private side of Gracie that knew about people. Some artistes know about audiences; Gracie knew *instinctively* about audiences, and she learned about people.

Gracie the woman—or Grace, as many of her friends called her—was her other self, and between the two were the gamut of images she created, the many-faced diamond that gave off sparks of colour and fire—that could be unpredictable and unfathomable, laughing and loving, practical and proper, noisy and nervous, innocent and inspired.

As long ago as February 1933, R. H. Naylor, the well-known astrologer, wrote:

'Speaking as a student of human nature I must confess that Gracie Fields fascinates me. In both her face and her horoscope there are unmistakale signs of unquenchable ambition, of a will that brooks no opposition.

'At her birth the sun was placed in the sign of Capricorn, a group of stars which is symbolised by an animal climbing to the mountain top; then one remembers that she is born with the moon in Leo, and Jupiter in Libra. Leo stands for a royal generosity, an indomitable pride.

'Jupiter's position in Libra adds a fierce sense of justice, but emphasises the prodigal generosity of Gracie's nature. Who, either among audiences or personal friends can resist such a battery of magnetic qualities?

'The older Gracie becomes the more Gracie will be a law unto herself. I am grateful to Gracie Fields, for her horoscope sheds light on a question that has long puzzled me. You see a sense of humour and a willingness to be funny at the expense of "refinement" is as rare among women as nuts in May.

'*Miss Fields has yet to experience her greatest successes*. About 1935 the sun in her progressed horoscope reaches the conjunction of Venus. This means money; it means still more fame; above all it means happiness. Somehow or other, the vivid, lovable, and strenuous thing which is the soul of Gracie Fields, will for a time find peace and content. But, mark you, only Gracie Fields will know about it!'

'Miss Fields strikes a bad patch about 1941 or 1942, but centres of propitious periods are marked as for (roughly) 1944 and 1949.'

1935 was the year she signed the contract for £50,000 a film, the year she saw and bought her Capri home, knew John Flanagan, met Monty Banks, toured South Africa and was blossoming rapidly from a rather naïve woman who did what others, 'the bosses', told her into a kind of maturity that could cope graciously with any situation, yet please herself. And of course the early forties brought the 'patch' mentioned when there was trouble over her marrying and leaving Britain and Monty Banks.

She did also become more 'a law unto herself as she grew older'. If Gracie hadn't gone on the stage, she would probably still have been involved with the welfare of others, because it was so much a part of her nature. She *cared* about humanity and did what she could to help when it came to her ears that help was needed—not just with money, although she gave plenty of that over the years, some with publicity, much without. Gracie gave her presence, her time and *herself*—for when she was there, every ounce of *her* was concentrating—she gave wholeheartedly. It sapped her, and, as was mentioned earlier, it very often exhausted the recipients, but it exhilarated them too—the full force of Gracie's dynamic personality cannot be denied.

Actor Roddy McDowall said, 'Being with Gracie was like having an inoculation, or a shot of oxygen about living, a good punch in the shoulder. She *lived*—everything that landed on her plate she took, and dealt with.'

Often very noisy, yet she loved tranquillity, and throughout all the jealousies within a family and among fans, which arose, as they do almost everywhere there are people, she strove to maintain a state of unity. More than anything else, she wanted everyone to live in peace together.

'Wendell Wilkie wrote a book called "One World",' she said in 1946 after her years of entertaining troops all over the globe, 'and if I ever get round to writing about my travels I think I'll call it "One Folk". A smile you know is the same in any language and among every nationality.'

Gracie is missed, not so much these days as an artiste (that in no way belittles her artistic standing because she gave only occasional concerts in the last years) but as a person.

She *did* change, because we all do change as we go through life, as we grow older and experience different emotions, turmoils and circumstances, but her instincts remained the same—to help *people*. At eighty she held a baby in her arms so it would not get crushed in the crowd surrounding her, and in that she had altered little from the seventeen-year-old who walked down a Rochdale Street with a young Nell Whitwell and stopped to wipe the nose of a child sitting in the gutter.

'It was a very dirty child,' Nell said, 'and she wiped its eyes and nose with her clean handkerchief.

'Isn't she lovely?' she said, smiling and chucking her under the chin.

Of all the different mediums in which Gracie worked, she loved the theatre best. Filming she hated at one time, although she grew to enjoy it more when Monty was directing her. Radio and television she took in her stride, especially if there was an audience, although as she grew older she admitted she liked it less. 'Television is for young people,' she said. 'It's cruel on artistes who are getting on in years a bit—not just the closeups but the whole business, getting dressed up, made up, the lot. I'd rather be with an audience than have a man pointing a black box at me.'

She was happy to sing for people anywhere—in a taxi, on a bus, outside in the street if the mood took her and them. She enjoyed singing for the sheer joy of it—but that didn't make it easy to have the career she had. 'Every time a song went over well I thought, good—that was all right, *but how do I top it?* Always it was a constant worry to keep up.' She never gave less than the best she was capable of, and she refused to do three shows a night as time went on, because 'I couldn't do justice to them.'

Her delicious humour often involved sending herself up. The words she wrote to 'Volare' always received a clap as well as a laugh when she sang them, for no-one begrudged her the rewards of her labour because she somehow made it seem that she took each of them with her to the top:

For a beautiful home by the sea,
You all helped to build it for me, (true, it's true)
(laughing with her audience)
Without you where would I be?
Most certainly not in Capri—Thank you.

Gracie touched many lives, and in the telling of her story—the facts and figures of her life, one is left with *gladness* because she lived. She drew from her audiences as they drew from her; mentally she always joined hands with them so that the stage and the auditorium became a huge circle singing together. She inspired loyalty to the utmost degree, kept up with the modern world and retained all that seemed best to her of the old.

Nobody could mix the fun and the seriousness so well—in neither did she ever lose the essence. The fun was no less funny for being underlined by the solemn, and the serious lost nothing by the merriment which had gone before, or would come after. Each was a perfect cameo which joined together to make a whole, each another link in the chain that swung out above all else to *people* to grasp and to continue.

In one of her *Working Party* broadcasts in 1947, Gracie told the story of a little old lady who called at her dressing-room after a show and said, 'You don't know me, and I don't know you personally, but you've given me so much enjoyment...'

'The darling little lady,' Gracie said, was songwriter Carrie Jacobs-Bond. 'We became strong friends, and among the many lovely songs she wrote is the perfect one for me to sing right now—"The End Of A

Perfect Day".'

At the end of Gracie's life on earth we are left with the magical memories of a long and perfect day. She was a master—and when that is said there is no substitute. A 'one off'. Anybody who can win a nation's love—a world's love, and keep it for over fifty years, in spite of vast differences of opinion because of personal choices, *must* have something extra; circumstances, character, temperament, talent, they all count for good or bad, but there is a spark in every one of us that can make us the person we want to be. We all have the power within us to turn that spark into a flame—Dame Gracie made it blaze. She had great strength, physical and mental, and to a remarkable degree the gentleness and heart that gave it meaning.

In assessing Gracie Fields the artiste, one has the achievements to go on; in assessing Gracie Fields the woman, we have the testimonial of the people, the mass of humanity which she loved above all else. Queen Elizabeth, the Queen Mother, said: 'I admired Dame Gracie very much.' Countless other fans said: 'We loved Our Gracie...'

She has been described as an astounding woman, an amazing, generous and kind woman—a consummate and magnificent artiste. She was all of this. Songwriter Jimmy Kennedy put it more simply. He called her 'a star human being'.

Shortly before she died a friend asked her which prayer she most identified with, and Gracie replied, 'The Prayer of St Francis'.

'Lord, make me an instrument of your
  peace
Where there is hatred—let me sow love.
Where there is injury—pardon.
Where there is discord—unity.
Where there is doubt—faith.
Where there is error—truth.
Where there is despair—hope.
Where there is sadness—joy.'
Where there is darkness—light.

Oh, Divine Master, grant that I may not
  so much seek
To be consoled—as to console.
To be understood—as to understand.
To be loved—as to love.

For
It is in giving—that we receive.
It is in pardoning—that we are pardoned.
It is in dying—that we are born to eternal
  life.'

Amen.

THE RECORD

Shows and Revues

Revues

1915 *Yes, I Think So*
1916 *It's A Bargain*
1918 *Mr Tower of London*
1925 *By Request*
1929 *The Show's The Thing*
1931 *Walk This Way*

Royal Variety Shows

1st March	1928	London Coliseum
11th May	1931	London Palladium
15th November	1937	London Palladium
3rd November	1947	London Palladium
13th November	1950	London Palladium
29th October	1951	Victoria Palace
3rd November	1952	London Palladium
4th November	1956	London Palladium

(cancelled due to Suez crisis)

18th November	1957	London Palladium
2nd November	1964	London Palladium
13th November	1978	London Palladium

Filmography

1931   *Sally In Our Alley*

Directed by Maurice Elvey. Cast included Ian Hunter, Florence Desmond, Fred Groves, Gibb McLaughlin, Ben Field.

1932   *Looking On The Bright Side*

Directed by Basil Dean. Cast included Richard Dolman, Julien Rose, Wyn Richmond, Toni De Lungo, Betty Shale, Bettina Montahners, Viola Compton.

1933   *This Week Of Grace*

Directed by Julius Hagen. Cast included Henry Kendall, John Stuart, Helen Haye, Marjorie Brooks, Frank Pettingell, Minnie Rayner, Douglas Wakefield, Nina Boucicault, Vivian Foster, Lawrence Hanray.

1934   *Sing As We Go*

Directed by Basil Dean. Cast included John Lodder, Dorothy Hyson, Stanley Holloway, Frank Pettingell, Lawrence Grossmith, Morris Harvey, Arthur Sinclair, Maire O'Neill, Ben Field, Olive Sloane, Margaret Yarde, Evelyn Roberts, Norman Walker, Richard Grey, Margery Pickard, James R. Gregson, Florence Gregson. The script was by J.B. Priestley.

1934 *Love, Life And Laughter*
Directed by Maurice Elvey. Cast included John Loder, Veronica Brady, Norah Howard, Allan Aynesworth, Esme Percy, Ivor Barnard, Bromley Davenport, Esme Church, Eric Maturin, Fred Duprez, Robb Wilton, Horace Kenney.

1935 *Look Up And Laugh*
Directed by Basil Dean. Cast included Robb Wilton, Harry Tate, Tommy Fields, Vivien Leigh. The script was by J.B. Priestley.

1936 *Queen of Hearts*
Directed by Monty Banks. Cast included John Loder, Enid Stamp-Taylor.

1937 *The Show Goes On*
Directed by Basil Dean. Cast included Owen Nares, John Stuart, Arthur Sinclair, Horace Hodges, Cyril Ritchards.

1937 *We're Going To Be Rich* (In USA called *He Was Her Man)*
Directed by Monty Banks. Cast included Victor McLaglen, Brian Donlevy, Coral Browne, Ted Smith, Gus McNaughton, Charles Carson, Syd Crossley, Hal Gordon, Robert Nainby, Charles Harrison, Tom Payne, Don McCorkindale, Joe Mott, Alex Davies.

1938 *Keep Smiling*
Directed by Monty Banks. Cast included Roger Livesey, Mary Maguire, Peter Coke, Edward Rigby, Jack Donahue, Mike John-

son, Eddie Gray, Nina Rosini, Tommy Fields.

1939   *Shipyard Sally*

Directed by Monty Banks. Cast included Sydney Howard, Bromley Davenport, Oliver Wakefield.

1943   *Stage Door Canteen*

Directed by Frank Borzage. Cast included brief appearance of many stars and top-line orchestras. Gracie sang 'The Lord's Prayer' and 'The Machine Gun Song'.

1943   *Holy Matrimony*

Directed by John Stahl (from the book *Buried Alive* by Arnold Bennett). Cast included Monty Woolley, Laird Cregar, Una O'Connor.

1945   *Mollie and Me*

Directed by Lewis Seiler. Cast included Monty Woolley, Roddy MacDowall, Reginald Gardiner, Clifford Brooke, Aminta Dyne, Edith Barrett, Queenie Leonard, Patrick O'Moore, Natalie Schafer, Doris Lloyd. Lewis L. Russell, Ethel Griffies, Eric Wilton, Jean Del Val.

1946   *Madame Pimpernel* (In USA called *Paris Underground)*

Directed by Gregory Ratoff. Produced by Constance Bennett. Cast included Constance Bennett, George Rigaud, Kurt Kreuger, Leslie Vincent, Charles Andre, Eily Malyon, Adrienne d'Ambricourt, Richard Ryan,

Gregory Gaye, Andre Charlot, Harry Hays Morgan, Roland Varno, Dina Symrnova, Otto Reichow, Fred Gierman, Eric von Morhardt.

Discography

Songs recorded by Gracie Fields between 1928 and 1978

Year of
Recording   *Song Title*

1932	After Tonight We Say Goodbye
1937	Ah! Sweet Mystery Of Life
1938	Alexander's Ragtime Band
1962	All At Once
1942	All For One And One For All
1950	All My Life
1936	Alone
1962	Always You
1950	And You Were There
1950	Angels Guard Thee
1935	Anna From Anacapresi
1935	Anna From Anacapresi (in medley)
1939	Annie Laurie (in medley)
1932	Antonio
1938	Any Broken Hearts To Mend (in medley)
1932	'appy 'ampstead
1962	April Love
1930	Around the Corner

1958	Around the World
1974	Around the World
1947	Arrivederci
1962	As Time Goes By
1934	At The Court Of Old King Cole
1951	At The End Of The Day
1951	At The End Of The Day
1947	Au Revoir
1965	Autumn Leaves
1934	Ave Maria (Gounod)
1934	Ave Maria (Gounod)
1941	Ave Maria (Gounod)
1938	Ave Maria (Gounod)
1971	Ave Maria (Gounod)
1933	Balloons
1931	Bargain Hunter
1930	Barmaids Song
1928	Because I Love You
1932	Because I Love You (in medley)
1936	Because I Love You (in medley)
1940	Begin the Beguine
1940	Bella Bambina
1947	Bella Bella Marie
1939	Bells of St Mary's (in medley)
1958	Belonging To Someone
1974	Best Things In Life Are Free
1949	Beware Of April Rain
1950	Bibbidi-Bobbidi-Boo (in medley)
1936	Bicycle Made For Two (in medley)
1938	Biggest Aspidistra In The World
1939	Biggest Aspidistra In The World (in

	medley)
1941	Biggest Aspidistra In The World (Special 'Hitler' version)
1941	Biggest Aspidistra In The World
1975	Biggest Aspidistra In The World
1951	Biggest Aspidistra In The World
1937	Bill (in medley)
1940	Birthday Song (What's The Good Of)
1942	Bleeding Heart
1947	Bless This House
1965	Blow The Wind Southerly
1948	Bluebird Of Happiness
1948	Bluebird Of Happiness
1930	Body And Soul
1950	Bon Voyage
1935	Born To Be A Clown
1948	Buttons And Bows
1937	Can't Help Lovin' That Man (in medley)
1932	Can't We Talk It Over?
1935	Can't We Talk It Over (in medley)
1959	Carefree Heart
1962	Certain Smile
1934	Charmaine (in medley)
1934	Cherie
1934	Cherie (in medley)
1933	Christmas Bells At Eventide
1949	Christmas Eve In Fairyland
1948	Christmas Love
1938	Christopher Robin

1940	Christopher Robin (in medley)
1975	Christopher Robin
1949	Chump Chop And Chips
1949	Church Bells On Sunday Morning
1965	Ciao Ciao Bambino
1950	Cinderella (in medley)
1930	Clatter Of The Clogs
1931	Clockwork Courtship
1935	Clogs And Shawl
1947	Come Back To Sorrento
1930	Coople o' Dooks
1947	Core 'ngrato
1937	Coronation Waltz
1930	Cottage For Sale
1948	Count Your Blessings
1975	Count Your Blessings
1939	Crash, Bang! I Want To Go Home
1930	Crying For The Carolines
1929	Cute Little Flat (with Archie Pitt)
1936	Daisy Daisy (in medley)
1930	Dancing With Tears In My Eyes
1939	Danny Boy
1939	Danny Boy
1933	Dear Little Shamrock
1937	Desert Song
1938	Dicky Bird Hop
1936	Did I Remember?
1936	Did Your Mother Come From Ireland?
1947	Doin' What Comes Naturally (in medley)

1938	Donkey Serenade
1952	Don't Let The Stars Get In Your Eyes
1961	Do Re Mi
1931	Down At Our Charity Bazaar
1935	Do You Remember My First Love Song?
1950	Dream Is A Wish Your Heart Makes
1930	Dream Lover
1949	Echoes (USA; LONDON label)
1928	Ee By Gum!
1932	Ee By Gum! (in medley)
1959	Ee By Gum!
1935	'erbert 'enery 'epplethwaite
1951	Everlasting (USA; LONDON label)
1939	Fairy On A Christmas Tree
1931	Fall In And Follow The Band
1935	Fall In And Follow Me (in medley)
1938	Fall In And Follow Me (in medley)
1930	Falling In Love Again
1938	Family Tree
1958	Far Away
1939	F.D.R. Jones (in medley)
1936	Feather In Her Tyrolean Hat
1933	Fiddler Joe
1937	First Time I Saw You
1932	Fly's Day Out
1938	Foggy Day
1930	'fonso My Hot Spanish Knight
1975	'fonso My Hot Spanish Knight

1959	'fonso (Ponzo) My Hot Spanish Knight
1969	'fonso My Hot Spanish Knight
1948	Forever And Ever
1950	Forgive Me Lord
1970	Forgive Me Lord
1930	Fred Fannakapan
1938	Fred Fannakapan
1935	General's Fast Asleep
1965	Getting To Know You (in medley)
1974	Getting To Know You
1937	Gianinna Mia
1938	Giddy Up
1937	Gipsy Lullaby
1938	Girl In The Alice Blue Gown
1947	Girl That I Marry (in medley)
1940	Give A Little Whistle (in medley)
1936	Glory Of Love
1931	Go Home And Tell Your Mother
1952	Golden Years
1938	Goodnight Angel
1940	Goodnight, Children, Everywhere
1937	Goodnight My Love
1959	Go 'way From My Window
1937	Gracie and Sandy At The Coronation (with Sandy Powell)
1939	Gracie's Thanks (to the nation, after illness)
1940	Grandest Song Of All
1935	Grandfather's Bagpipes
1939	Grandfather's Bagpipes (in medley)

1931	Grannie's Little Old Skin Rug
1937	Greatest Mistake Of My Life
1948	Green Up Time (USA; LONDON label)
1933	Happy Ending
1965	Happy Talk
1949	Happy Valley (USA; LONDON label)
1937	Have You Forgotten So Soon?
1933	Heaven Will Protect An Honest Girl
1938	Heaven Will Protect An Honest Girl
1932	He Forgot To Come Back
1959	He Forgot To Come Back
1938	Heigh Ho! Heigh Ho! (in medley)
1935	Hello, Hello, Who's Your Lady Friend? (in medley)
1948	Here I'll Stay (USA; LONDON label)
1932	He's Dead But He Won't Lie Down
1941	He's Dead But He Won't Lie Down
1938	He's Dead But He Won't Lie Down
1945	He Wooed Her And Wooed Her And Wooed Her
1962	Hey There!
1940	Hi Diddle Di Dee (in medley)
1938	Holy City

	World (in medley)
1935	I Give My Heart
1947	I Got The Sun In The Morning
1933	I Had To Go And Find Another Job
1932	I Hate You
1935	I Haven't Been The Same Girl Since
1940	I Hear A Dream (in medley)
1940	I Hear A Dream (in medley)
1930	I Just Can't Figure It Out At All
1929	I Lift Up My Finger And I Say Tweet Tweet
1931	I'll Always Be True
1930	I'll Be Good Because Of You
1975	I'll See You Again
1939	I Love The Moon
1975	I Love The Moon
1965	I Love The Moon
1938	I Love To Whistle
1929	I'm A Dreamer, Aren't We All?
1934	I'm A Failure
1930	I'm In The Market For You
1935	I'm Ninety Nine Today
1935	I'm Only Her Mother
1933	I'm Playing With Fire
1939	I'm Sending A Letter To Santa Claus
1939	I'm Sending A Letter to Santa Claus (in medley)
1938	I'm Wishing (in medley)

1937	In The Chapel In The Moonlight
1936	Indian Love Call
1940	Indian Love Call (in medley)
1940	Indian Summer (in medley)
1965	Indian Summer
1937	I Never Cried So Much In All My Life
1940	I Never Cried So Much In All My Life
1939	I Never Cried So Much In All My Life (in medley)
1938	I Never Cried So Much In All My Life
1951	I Never Cried So Much In All My Life
1936	In A Little Lancashire Town
1960	In Jerusalem
1938	In Me 'oroscope
1938	In Me 'oroscope
1943	In My Arms
1934	In My Little Bottom Drawer
1938	In My Little Bottom Drawer
1959	In My Little Bottom Drawer
1933	In Old Siberia
1928	In The Woodshed She Said She Would
1939	I Promise You (in medley)
1934	Isle Of Capri
1974	Isle Of Capri
1934	I Taught Her How To Play Broop Broop

1947	It Began With A Tango
1928	I Think Of What You Used To Think Of Me
1933	It Isn't Fair
1937	It Looks Like Rain In Cherry Blossom Lane
1933	I Took My Harp To A Party
1949	I Took My Harp To A Party
1940	It's A Hap-Hap-Happy Day
1935	It's A Long Way To Tipperary (in medley)
1930	It's Nothing To Do With You
1936	It's A Sin To Tell A Lie (in medley)
1965	It's So Nice To Have A Man About The House
1928	I've Always Wanted To Call You Sweetheart
1929	I've Got A Code In By Doze
1939	I've Got The Jitterbugs
1929	I've Got A Man
1940	I've Got No Strings (in medley)
1962	I've Grown Accustomed To His Face (Lancashire dialect)
1962	I've Grown Accustomed To His Face
1965	I Whistle A Happy Tune (medley)
1938	I Won't Tell A Soul (in medley)
1965	Jealousy
1939	Jeepers Creepers (in medley)
1932	John Willie's Farm
1934	Just A Catchy Little Tune

1931	Just A Dancing Sweetheart
1931	Just One More Chance
1934	Keep It In The Family Circle
1943	Kerry Dance
1959	Kerry Dance
1931	Kiss Waltz
1938	Lambeth Walk (in medley)
1930	Lancashire Blues
1938	Lancashire Blues
1938	Land Of Hope And Glory
1951	Land Of Hope And Glory
1933	Land Of My Fathers (in medley)
1949	Last Mile Home
1962	Last Mile Home
1939	Last Rose Of Summer
1933	Laugh At Life
1928	Laugh, Clown, Laugh
1932	Laugh, Clown, Laugh (in medley)
1936	Laughing Irish Eyes
1948	La Vie En Rose (Take Me To Your Heart Again)
1935	Let The Great Big World Keep Turning (in medley)
1932	Let's All Go Posh
1956	Letter To A Soldier
1948	Let Us Be Sweethearts Over Again
1935	Life Is A Song (in medley)
1931	Life's Desire
1928	Like The Big Pots Do
1938	Like The Big Pots Do
1958	Little Clockmaker

1940	Little Curly Hair In A High Chair
1959	Little Donkey
1938	Little Drummer Boy
1938	Little Lady Make Believe
1930	Little Love A Little Kiss
1934	Little Man You've Had A Busy Day
1937	Little Old Lady
1937	Little Old Lady
1938	Little Old Lady
1974	Little Old Lady
1929	Little Pal
1930	Little Pudden Basin
1939	Little Sir Echo (in medley)
1939	Little Swiss Whistling Song (in medley)
1940	Little Wooden Head (in medley)
1933	Loch Lommond (in medley)
1950	Lock, Stock And Barrel
1938	London Is Saying Goodnight
1959	London Pride
1932	Looking On The Bright Side
1938	Looking On The Bright Side
1936	Looking On The Bright Side (in medley)
1935	Look To The Left And Look To The Right
1935	Look Up And Laugh
1935	Look Up And Laugh (medley)
1935	Look Up And Laugh (medley)
1943	Lord's Prayer

1959	Lord's Prayer
1975	Lord's Prayer
1934	Love In Bloom
1935	Love Is Everywhere (with Tommy Fields)
1935	Love Is Everywhere (medley)
1962	Love Is A Many Splendoured Thing
1962	Loveliest Night Of The Year
1934	Love, Life And Laughter
1935	Love Me Forever
1938	Love Walked In
1934	Love, Wonderful Love
1930	Lovely Aspidistra In The Old Art Pot
1934	Love's Last Word Is Spoken
1930	Love's Old Sweet Song (in medley)
1935	Lullaby Of Broadway
1947	MacNamara's Band
1935	Mademoiselle From Armentieres (in medley)
1937	Make Believe (in medley)
1932	Mary Ellen's Hot Pot Party
1933	Mary Rose
1957	Mary's Boy Child
1933	May Morn (in medley)
1933	Melody At Dawn
1962	Mistakes
1951	Mocking Bird Hill
1931	Mocking Bird Went Cuckoo
1965	Moon River

1929	Moscow
1939	Mrs Binn's Twins
1959	Mrs Binn's Twins
1938	Music, Maestro, Please
1928	My Blue Heaven
1932	My Blue Heaven (in medley)
1936	My Blue Heaven (in medley)
1948	My Darling, My Darling (USA; LONDON (label)
1961	My Favourite Things
1938	My Heaven In The Pines
1937	My Love For You
1933	My Lucky Day
1933	My Mother's Name Was Mary (in medley)
1928	My Ohio Home
1932	My Ohio Home (in medley)
1970	Mysterious People
1970	My Way
1929	Nagasaki
1959	Nature Boy
1975	Never, Never, Never
1937	Nice Cup Of Tea
1942	Nighty Night Little Sailor Boy (USA; DECCA Label)
1947	Now Is The Hour
1974	Now Is The Hour
1962	Now Is The Hour
1938	Now It Can Be Told
1930	Nowt About Owt
1932	Now That You've Gone

1949	Nun's Chorus
1931	Obadiah's Mother
1942	O'Brien Has Gone Hawaiian
1938	O Come All Ye Faithful
1939	O Come All Ye Faithful (in medley)
1931	Oh! Glory
1929	Oh!? Maggie, What Have You Been Up To?
1938	Oh! Ma Ma
1949	Oh! My Beloved Father
1931	Oh! Sailor, Behave
1947	Oh! What A Beautiful Morning (in medley)
1974	Oh! What A Beautiful Morning
1928	Oh! You Have No Idea
1947	Oklahoma (in medley)
1938	Old Father Thames
1939	Old Lady From Armentieres (in medley)
1935	Old Soldiers Never Die (in medley)
1938	Old Violin
1939	Old Violin (in medley)
1941	Old Violin
1970	Old Violin
1975	On A Clear Day
1937	On A Little Dream Ranch
1939	One Day When We Were Young
1932	One Little Hair On His Head
1935	One Night Of Love
1938	One Night Of Love
1935	One Night Of Love (in medley)

411

1934	Riding On The Clouds
1936	Ring Down The Curtain
1931	River Stay'way From My Door
1932	Rochdale Hounds
1933	Rochdale Hounds (in medley)
1936	Rochdale Hounds (in medley)
1938	Rochdale Hounds
1947	Rochdale Hounds
1935	Roll Along Prairie Moon
1939	Romany
1939	Romany (in medley)
1938	Rosalie
1936	Rose Marie
1942	Rose O'Day
1940	Roses Of Picardy
1932	Round The Bend Of The Road
1970	Round The Bend Of The Road
1939	Run, Rabbit, Run (in medley)
1938	Sailing Home
1931	Sally
1931	Sally (in medley)
1941	Sally
1936	Sally (in medley)
1937	Sally (in medley)
1933	Sally (in medley)
1935	Sally (in medley)
1934	Sally (in medley)
1952	Sally (in medley)
1959	Sally
1938	Sally (chorus)
1974	Sally

1975	Sally
1932	Say It Isn't So
1957	Scarlet Ribbons
1970	Scarlet Ribbons
1929	Scented Soap
1937	September In The Rain (in medley)
1959	September Song
1969	September Song
1929	Serenade (Toselli)
1947	Serenade Of The Bells
1936	Serenade In The Night
1935	Shall I Be An Old Man's Darling?
1938	Shall I Be An Old Man's Darling?
1936	She Came From Alsace Lorraine
1935	She Fought Like A Tiger For 'er 'onour
1949	She Fought Like A Tiger For 'er 'onour
1949	Shepherd
1929	She's Funny That Way
1934	Sing As We Go
1938	Sing As We Go
1936	Sing As We Go (in medley)
1936	Sing As We Go (in medley)
1937	Sing As We Go (in medley)
1935	Sing As We Go (in medley)
1939	Sing As We Go (in medley)
1951	Sing As We Go
1959	Sing As We Go
1930	Singin' In The Bathtub

1934	Singin' In The Bathtub (in medley)
1932	Singin' In The Bathtub (in medley)
1931	Siting On A Five Barred Gate
1962	Small World
1937	Smile When You Say Goodbye
1935	Smilin' Thro'
1965	Smoke Gets In Your Eyes
1951	So In Love
1933	So Long, Lads, We're Off!
1938	Somebody's Thinking Of Me To-night
1933	Somebody's Waiting For Me (in medley)
1938	Some Day My Prince Will Come
1965	Something Wonderful (in medley)
1978	Sometimes
1962	Somewhere
1969	Somewhere My Love
1974	Somewhere My Love
1951	Somewhere, Somehow, Someday
1932	Song Of The Bells
1931	Song Of The Highway
1949	Song Of The Mountains
1959	Song Of The Mountains
1937	Song In Your Heart
1929	Sonny Boy
1950	So This Is Love
1928	So Tired
1935	South American Joe
1975	Speak Softly, Love
1930	Stop And Shop At The Co-op Shop

1940	Stop And Shop At The Co-op Shop
1947	Stop And Shop At The Co-op Shop
1933	Stormy Weather
1933	Stormy Weather (in medley)
1970	Story Of The Sparrows
1952	Story Of The Sparrows
1969	Strangers In The Night
1956	Summertime In Venice
1947	Surrey With The Fringe On Top (in medley)
1948	Susy
1974	Swanee
1956	Sweetest Prayer In All The World
1938	Sweetest Song In The World
1938	Sweetest Song In The World (in medley)
1936	Sweetheart Let's Grow Old Together
1939	Sweethearts (in medley)
1938	Swing Your Way To Happiness
1937	Sympathy
1929	Take A Look At Mine
1935	Take Me Back To Dear Old Blighty (in medley)
1959	Take Me To Your Heart Again (La Vie En Rose)
1974	Tea For Two
1952	Thankyou, My Dear
1942	That Lovely Weekend (USA; DECCA Label)
1931	That Must Have Been Our Walter

1929	That's How I feel About You Sweetheart
1929	That's What Put The Sweet In 'Home Sweet Home'
1938	There Is A Tavern In The Town (in medley)
1939	There'll Always Be An England (in medley)
1933	There's A Cabin In The Pines
1933	There's A Cabin In The Pines (in medley)
1935	There's A Long Long Trail (in medley)
1935	There's A Lovely Lake In London
1934	There's Millions And Millions Of Women
1947	There's No Business Like Show Business (in medley)
1937	There's A Small Hotel
1931	They All Make Love But Me
1940	They Can't Ration Love (in medley)
1939	They Say (in medley)
1947	They Say It's Wonderful (in medley)
1935	Things Might Have Been So Different
1942	Thingummy Bob (USA; DECCA Label)
1929	This Is Heaven
1929	Thoughts Of You

1962	Three Coins In The Fountain
1930	Three Green Bonnets
1970	Three Green Bonnets
1975	Three Green Bonnets
1952	Till They've All Gone Home
1938	Tisket A Tasket (in medley)
1935	Trees
1938	Trek Song
1975	Trek Song
1935	Turn 'erbert's Face To The Wall Mother
1938	Turn 'erbert's Face To the Wall Mother
1940	Turn On The Old Music Box (in medley)
1960	Twelfth Of Never
1956	Twenty
1939	Two Sleepy People (with Tommy Fields)
1939	Una Voce Poco Fa (guyed; in medley)
1947	Una Voce Poco Fa (guyed; in medley)
1959	Ugly Duckling
1975	Ugly Duckling
1939	Umbrella Man (with Tommy Fields)
1928	Under The Moon
1932	Underneath The Arches
1948	Underneath The Linden Tree
1929	Unlucky Number Thirteen

1969	Volare (adaptation)
1947	Waiata Poi
1959	Waiata Poi
1943	Wait For Me Mary
1938	Walter, Walter
1939	Watler, Walter (in medley)
1938	Walter, Walter
1932	Waltzing Time In Old Vienna
1937	We're All Good Pals Together (in medley)
1928	We're All Living At The Cloisters
1940	We're All Together Now
1935	We've Got To Keep Up With The Jones'
1959	We've Got To Keep Up With The Jones'
1959	We've Got To Keep Up With The Jones'
1930	What Archibald Says, Goes
1934	What Can You Buy A Nudist For His Birthday?
1962	Whatever Will Be Will Be
1930	What Good Am I Without You?
1959	What's The Good Of A Birthday?
1975	What's The Good Of A Birthday?
1933	When Cupid Calls
1937	When The Harvest Moon Is Shining (in medley)
1935	When I Grow Too Old To Dream
1974	When I Grow Too Old To Dream
1939	When I Grow Too Old To Dream

(in medley)

1938	When Mother Nature Sings Her Lullaby (in medley)
1937	When My Dreamboat Comes Home (in medley)
1938	When The Organ Played 'O Promise Me'
1940	When Our Dreams Grow Old
1932	When The Rest Of The Crowd Goes Home
1935	When The Robin Sings His Song
1929	When Summer Is Gone
1932	When We All Went To The Zoo
1935	When You Grow Up Little Lady
1950	When You Return
1929	When You've Gone
1940	When You Wish Upon A Star (in medley)
1937	Where Are You?
1937	Where Is The Sun? (in medley)
1933	Whiskers An' All
1933	Whiskers An' All (in medley)
1938	Whistle While You Work
1948	White Christmas
1934	Who Made Little Boy Blue? (in medley)
1929	Why Can't You?
1935	Why Did I Have To Meet You?
1936	Why Did She Fall For The Leader Of The Band?
1928	Why Does The Hyena Laugh?

1935	You Haven't Altered A Bit
1935	You And The Night And The Music
1959	Young At Heart
1975	Young At Heart
1935	Your Dog's Come Home Again
1965	Your Dog's Come Home Again
1952	Your Mother And Mine
1965	You're Breaking My Heart
1930	You're Driving Me Crazy
1932	You're More Than All The World To Me
1934	You're More Than All The World To Me (in medley)
1948	You're Too Dangerous, Cherie (USA; LONDON label)
1938	You've Got To Be Smart In The Army Nowadays

If any reader who has tapes or memorabilia about Gracie Fields will write to me c/o Messrs Robert Hale, Clerkenwell House, Clerkenwell Green, London, it will help in locating tapes, films, records, photographs etc. which exist outside of already known sources for exhibition purposes.

Musical Appreciation

Gracie Fields first recorded, on an acoustic disc, for the HMV label in 1923, but this was never issued to the general public, and the masters were unfortunately destroyed some time in the 1930s by an unthinking employee of the company. The two items recorded were 'Romany Love' and 'Tweedle-eedle Dum', and Madam Adani was the accompanist.

The straight singing voice was a distinctive and powerful operatic-style soprano: very beautiful in tone, pure and crystalline as a choirboy's, but with emotional overtones of great warmth and colour. For such a large voice the range was exceptional. On record the highest note is E above top C (example on HMV C2378 in the song 'Because I Love You'.) In later years the lower end of the voice became more evident in recordings. (On Columbia CLP1824 in 'Indian Summer' it ranges down to G below middle C several times, and just touches one note even lower.)

Top C is a proud achievement for operatic singers with extensive musical training

(Gracie never had a lesson in her life), but she sang it effortlessly and often in different types of songs. (On Regal Zono MR2917 'Snow White Medley', the song 'I'm Wishing' runs for sixty-five seconds during which top C is sung with ease no less than fourteen times.) She could still sing this note in her late sixties and used it in live performances at that time.

Technically speaking, although the musical repertoire was different, the vocal method of Gracie Fields, with the manner of singing high in the chest register, and precise forward attack into the upper notes, was remarkably similar to that of the historic operatic soprano who had admired her so much, Madame Luisa Tetrazzini.

For genuine old-time music hall style there is 'Oh! You Have No Idea' on HMV B2795; hilarious sob-stuff comedy with phenomenal vocal pyrotechnics (in Lancashire Spanish) with the song 'Because I Love You' on HMV C2378; straight operatic-style singing of 'The Nuns' Chorus' on Decca F9219. A sample of yodelling in 'I Love To Whistle' on REX 9328; concert soprano straight voice with Toselli's 'Serenade' on HMV B3104; clean whistling in 'Bluebird Of Happiness' on Decca F8996; a superb violin impression in 'An Old Violin' on Decca F8015, showing marvellous vocal control on extreme high notes.

424

Accurate coloratura-opera-style singing in the Galli-Curci manner in the funny 'Stop And Shop At The Co-op Shop' on the very rare disc Columbia FB2449; vocal impressions of farmyard animals with 'You Can't Kill Flies By Scratching Them' on HMV B3383; male voice in the Scottish accent and manner of that great music hall personality Will Fyffe in 'I Belong To Glasgow' on Columbia 33SX1198, and a child character voice in 'The Birthday Song' on Columbia FB2448. Gracie gives a full-blooded laughter-song to music in 'Laugh At Life' on HMV 8064; swing music in 'I've Got The Jitterbugs' on Regal MR3119; emotional acting in the monologue 'It's Nothing To Do With You' on HMV B3505.

She recorded many holy songs, of which one of the best known is Gounod's 'Ave Maria' on HMV C2705 (it was Gracie Fields who made this song *really* popular with the general public; she sang it 'by special request' hundreds of times). The three record set 'Gracie In The Theatre', on HMV C2625/2626/2627, was the first recording of a live variety performance and was made in October 1933 at the Holborn Empire. (You can hear the engineer laughing at her antics on this recording.)

Gracie Fields wrote the lyrics of 'Thank You, My Dear'; put her own words to *'Volare'* to suit numerous occasions; wrote the words and music of 'Lancashire Blues' (sometimes known as 'Rochdale Blues'), and wrote English lyrics for *'Core'ngrato'* and 'Song Of The Mountains'.

Unfortunately we have no recording of the 'rock and roll' style which featured in 'Rockin' On The Green' in her 1950s stage shows. However, there *is* reputed to be an athletic cartwheel in 'South American Joe' which she included with a burst of enthusiasm while recording the song for REX 8585!

Advancing years that brought with them the usual breathing difficulties made inevitable inroads on the voice itself, although it still held many notes of remarkable beauty and purity to the end of her life. However, the superb artistry never diminished, and all who had technical knowledge of her life in music marvelled at the way she adapted her songs and technique to match the vocal resources still left to her. Gracie Fields has no peer in the art of vocally colouring a song, a fine example is the 'Never, Never, Never' on Warwick WW5007 which was recorded in her seventy-seventh year. The recording studio musicians and technicians rose to their feet with a spontaneous burst of prolonged applause in appreciation of her unique professional artistry.

WALLY SINGER